MAY '89 X 66 X X 16

S0-ABD-756

LIFE STYLE

By the authors:

THE ABC'S OF CLASSROOM DISCIPLINE
LIFE STYLE: Theory, Practice, and Research
LIFE STYLE: What It Is and How to Do It
A SINGLE PARENT'S SURVIVAL GUIDE:
How to Raise the Children

LIFE STYLE
Theory, Practice, and Research
Second Edition

Leroy G. Baruth
Daniel G. Eckstein

Also distributed by: Alfred Adler Institute
159 North Dearborn Street
Chicago, IL. 60601

KENDALL/HUNT PUBLISHING COMPANY
Dubuque, Iowa, USA • Toronto, Ontario, Canada

Copyright © 1978, 1981 by Kendall/Hunt Publishing Company

ISBN 0-8403-2375-1

All rights reserved. No part of this publication may be reproduced,
stored in a retrieval system, or transmitted, in any form or by any
means, electronic, mechanical, photocopying, recording, or otherwise,
without the prior written permission of the copyright owner.

Printed in the United States of America
10 9 8 7 6 5 4

Dedication

To our parents, George and Helen Baruth, and Oscar, Jr. (deceased) and Frances Eckstein, and to our siblings Carroll Baruth, and Donna, Dave and Doug Eckstein, for their formative influences on our own life styles.

Contents

Preface

After introducing the term "life style" in *The Science of Living* (1929), Alfred Adler later wrote (in Ansbacher and Ansbacher, 1956) that "The style of life is the more general concept comprising, in addition to the goal, the individual's opinion of himself and the world and his unique way of striving for the goal in his particular situation" (p. 172). In the Research section of this book, Gushurst defines a life style as "The total system which accounts for the consistency and directionality of an individual's life movement" (p. 97). Other writers have equated life style with the unity of personality, self, ego, individuality, or individual creative ability and opinion about oneself and the problems of life.

In *Life Style: What It Is and How to Do It* (1978) we have introduced basic guidelines for completing, interpreting, and modifying one's life style. The purpose of the present book has been to compile in a single volume important manuscripts by leading Adlerian therapists relative to the actual theory applications and relevant life style research. A brief biographical sketch of each contributor to this book has been included in Appendix A, p. 171.

In the initial section of this book pertaining to Theory, life style is discussed from a historical and systematic point of view, focusing specifically on consistency, family constellation influences, and dream analysis. Several practical applications of the life style techniques comprise the Practice section including vocational counseling, correctional counseling, psychodrama, working with children, moral dimensions of life style, pictorial illustration of life styles, and methods of utilizing early recollections. The Research section investigates the validity of life style analysis, studies the use of early recollections, and examines the relationship of birth order to intellectual attainment and antisocial behavior.

As a final overview to life styles, specific assumptions and possible limitations for counseling should be noted. An important theoretical construct of a life style concerns the philosophical concept of phenomenology, an individual's subjective impression of his or her early family influences. Another member of the family could have an entirely different opinion regarding the prevailing atmosphere, but the counselor is only interested in the client's personal perception of self, others, and life in general. Thus, any self report data shared in an interpersonal process between two or more individuals may introduce a certain amount of bias. As Gushurst (1977) speculates, interpersonal sharing is influenced by the following:

1. How much a person actually knows about himself or herself. The greater the amount of self-awareness and introspection, the more chance there is of "psychologically relevant" data the person can share. Similarly, the earlier a pattern is established the less likely an individual may be able to identify and discuss it. Thus, adequate intellectual, verbal, and introspective abilities are favorable factors.
2. What a person shares in a life style interview depends upon what one chooses to tell the counselor. Individuals often consciously and selectively decide to omit, emphasize, or distort data in a manner consistent with their life style. Avoidance behaviors and "gaming" motives affect the amount of conscious distortion of data by clients. The former behavior is used to avoid embarrassment, manipulation, harm, or even protect the civil liberties of self or significant others (i.e., not discussing alcoholism or child abuse); conversely, "gaming" may involve attempts to seduce, discourage or praise the person recording the data.

3. Two frequently occurring themes which emerge include (1) the individual's need to be liked by the therapist, and (2) the individual's desire to avoid pain and hurt whenever possible. Both themes are positively or negatively affected by the perceived characteristics of the individual toward the therapist. The client's believing a therapist is more likely to be helpful should minimize the fears of being hurt.

Although a standard suggested life style interview guide is included in this book (see appendix G, p. 145), it should be noted that many different versions exist. For example, as a means of de-emphasizing the procedure of focusing initially on one's sibling interactions, Gushurst merely asks "who was the more influential person in your life?" Willhite makes extensive use of early recollections by contrasting one's self concept and self ideal, Coker adds psychodrama to the process, while the Kvols-Riedlers pictorially represent one's life style.

Thus, our approach in this book is based upon the belief that self report data is valid, that a significant Adlerian contribution to the helping professions is the concept of life style, but that different therapists employ a variety of approaches and techniques to obtain and analyze data.

We are interested in hearing about other innovative applications and research studies of the life style analysis for inclusion in future publications.

Leroy G. Baruth
Daniel G. Eckstein

January 1981

Adler, Alfred. *The Science of Living.* New York: Greenberg Publishers, 1929.
Ansbacher, Heinz, and Ansbacher, Rowena. *The Individual Psychology of Alfred Adler.* New York: Harper & Row, 1956.
Eckstein, Daniel, Baruth, Leroy, and Mahrer, David. *Life Style: What It Is and How to Do It.* Dubuque, Iowa: Kendall/Hunt Publishing Company, 1978.
Gushurst, Robin. "A Life Style Demonstration," Southern Regional NASAP Convention, Atlanta, Ga., Sept. 24, 1977.

Acknowledgments

We would like to express our grateful appreciation to the following individuals:

Carmella Baruth and Judy Eckstein, for encouragement, suggestions, and support;

Albino Hinojosa for his illustrations that helped make our words come to life;

All the authors who permitted us to reprint their previously published articles or who worked diligently to complete original manuscripts;

Guy Manaster, Editor of the *Journal of Individual Psychology* and B. Udelle Freidland, Past Editor, and Jon Carlson, Editor of *The Individual Psychologist* for permission to reprint articles originally published in their respective journals.

Joyce Metz-Roberts, for administrative assistance.

PART I: THEORY

Life Style: A Historical and Systematic Review

Heinz L. Ansbacher

The term life style, which has for 40 years described a central concept of Adlerian psychology, has recently gained greatly among psychologists and sociologists in general and has even become part of the everyday vocabulary. It has now been included in the glossary of an important introductory psychology textbook (61); it is to be found in the new Webster International Dictionary (72); a recent newsmagazine story referred to the "hippies" as "more than a choice of life style" (40); and a whimsical newspaper headline spoke of "the life style of some favorite inhabitants of the Zoo" (52).

In view of this new importance we propose here to trace the origin and history of the term, review in outline form its various uses, show what they have in common, and conclude with observations regarding the theoretical significance of this development.

Adler's Concept of Life Style

For Adler life style represented the organismic ideas of the individual as an actor rather than a reactor; of the purposiveness, goal-directedness, unity, self-consistency, and uniqueness of the individual; and of the ultimately subjective determination of his actions. The following quotations may illustrate this.

We must refute the causal significance of situation, milieu, or experiences of the child. Their significance and effectiveness develop only in the intermediary psychological metabolism, so to speak. They are assimilated by the early derived style of life of the child (19, p. 178). In considering the structure of a personality, the chief difficulty is that its unity, its particular style of life and goal, is not built upon objective reality, but upon the subjective view the individual takes of the facts of life (19, p. 183). The goal of superiority with each individual is personal and unique. It depends upon the meaning he gives to life. This meaning . . . is built up in his style of life and runs through it like a strange melody of his own creation (19, p. 181).

From the concept of unity there followed the principle that specific manifestations must be considered with reference to the context (*Zusammenhang*) of the whole individual. Disregard for this context, or coherence, was one of Adler's main quarrels with psychoanalysis. Thus he stated:

To deny the context (*Zusammenhang*) is like picking single notes out of a melody to examine them for their significance, their meaning. A better understanding of this coherence is shown by Gestalt psychology which uses this metaphor frequently, as we do. The difference is only that we are not satisfied with the "Gestalt," or as we prefer to say with the "whole," when we refer all the notes to the melody. We are satisfied only when we have recognized in the melody the originator and his attitudes as well, for example Bach, Bach's life style (8, p. 205).

The relationship of life style to style in general is expressed in the passage, "The life style can come about only through elimination of less suitable forms of expression, through acts of abstraction. This is the same as in the style in painting, architecture, or music" (8, p. 203).

In the opening paragraph of a chapter on "Psychological Means and Ways for the Investigation of the Life Style" Adler points out that poets have in fact always described life styles, although what they did was not formulated in this way.

Our knowledge of the individual is very old. To name only a few instances, the historical and personality descriptions of the ancient peoples, the Bible, Homer, Plutarch, all the Greek and Roman poets, sagas, fairy tales, and myths, show a brilliant understanding of personality. Until recent times it was chiefly the poets who best succeeded in getting the clue to a person's life style. Their ability to show the individual living, acting, and dying as an *indivisible* whole in

Heinz Ansbacher, Life Style: A Historical and Systematic Review, *Journal of Individual Psychology*, 23(2), 1967, 191–212. Reprinted from the *Journal of Individual Psychology* with permission of the author and publishers.

closest context with the tasks of his sphere of life rouses our admiration for their work to the highest degree (10, pp. 32–33; translation modified from 9, p. 20).

Adler generally prided himself in not having made any new "discoveries" but only in having contributed toward "understanding what mankind had known in the main parts long ago"(11).

But beyond personality description and comprehension, Adler was primarily concerned with personality change, and the concept of life style permeates his writings on psychotherapy (19, pp. 326–336). Dreikurs, describing how the concept of life style is employed in Adlerian psychotherapy, makes in this respect a distinction between counseling and psychotherapy. "In counseling we remain on the present level of functioning" whereas in psychotherapy we start with the exploration of the patient's "present field of action and then proceed to his general movement through life, to his life style" from childhood on (28, p. 89). Within a given life style and its long-range goals many sub-goals or immediate goals and a wide choice of actions are possible (28a).

Whereas Adler stressed the individual uniqueness, he nevertheless recognized similarities among individuals and their life styles. Thus he used life style also as a generic term, especially in reference to mental disturbances. "The nervous individual formulates his style of life more rigidly, more narrowly; he is nailed to the cross of his narrow, personal, noncooperative fiction" (19, p. 279). Generic uses of life style by Adler and others are reported below.

Development of the Concept in Adler

Adler's active career in psychology can be said to have extended over the 30-year period from 1907 when he published his *Study of Organ Inferiority* until his death in 1937. It was not until 1926 that the term life style appears in his writings, roughly the last third of this period, although the main thoughts referred to by this term were present from the beginning. These were the assumptions of the unity of the organism, and its continuous forward orientation. The latter is often described as the striving toward a goal—a "fictitious" goal in the sense that it is the creation of the subject, or perhaps the inference of the psychologist (19, pp. 87–100). Every expression of the individual would be influenced by his guiding principle.

Guiding Image

Adler used a series of terms to express these ideas, the first of which probably was that of the "guiding image" (*Leitbild*). He wrote in 1912:

Toward the end of infancy when the child has become capable of achieving independent, goal-directed actions which do not merely aim at drive satisfaction, when he occupies his place in the family and arranges himself in his environment, he has already acquired certain skills, psychological gestures and readinesses. Furthermore his action has become unified and one sees him on the way to conquer for himself a place in the world. Such unified action can be understood only if one assumes that the child has found a fixed point outside himself toward which he strives with his psychological growth energies. In other words the child must have formed a guiding line (*Leitlinie*), a guiding image (*Leitbild*) in the expectation thus best to be able to orient himself in his environment and to achieve satisfaction of his needs, the avoidance of displeasure, and the attainment of pleasure (1, p. 33).

The term *Leitbild* was used six years earlier by Ludwig Klages (43).[1] According to Klages, who was interested in the interpretation of expressive movements, primarily handwriting, certain strivings press for expression which they achieve through selecting kindred forms and movements. The constant in this selection process is what Klages calls "the personal guiding image." The final formulation of his doctrine of the expressive principle was: "Every spontaneous movement of man is unconsciously co-determined by his personal guiding image" (44, p. 38).

Adler was well acquainted with the work of Klages and greatly admired it. He concluded his paper on "Organ Dialect, by reprinting over three pages (about 1200 words) from Klages on the interpretation of expressive movements, introducing them with the tribute: "Already in 1905 (42, pp. 7–8) this scholar developed thoughts regarding the personal form of expression which we want to present here, with the author's consent, on account of their significance and classical form" (2, p. 136).[2] In view of this relationship it seems reasonable to assume that Adler adopted the term guiding image from Klages.

Guiding Line

But Adler was very sensitive to the danger of the reification of a term and thus tended to use different terms simultaneously and over a period of time to express the same concept. In the first passage quoted in the preceding section we find guiding line (*Leitlinie*) used interchangeably with guiding image (*Leitbild*), and the chapter from which the passage is taken carries the term guiding idea (*leitende Idee*) in its title (1, p. 33), a third term.

1. We became aware of this through a paper by Adolf Diumling (25) in which he compares four individual guiding-image theories, those of Klages, Adler, Spranger and Jung; and discusses three kinds of collective guiding images (social, public and of a period).
2. Part of this selection from Klages by Adler has been translated elsewhere (19, pp. 220–221).

Two years later Adler speaks no longer of a guiding line as the principle of unity of the individual. Instead he says that in order to arrive at a unified conception of a particular person one must compare his various traits and bring them down to their common base line (3, p. 1). The unifying principle is "the line which a person pursues" (*die Linie, die einer verfolgt*) (3, p. 2).

Life Plan

In the same paper Adler also speaks of life plan (*Lebensplan*), a term subsequently used extensively by him. "Once I have recognized the goal of a psychological movement, of a life plan, I must expect that all partial movements will correspond to the goal and the life plan" (3, p. 4). And reciprocally: "The partial movements properly understood must in their coherence give an image of a unitary life plan and its final goal" (3, p. 4).

Life plan was then used in some of Adler's most important writings (4, pp. 37, 41, 42, 100–103, 106, 108). But at times he also used such terms as life line, line of movement, total life attitude, total personality (*Lebenslinie, Bewegungslinie, Gesamtlebenshaltung, Gesamtpersonlichkeit*), all these terms, incidentally, within three pages of one publication (5, pp. 20–22).

While the term life plan was later de-activated by Adler, it has recently assumed new significance. In their provocative book, *Plans and the Structure of Behavior*, the authors Miller, Galanter and Pribram present the thesis that the notion of a plan which guides behavior is "quite similar to the notion of a program that guides an electronic computer" (48, p. 2) although, as we would add, the computer, in contrast to the human organism, does not write its own program. A plan is defined simply as "any hierarchical process in the organism that can control the order in which a sequence of operations is to be performed" (48, p. 16).

Life Style

In 1929 Adler formally and cryptically announced that he now preferred style of life (*Lebensstil*) to life plan (*Lebensplan*). "Individual Psychology has long called the consistent movement toward the goal a plan of life. But because this name has sometimes led to mistakes among students, it is now called a style of life" (19, p. 173).

To our knowledge, Adler used the term for the first time, informally, in 1926. The particular circumstances under which this occurred will be described in the section after the following.

Adler decided on life style probably because it was the broader term under which all the others could

well be subsumed. Thus he once defined the individual's life style rightly conceived as "the wholeness of his individuality" (10, p. 189). Another advantage of this term is that it should be most resistant to reification, style of life being easily changed to style of living, which becomes very similar to the extentialists' mode-of-being in the world. In this endeavor to avoid reification Adler occasionally also modified the phrasing as in the epitome, "Not heredity and not environment are determining factors. Both are giving only the frame and the influences which are answered by the individual in regard to his styled creative power" (19, frontispiece). Finally, life style is more organismic and humanistic than life plan which it superseded. While a computer can be said to proceed according to a plan, one would not say that it is prone to develop its own particular style.

From Max Weber via Folkert Wilken to Adler

When and how the term life style originated has not yet become clear. Already 200 years ago the French naturalist and writer Georges-Louis de Buffon (1707–1788) stated, "The style is the man himself" (*Le style est l'homme meme*). And still another 150 years earlier the English philosopher and author, Robert Burton (1577–1640) observed, "It is most true, *stylus virum arguit*—our style betrays us" (20, p. 122). These statements presuppose an underlying personality style or life style corresponding to style in the sense of "manner of expression." The actual phrase "stile of living" is found in the foreword of the English translation, dated 1811, of *Moralische Geschichten* by a quite obscure German author named Adlerjung, "stile" being an older way for style.[3]

Max Weber

In more recent times it was the sociologist Max Weber (1864–1920) who used the term life style before Adler. However, Weber used life style collectively so that its meaning was quite similar to that of subculture.

In the absence of a specific definition we shall show the contexts in which the term is found. Differences in life styles of groups are determined "chiefly by differences in education" (70, p. 300). The most important source of development of distinct social strata is "the development of a peculiar style of life including, particularly, the type of occupation pursued" (71, p. 429). On the other hand, speaking about status,

3. Personal communication, December 23, 1961, by Paul Rom who found this book in the British Museum.

Weber notes that this "is normally expressed by . . . a specific style of life [of] all those who wish to belong to the circle" (70, p. 187). A given status group develops a specific life style and demands its members to adhere to it. "All 'stylization' of life either originates in status groups or is at least conserved by them" (70, p. 191).

Although Weber, the sociologist, was concerned with collective life styles and the concept was of only minor importance in his writings, whereas Adler, the psychologist, was concerned with individual life styles as the most central concept in his system, they both built their theories on essentially the same methodological foundations, the same basic assumptions. Thus it also turns out that the two concepts of life style are not as different as might appear at first, but are rather the extension of the same concept from one area to another.

Like Adler, Weber was concerned with understanding human action, that is, behavior which has a "teleological orientation" (71, p. 94), an "intended purpose" (71, p. 93), a subjectively intended meaning for the actor (71, p. 93). Furthermore, "In no case does meaning refer to an objectively 'correct' meaning or one which is 'true' in some metaphysical sense" (71, p. 89). Consequently also, the presence of objective factors such as "hereditary biological constitution" does not in the least alter the specific task of any of the sciences of action, which is "the interpretation of action in terms of its subjective meaning" (71, p. 94).

Understanding involves observation of the subjectivity of the actor and the motivational interpretation of the action. What counts in the interpretation is the operational applicability of the "subjective categories" which the investigator has developed, not whether these are "true," as just stated, or whether the actor is conscious of the meanings that have been imputed to him, or whether he had "intended" in the ordinary sense a given course of action. Thus Weber is quite pragmatic, like Adler (see 18).

Interpretation in terms of motive, which is also called explanatory understanding, is achieved by "placing the act in an intelligible and more inclusive context of meaning" (71, p. 95). The German term for context is *Zusammenhang*. The necessity for regarding individual manifestations of action in their *Zusammenhang* was, of course, also greatly stressed by Adler as his principal methodological tool (18, p. 347). Correspondingly, "Weber found of no use for his purposes" a concept such as instinct (53, p. 26). If one explains on the basis of instinct one is likely to disregard the particular context of a phenomenon.

This may suffice to support the contention that in the distinction between objectifying and subjectifying psychology established by Jaspers, Weber, like Adler, belongs to the second alternative where we find an organismic conception, immanent teleology, a holistic approach, phenomenological description, field theory, and "soft" determinism (19, pp. 4–5)—altogether what is today often designated as organismic-humanistic psychology.

The principal translator and interpreter of Weber has been Talcott Parsons (53, 71) who has had a considerable influence on American sociology. Life style is frequently used by present-day sociologists who have had some relationship to Parsons.

Folkert Wilken

In 1926 a handbook of Individual Psychology (73) was published, edited by Erwin Wexberg. It contained a paper by Folkert Wilken (76), then lecturer (*Privatdozent*) in political science at the University of Freiburg, which was essentially concerned with the problem of the mental health hazard represented by the increasing liberation of modern man from the communal ties of previous ages.

The author had become interested in Individual Psychology through Leonhard Seif in Munich with whom he was in treatment in 1918. When Max Weber came to the University of Munich in 1919, Wilken, having been a great admirer of his, began his doctoral disertation under him. This was interrupted through Weber's untimely death in 1920, but the study eventually became Wilken's *Habilitationsschrift* at Breiburg and was published under the title of *Outline of a Personalistic Value Theory* (75).[4]

In Wilken's handbook article the term life style is frequently used, always in the sense of Weber, referring to a collective phenomenon. It is introduced through the sentence: "Modern times have developed their own life style which reflects how mankind has undertaken to found its autonomy of personality" (76, p. 72); this must be followed by a new kind of community (76, p. 73). From then on Wilken speaks of the "modern life style" (*der neuzeitliche Lebensstil*), using also the terms "nervous life style" (76, p. 83) and "materialistic life style" (76, p. 87). He refers to Weber's writings several times, once with the footnote: "Regarding the recognition of the significance of rationality in the modern life style first of all the writings of Max Weber must be mentioned" (76, p. 74).

---

4. These data were kindly supplied to us by Professor Wilken in a personal communication, June 28, 1967. The larger part of the career of Professor Wilken, who was born in 1890, was centered in Freiburg where, since 1952, he was full professor of political science and sociology, until his retirement in 1958.

The following year a monograph by Wilken on neurosis and present-day culture (77) appeared in a series, *Individuum und Gemeinschaft*, edited by Adler, Seif, and Otto Kaus, with chapters on "The Formative Forces of the Modern Life Style," and "The Nervous Basic Attitude as a First but Failing Attempt to Overcome the Modern Life Style."

Most interestingly when in the handbook article he mentions Adler, Wilken uses not "life style," but "life plan"—the term which Adler three years later replaced by life style (see above). Wilken credits Adler for having found that in the case of neurosis "the life plan . . . contains the characteristic roots of the entire disturbance" (76, p. 69).

Adler

The handbook in which Wilken's paper appeared is a work of nearly 900 pages by some 30 contributors, and Wilken mentioned life style on at least 15 pages. Still the term is not to be found in the index. This would indicate that the index was not too carefully made, but certainly also that "life style" was not yet a concept in Individual Psychology. Else such an oversight would be unthinkable. What we do find in the index instead are numerous entries under life plan, life line, and guiding line.

And yet, it is Adler in addition to Wilken who uses the term life style—once, and perhaps for the first time, in the introduction to the handbook, as follows:

It is always a matter of comprehending the individual life style which results in a formal line of movement. We arrive at it when we divest the forms of expression, which we have come to know, of their content, because all comprehensible psychological phenomena are in the last analysis concretizations of the unitary action line of the individual. From the level he reaches in this creative activity of concretizing, and from the extent to which this falls on the side of the generally useful, each individual draws his feeling of personal worth (6, p. vi).

From these circumstances we venture the hypothesis that the work of Wilken, the student and admirer of Weber, was somehow instrumental in Adler's adopting the term life style. This hypothesis is strengthened by the fact that Adler speaks of "individual life style," which would be in distinction to the previous usage of the term as collective life style.

Adler may have become aware of the new term not only through Wilken's writing but also through personal contact. As Wilken recalls today: "At that time I was very active in Individual Psychological circles, gave many talks and . . . had personal contacts and conversations with Adler. Thus it is possible that the phrase of the modern life style, which I used, informally entered the many talks given by Adler. This was actually not remarkable since the concept of life style was not a particular neologism, or was at least not regarded by me as such."[5]

Different Uses of Life Style

The concept of life style can be used in three different ways according to who is the actor or author. This may be an individual; or a group, where the members bear a psychological relationship to each other, and which has stability over time; or a class or category, where the members have only the property in common on the basis of which they are classified. The concept may vary further with regard to content, inclusiveness, and centrality in the theory of the user.

Individual Life Style

This is, of course, the way the term is used in Adlerian psychology, but by other psychologists as well.

Allport describes the individual life style as functionally autonomous and as the highest level of organization of a personality, "the complex propriate organization that determines the 'total posture' of a mature life-system." The life style "evolves gradually in the course of life, and day by day guides and unifies all, or at least many, of a person's transactions with life" (15, p. 237).

Coleman holds that "the individual's pattern of assumptions leads to consistent ways of perceiving, thinking, and acting—to a characteristic *modus operandi* or *life style*" (24, p. 63). "Each individual tends to establish a unique relatively consistent life style. He has a characteristic way of going, thinking, reacting, and growing that tends to distinguish him from everyone else. He puts his personal stamp on every role he plays and every situation he encounters . . . consistent with his self-concept" (23, p. 69). Coleman gives as an example *The Diary of Anne Frank* where "each member is portrayed as behaving in ways consistent with his life style before the episode began" (23, p. 138).

Revers (58) connects individual and generic life style (see below) saying that at first the style of the period shapes the individuality, while the mature personality is so to speak the personalization of the interiorized life style.

5. F. Wilken, personal communication, June 14, 1967.

Group Life Style

Life style can be used collectively in reference to the behavioral and cognitive aspects of a relatively permanent, small group, down to a dyad, where the members are interacting with one another. Life style in this sense belongs to the area of group dynamics.

"Family life style" as used by Danica Deutsch (26, 27) would be an example. It is so to speak the behavioral or action aspect of "family constellation" in the Adlerian sense as explored methodologically by Shulman (64). "Family theme" is a term used by Hess and Handel (39) which Ferreira (31) considers practically equivalent to family life style, while Handel is among authors using life style itself in the generic sense below (36, 56). Finally, "family myth" described by Ferreira (31) would seem to belong here, as part of the family life style.

When Parsons speaks of the style of life of a family he has less the group-dynamic than the classificatory description in mind as he states that the husband's occupation is the primary determiner of the family's style of life and status in the community (54, p. 13).

Erikson, again, touches on the group-dynamic aspect, although only briefly, when he speaks of an infant participating "zestfully in the style of life of his cultural milieu" (29, p. 282). He uses the term also with regard to a loving couple where he talks of a "polarization of the two sexes within a joint life-style" (30, p. 129).[6] Another instance of a dyadic group life style would be what is commonly called folie a deaux.

As in the case of individual life styles, excellent examples and descriptions of group life styles are also found in good literature. Particularly the plays of Chekhov and Ibsen come to mind. Also *The Diary of Anne Frank* could be mentioned in this connection again.

Life Style as a Generic Term

Two kinds of generic uses of life style are possible: (a) referring to relatively natural categories, such as the lower class, and (b) referring to such pure abstractions as the generalized neurotic. The first use is that made by sociologists, while the second is made mostly by psychologists although by sociologists also.

1. The first generic use covers life styles of cultures, subcultures, status or occupational groups, or time-bound subcultures as mentioned by Weber and also by Wilken.

Some authors simply equate culture with life style, as does Rothacker (60), author of the stratification theory of personality (*Schichtentheorie*). He maintains that cultures *are* life styles, emerging from a more primitive state of life-communities (*Lebensgemeinschaften*), and possibly developing into a higher state of cultural styles. Johannes Neumann (51, p. 118), an Adlerian psychotherapist, in a special connection made the analogy that culture is to the larger group what life style is to the individual.

Recent usages of life style pertaining to subcultures are to be found in papers on suburban life style (21, 22), working-class life style (36, 50), and lower-class life style as distinguished from the former (49). Without actually having used the term, a good many of the descriptions from cultural anthropology would also belong here.

2. The second generic use covers the more abstract categories of individuals in everyday life and among the mentally disturbed or problem cases. Regarding the former there are studies on the life style of the workingman's wife (56) and life styles of educated women (34).

Regarding the latter, Adler spoke of "the negative life style" of the patient in general (12, p. 192), "the life style of the compulsion neurotic" (12, p. 137), "the life style of the potential suicide" (19, pp. 323–324), and others. Greatest importance in Adler's system became attributed to the pampered life style which he found common to all neuroses (19, pp. 241–242) and crime, forming the basis of a criminal style of life (10, p. 137). Life style being the central term in Adler's theory, all generalizations about individuals were with respect to life style. Recently Kurt Adler outlined the schizophrenic life style (13).

Life style in the generic sense has come into use also by ego-oriented psychoanalysts. Thus David Shapiro recognizes among neurotics an obsessive-compulsive style, a paranoid style, a hysterical style and an impulsive style (62). Incidentally, Adler had said "What is frequently labeled the ego is nothing more than the style of the individual" (19, p. 175), so that a book by a Freudian ego psychologist on *Neurotic Styles* (62) is almost like a prophesy come true.

These generalized life styles bear a certain similarity to the character sketches of Theophrastus. But these depict "ideal types," not empirical generalizations, as Allport has pointed out (15, pp. 31 & 44) and lack the dynamic, teleological quality. The same goes for types. If, however, a typology includes dynamic principles and is empirically derived, it comes very close to generic life style. Adler actually suggested what might be called a life-style typology. When he spoke of the ruling, leaning, getting, and

---

6. We wish to express our appreciation to Professor M. M. Nawas for having made us aware of the last three references. He also kindly read the finished manuscript and we are indebted to him for valuable suggestions.

avoiding types (19, pp. 167–168) he meant individuals whose styles of living in relationship to others are characterized by one of these four traits.

Content and Range

Among psychologists the concept of style may vary in range from a relatively limited segment to the totality of behavior when it becomes life style. In the restricted range, in respect to individuals, characteristic perceptual styles, also known as cognitive styles, and response styles, as well as complex response styles have been discerned. This area of investigation has been summarized by Stagner under "personality style" (65, pp. 137–155). The amount of current interest in cognitive style can be seen from the index of the *Psychological Abstracts* for 1966 which lists 32 entries under this topic, many referring to dissertations.

The broad range of life style includes cognitive style and response style. Thus according to Coleman life style is "the general pattern of assumptions, motives, cognitive styles, and coping techniques that characterize the behavior of a given individual and give it consistency" (24, p. 664). As Adler's counterpart to cognitive style one may take his "schema of apperception" (19, pp. 181–186), as counterpart to response style or coping techniques, his "law of movement" of the individual (19, pp. 195–196). But at the beginning of one of his books Adler also spoke of "style of acting, thinking and perceiving" as a patient's "way of life" (6a, p. 1). Adler's concepts are, however, more individualized than those currently in greater use.

Among sociologists the term life style itself may refer to such limited areas as cultural tastes and ideology (74); any kind of value orientation (35); "a characteristic way of distributing one's time, one's interest, and one's talent among the common social roles of adult life" (37, p. 333); "attitudes and behavior in the areas of family relationships and consumption patterns" (49, p. 13); or it may approach the broadness of subculture (50).

The concept may also be relatively central in the theory of its user as was certainly the case with Adler, or more peripheral as in the case of Weber. This is to some extent related to the broadness versus the limitation of the concept.

Common Properties of Life Style

In spite of the diversity discussed above, important common properties are to be found in all the uses of life style and even simply, style. By considering these, instead of dwelling on the differences, one is moving toward an eventual, desirable synthesis. The common properties we wish to point out are the unifying, the unique, and the operational aspects.

Unifying Aspect

This is the most important aspect, overshadowing the others by far. Even with regard to cognitive or response styles which are quite particularistic, Stagner comments that they "are the sources of internal consistency and unity . . . Entirely aside from specific percepts or specific responses, the person may show a characteristic *pattern of perceiving* or of responding. . . . Particular perceptual styles and response styles help us comprehend the organized unity of the individual personality" (65, p. 137).

The word "style" includes the characteristic of cutting across ordinary boundaries and uniting what might otherwise be quite separate entities. Thus in the case of Bach, Beethoven and Mozart, if one knows their music at all, one can easily match the musical manuscripts with the composer (80). It is such self-consistency which also characterizes style or life style when used in connection with culture or subculture.

Shapiro, who was mentioned earlier, also includes the unifying aspect in his definition of style. It is "a mode of functioning . . . that is identifiable, in an individual, through a range of his specific acts" (62, p. 1). Shapiro recognizes in a footnote that "this point is emphasized in Alfred Adler's psychology also" (62, p. 17n).

It was indeed Adler's main thesis that life style is the unifying principle on which the various behaviors will depend rather than on other variables. (See the opening section of this paper.)

Thorne, who accepts the Adlerian concept of life style in his system of personality, also emphasizes the self-consistency aspect, of which he was first made aware through Lecky (45). According to Thorne, "The factor which contributes to the internal consistency and totality of behavior is the existence of a life style which organizes a unified approach to the goals of life" (66, p. 68).

Today several studies in different areas and by people of quite diverse convictions, with different understandings of the exact meaning of life style, all support the contention that the life style determines the partial functions of the individual. Sexual behavior will be in accordance with the life style (55, 57), a finding which applies also to homosexual behavior (14, 41). Consumption choices and the use of leisure time will be in accordance with life style (35, 37, 38), as will be the response to mass media (74). Finally, people will grow old and face death in accordance with their life styles (63, 78, 79).

But also methodologically life style is unifying. Allport describes it as a "synoptic concept" which "allows for positivist principles . . . as well as for the basic formulations of existentialism" (15, p. 566).

Unique and Creative Aspects

A second important characteristic of style is a differentiating property. One style is always different from others, although there are similarities between styles. This applies whether the actor is an individual or a group; style is an idiographic concept referring to an irreproducible phenomenon which is sui generis whether it be the creation of a person or of a culture.

As the term was used in connection with artistic creations before it became a term in the social sciences, it always implied originality, spontaneity and creativity on the part of the actor. To illustrate this with an everyday example, a child learns to write according to the cultural model that is put before him, but he varies this spontaneously, developing his own style of handwriting, as a special aspect of his general style. Behavior which is spontaneous and unique involves choice on the part of the actor. And choice is a function of preferences, values, and goals which are the basis for hopes for the future. In this way, style, in anyone's usage, is likely to be associated with a forward-oriented, purposive, value psychology rather than with a causalistic, reductionistic psychology. It would be difficult to think of a robot doing his assigned work in a style of his own (see above).

Operational, Functional and Constancy Aspects

Style is very much tied to operations and actions. It was in the action theory of Weber that the term life style was used first, and it was Adler, who proclaimed a "psychology of use" (19, p. 205), who elevated the term to a central position. The reason may be that style of life lends itself perhaps less to reification than other terms, because it can easily be made into an adverbial phrase in the form of "style of living" as pointed out above. Therefore it fits well into a truly functional psychology, a psychology of use rather than possession. Objective conditions or stimuli will be responded to, will be used, in accordance with the style of living, be it an individual style that is meant or the group style of a culture or subculture. This aspect is well reflected in the definition found in the new Webster International Dictionary as "an individual's typical way of life: his attitudes and their expression in a self-consistent manner as developing from childhood" (72).

Style as an operational characteristic has also an aspect of constancy. If a person would not typically respond in a certain way again and again on different occasions, style would not have the other functions which are attributed to it. For Adler particularly the life style was relatively constant from early childhood on (19, pp. 189–191) which is also reflected in the Webster definition above.

When the Adlerian explores a person's past, it is not so much to find out what happened to him, as it is how he typically responded to situations to which a person with another life style would have responded quite differently. This is also what Thorne means when he says that life style is the principle which accounts "for the observed reliability of behavior" (66, p. 65).

Examples

Let us take two specific instances to show that the above aspects are apparently really common to various life-style conceptions, despite different origins, or that the term life style is likely to be adopted when all these aspects are recognized.

1. Williams, principal author of a book subtitled *Styles of Life and Successful Aging* (79), writes: "The concept of style of life seems inherent in a theory of action defined as meaningful behavior. Action is a series of projects with means related to goals and governed by certain norms. The over-all pattern of the projects and their interrelationships can well be called style" (78, p. 100).

The similarity with Adler regarding the *unifying* aspect is pointed out by the author himself. "We also think of style of life as a unifying principle or, as Adler would put it, as the 'self-consistency' of the actor" (78, p. 102). As to the aspect of *uniqueness and creativity* with its forward and goal orientation, this is represented by Williams when he speaks of "meaningful behavior" in terms of "projects" and "goals," while "the focus throughout was on the social systems of individual actors as they move and evolve through time" (78, p. 100). Regarding the *operational* aspect so important in the Adlerian conception, this is reflected in the statements by Williams of individual actors moving and evolving through time, and that "style can be most readily judged when the individual is faced with major decisions" (78, p. 101).

2. The history of the adaptation of the term life style by one research group (33) is another even more interesting example in that it shows practically the same sequence of steps that Adler had taken. The director of the group is Eli Ginzberg, an economist who has done interdisciplinary research on human resources and manpower for the past three decades. Ginzberg noted first that even sexual behavior depends on the values men live by—which realization on the part of Adler was at the root of his

person's life are patterned—as one of Adler's later books, a collection of child-guidance cases, was entitled *The Pattern of Life* (7). This was followed by Ginzberg's use of the term life plan, until finally life style was adopted—just as with Adler, who eventually substituted for life plan the more comprehensive and more dynamic term.

Ginzberg reports that all along he tried to avoid specialized terms and that he is concerned with man's interaction with his environment, ego development, performance, and, once more, the importance of values in determining behavior. In all this, too, parallels with Adler can be seen. It is most noteworthy that from this common basis the two men quite independently and over a generation apart were led, obviously by the compelling logic of the data themselves, finally to adopt the term life style.

Parallel Constructs

Actually the concept of life style even without the use of the term is in a sense the common property of all clinical psychology where the aim of appraisal is to arrive at a self-consistent understanding of the person studied. According to McArthur the aim of a clinical study is "to build from the data a clinical construct, . . . a special theory applicable to one person, a model of the person . . . a formulation of the premises governing all of S's behavior . . . with which the person being studied had learned to face the world" (46, p. 101). Similarly, the clinician's aim in personality assessment, according to Meehl, is to arrive at an "idiographic conceptualization" of the person (47, p. 139). These statements are not too different from saying that we want to arrive at a formulation of the person's unique and self-consistent life style.

Furthermore, idiographic life-style description is implicit in good literary biography, autobiography and character fiction, as Gilbert (32) has pointed out. This is also the reason why Adler, as quoted above, felt that he had learned much from the great works of literature. He did not analyze these to "discover" what were the forces underneath the actions described, but studied them for their self-consistency and goal directedness.

Finally the mode-of-being or mode-of-existence of the existentialists, mentioned earlier, runs parallel to life style in all its three aspects, as pointed out in several papers (e.g., 67). The unifying, unique and operational aspects of the mode-of-existence can be seen particularly from the description by Van Kaam. According to him, "Existence differentiates itself in various modes-of-existence. . . . Each mode-of-existence integrates various modalities-of-existence such as perceiving, feeling, touching, and thinking" (68, p. 239).

And so we find that Allport treats mode of being-in-the-world and life style quite interchangeably (16, p. 173), and judges that style, although a difficult concept to define, "is highly relevant to the morphogenesis of personality, and as such will have to be dealt with by psychology in the future" (15, p. 566n).

Summary and Conclusion

With the increased general use of the term life style a review of its origin and the variety of its uses appeared called for. The term seems to have been used in modern times first by Max Weber, and was accepted by Adler replacing previous similar terms. Life style has been employed with regard to individuals, groups, or abstract categories of actors, by sociologists and psychologists. The different applications of the term have in common, reference to the unifying functions of the individual or culture; to uniqueness, creativity, value and goal orientation; to operational description; and to individuals or groups conceived as actively shaping their lives through preferences and corresponding choices.

Growing use of the term would indicate that a corresponding concept of man is gaining. That is, an organismic, holistic and purposive conception seems to be gaining over a mechanistic, elementaristic and strictly deterministic conception. Man is increasingly understood as a self-consistent and self-directed unity whose central theme is reflected in all his actions, as forward oriented, purposive, determined by his own values rather than physiological factors, and in interaction with his environment.

In accordance with this development Weber and Adler who both advanced such a conception of man, and incidentally sponsored the term life style, are themselves gaining in recognition. Thus a recent judgment of Weber contends that "Whereas the influence of men like Marx, Nietzsche and Freud . . . appears to have passed its apex, that of Max Weber still seems to be in the ascendancy" (59, p. 6). And of Adler a recent evaluation points out that he "emphasized ego functions and . . . the individual unity of each person. In these two emphases Adler was prophetic of much current thinking" (69, p. 484).[7]

---

7. Adler's increasing recognition has been the subject of a separate review (17).

References

1. Adler, A. *Ueber den nervösen Charakter* (1912). 4th ed. Munich: Bergmann, 1928.

2. Adler, A. Organdialekt (1912). In A. Adler & C. Furtmuller (Eds.), *Heilen und Bilden*. Munich: Reinhardt, 1914. Pp. 130–139.

3. Adler, A. *Praxis und Theorie der Individualpsychologie* (1920). 2nd ed. Munich: Bergmann, 1924.

4. Adler, A. *The practice and theory of Individual Psychology* (1925). Paterson, N.J.: Littlefield, Adams, 1959.

5. Adler, A. *Liebesbeziehungen und deren Storungen*. Vienna: Moritz Perles, 1926.

6. Adler, A. Vorrede. In E. Wexberg (Ed.), *Handbuch der Individualpsychologie*. Vol. I. (1926). Amsterdam: Bonset, 1966. Pp. v–vi.

6a. Adler, A. *Problems of Neurosis* (1929). New York: Harper Torchbooks, 1964.

7. Adler, A. *The pattern of life*. Ed. by W. B. Wolfe. New York: Cosmopolitan Book, 1930.

8. Adler, A. Nochmals—die Einheit der Neurosen. *Int. Z. Indiv. Psychol.*, 1930, 8, 201–216.

9. Adler, A. *Der Sinn des Lebens*. Vienna, Leipzig: Passer, 1933.

10. Adler, A. *Social interest* (1933). Transl. by J. Linton & R. Vaughan. New York: Capricorn Books, 1964.

11. Adler, A. A Note to a clergyman (1933). *J. Indiv. Psychol.*, 1966, 22, 234.

12. Adler, A. *Superiority and social interest*. Evanston, Ill.: Northwestern Univer. Press, 1964.

13. Adler, K. A. Life style in schizophrenia. *J. Indiv. Psychol.*, 1958, 14, 68–72.

14. Adler, K. A. Life style, gender role, and the symptom of homosexuality. *J. Indiv. Psychol.*, 1967, 23, 67–78.

15. Allport, G. W. *Pattern and growth of personality*. New York: Holt, Rinehart & Winston, 1961.

16. Allport, G. W. (Ed.) *Letters from Jenny*. New York: Harcourt, Brace & World, 1965.

17. Ansbacher, H. L. Introduction: the increasing recognition of Adler. In A. Adler, *Superiority and social interest*. Evanston, Ill.: Northwestern Univer. Press, 1964. Pp. 3–19.

18. Ansbacher, H. L. The structure of Individual Psychology. In B. B. Wolman & E. Nagel (Eds.), *Scientific psychology*. New York: Basic Books, 1965. Pp. 340–364.

19. Ansbacher, H. L., & Ansbacher, Rowena R. (Eds.) *The Individual Psychology of Alfred Adler*. New York: Basic Books, 1956.

20. Bartlett, J. *Familiar quotations*. 12th ed. Ed. by C. Morley & Louella D. Everett. Boston: Little, Brown, 1951.

21. Bell, W. Social choice, life styles, and suburban residence. In W. Dobriner (Ed.), *The suburban community*. New York: Putnam, 1958. Pp. 225–242.

22. Berger, B. M. *Working class suburb*. Berkeley, Calif.: Univer. Salif. Press, 1960.

23. Coleman, J. C. *Personality dynamics and effective behavior*. Chicago: Scott, Foresman, 1960.

24. Coleman, J. C. *Abnormal psychology and modern life*. 3rd ed. Chicago: Scott, Foresman, 1964.

25. Daeumling, A. Psychologische Leitbildtheorien. *Psychol. Rundsch.*, 1960, II, 92–108.

26. Deutsch, Danica. Group therapy with married couples: the birth pangs of a new family life style in marriage. *Indiv. Psychologist*, 1967, 4, 56–62.

27. Deutsch, Danica. Family therapy and family life style. *J. Indiv. Psychol.*, 1967, 23, 217–223.

28. Dreikurs, R. The Adlerian approach to therapy. In M. I. Stein (Ed.), *Contemporary psychotherapies*. New York: Free Press of Glencoe, 1961. Pp. 80–94.

28a. Dreikurs, R. The meaning of behavior. *J. Indiv. Psychol.*, 1967, 23, 237. (Abstract)

29. Erikson, E. H. *Childhood and society* (1950). 2nd ed. New York: Norton, 1963.

30. Erikson, E. H. *Insight and responsibility: lectures on the ethical implications of psychoanalytic insight*. New York: Norton, 1964.

31. Ferreira, A. J. Family myth and family life style. *J. Indiv. Psychol.*, 1967, 23, 224–225.

32. Gilbert, A. R. The concept of life style; its background and its psychological significance. *Jahrb. Psychol. Psychother. med. Anthropol.*, 1960, 7, 97–106.

33. Ginzberg, E. Choice of the term "life style" by one research group. *J. Indiv. Psychol.*, 1967, 23, 213–216.

34. Ginzberg, E., et al. *Life styles of educated women*. New York: Columbia Univer. Press, 1966.

35. Hamilton, R. F. The behavior and values of skilled workers. In A. B. Shostak & W. Gomberg (Eds.), *Blue-collar world*. Englewood Cliffs, N.J.: Prentice-Hall, 1964. Pp. 42–57.

36. Handel, G., & Rainwater, L. Persistence and change in working-class life style. In A. B. Shostak & W. Gomberg (Eds.), *Blue-collar world*. Englewood Cliffs, N.J.: Prentice-Hall, 1964. Pp. 36–41.

37. Havighurst, R. J. The nature and values of meaningful free-time activity. In R. W. Kleemeier (Ed.), *Aging and leisure*. New York: Oxford Univer. Press, 1961. Pp. 309–344.

38. Havighurst, R. J., & Feigenbaum, K. Leisure and life style. *Amer. J. Sociol.*, 1959, 64, 396–404.

39. Hess, R. D., & Handel, G. *Family worlds: a psychosocial approach to family life*. Chicago: Univer. Chicago Press, 1959.

40. The hippies. *Time*, July 7, 1967, pp. 18–22.

41. Hooker, Evelyn. Male homosexual life styles and venereal disease. *Publ. Health Serv. Publ.*, No. 997. Proceedings of the World Forum on Syphilis and other Treponematoses, Washington, D.C., September 4–8, 1962. Pp. 431–437.

42. Klages, L. Graphologische Prinzipienlehre. In *Graphol. Monatshefte*. Munich: Ackermann, 1905.

43. Klages, L. Das personliche Leitbild. In *Graphol. Monatshefte*. Munich: Ackermann, 1906.

44. Klages, L. *Graphologie*. Leipzig: Quelle & Meyer, 1932.

45. Lecky, P. *Self-consistency*. 2nd ed. New York: Island Press, 1951.

46. McArthur, C. C. Clinical versus actuarial prediction. In R. F. Berdie (Chm.), *Proc. 1955 Invitational Conf. on Testing Problems*. Princeton, N.J.: Educ. Testing Serv., 1956. Pp. 99–106.

47. Meehl, P. E. Clinical versus acutarial prediction. In R. F. Berdie (Chm.), *Proc. 1955 Invitational Conf. on Testing Problems*. Princeton, N.J.: Educ. Testing Serv., 1967. Pp. 136–141.

48. Miller, G. A. Galanter, E., & Pribram, K. H. *Plans and the structure of behavior.* New York: Holt, 1960.

49. Miller, S. M. The American lower classes: a typological approach. In A. B. Shostak & W. Gomberg (Eds.), *Blue-collar world.* Englewood Cliffs, N.J.: Prentice-Hall, 1964. Pp. 9–23.

50. Miller, S. M., & Riessman, F. The working-class subculture: a new view. In A. B. Shostak & W. Gomberg (Eds.), *Blue-collar world.* Englewood Cliffs, N.J.: Prentice-Hall, 1964. Pp. 24–36.

51. Neumann, J. *Der nervose Charakter und seine Heilung.* Stuttgart: Hippokrates Verlag, 1954.

52. *New York Times,* April 5, 1967, p. 41.

53. Parsons, T. Introduction. In M. Weber, *The theory of social and economic organization.* New York: Oxford Univer. Press, 1947. Pp. 3–86.

54. Parsons, T., & Bales, R. F. *Family, socialization and interaction process.* Glencoe, Ill.: Free Press, 1955.

55. Rainwater, L. Some aspects of lower class sexual behavior. *J. soc. Issues,* 1966, 22, 96–108.

56. Rainwater, L., Coleman, R. P., & Handel, G. *Workingman's wife: her personality, world and life style.* Dobbs Ferry, N.Y.: Oceana Publications, 1959.

57. Reiss, I. L. Social class and premarital sexual permissiveness: a re-examination. *Amer. sociol. Rev.,* 1965, 30, 747–756.

58. Revers, W. J. Uber das Problem des Stils im personlichen Lebenslauf. *Studium Generale,* 1955, 8, 151ff.

59. Roth, G., & Berger, B. M. Max Weber and the organized society. *N.Y. Times Book Rev.,* April 3, 1966, pp. 6, 44 & 45.

60. Rothacker, E. *Probleme der Kulturanthropologie.* 2nd ed. Bonn: Bouvier, 1948.

61. Ruch, F. L. *Psychology and life.* 7th ed. Glenview, Ill.: Scott, Foresman, 1967.

62. Shapiro, D. *Neurotic styles.* New York: Basic Books, 1965.

63. Shneidman, E. S. Orientations toward death: a vital aspect of the study of lives. In R. W. White (Ed.), *The study of lives: essays on personality in honor of Henry A. Murray.* New York: Atherton, 1963. Pp. 200–227.

64. Shulman, B. H. The family constellation in personality diagnosis. *J. Indiv. Psychol.,* 1962, 18, 35–47.

65. Stagner, R. *Psychology of personality.* 3rd ed. New York: McGraw-Hill, 1961.

66. Thorne, F. C. *Personality: a clinical eclectic viewpoint.* Brandon, Vermont: Journal of Clin. Psychol., 1961.

67. van Dusen, W. Adler and existence analysis. *J. Indiv. Psychol.,* 1959, 15, 100–111.

68. Van Kaam, A. *Existential foundations of psychology.* Pittsburgh: Duquene Univer. Press, 1966.

69. Watson, R. I. *The great psychologists: from Aristotle to Freud.* Philadelphia: Lippincott, 1963.

70. Weber, M. *Essays in sociology.* Trans. & edited by H. H. Gerth & C. W. Mills. New York: Oxford Univer. Press, 1946.

71. Weber, M. *The theory of social and economic organization.* Transl. by A. M. Henderson & T. Parsons; edited by T. Parsons. New York: Oxford Univer. Press, 1947.

72. *Webster's third new international dictionary.* Springfield, Mass.: Merriam, 1961.

73. Wexberg, E. (Ed.) *Handbuch der Individualpsychologie* (1926). Amsterdam: Bonset, 1966. 2 vols.

74. Wilensky, H. L. Mass society and mass culture: interdependence or independence? *Amer. sociol. Rev.,* 1964, 29, 173–197.

75. Wilken, F. *Grundzuge einer personalistischen Werttheorie.* Jena, 1924.

76. Wilken, F. Staats- und Sozialwissenschaften. In E. Wexberg (Ed.), *Handbuch der Individualpsychologie.* Vol. 2 (1926). Amsterdam: Bonset, 1966. Pp. 67–96.

77. Wilken, F. *Die nervose Erkrankung als sinnvolle Erscheinung unseres gegenwartigen Kulturzeitraums: eine Untersuchung uber die Storungen unseres heutigen Soziallebens.* Munich: Bergmann, 1927.

78. Williams, R. H. A concept of style of life induced from a study of aging. *J. Indiv. Psychol.,* 1966, 22, 100–103.

79. Williams, R. H., & Wirths, Claudine G. *Lives through the years: styles of life and successful aging.* Foreword by T. Parsons. New York: Atherton Press, 1965.

80. Wolff, W. *The expression of personality.* New York: Harper, 1943. (15 above, pp. 388–389, 474).

Life Style Identification and Assessment

Manford Sonstegard

An individual's character is the manifestation of a plan for life which developed during childhood. The pattern of life which is formulated by age four or five is adhered to for life. Adler (1935) wrote, "Character traits are the external aspects of the relationship of an individual to the problem of the outside world, and are to be regarded as indexes to how the style of life of a certain individual will express itself in reaction to an external stimulus or to a stimulus which may even originate within himself."

Neither does the strategy of life just occur, nor does it develop from peculiarities or isolated experiences. The scheme for living emerges by repetition of the difficulties an individual encounters in the family which is the first group in which he attempts to find a place. Later the social environment plays an equally vital role in establishing the life plan. "Each individual will find special ways and means which appear to be serviceable for his special plan. Out of the individual's special life plan develops the life style which characterizes him and everything he does" (Dreikurs, 1953).

The individual may pursue a great variety of immediate and sometimes temporary goals with reference to his life style. Basic goals form the foundations for his personality. Immediate goals are the individual's conception of finding a place in society. They may be "fictitious" as Adler (1956) points out. The individual is not aware of his basic concepts nor his personal bias, that is, his fictitious goals. Nevertheless, his actions are congruent with the goals he has set for himself.

Although the individual is unaware of the goals he pursues, his life style may be recognized. The identification may be made by observing the individual in action, exploring the family constellation, and eliciting the early recollections.

Through direct observation it is not difficult to recognize the goals of behavior. Actions are usually in harmony with his goals (Grunwald, 1970). As Dreikurs (1957) points out, "The individual may be convinced that he does not want what he brings about, but then he is merely not aware of the objectives he sets for himself. It is more difficult to recognize his basic goals which are the foundation of his life style, the fictitious goals. They represent a scheme of action by which the individual hopes to find his place in society. A set of convictions about himself and life which underlie his social movements."

The exploration of the family constellation and the interaction of the individual with all the members of his family during early childhood permits a clear picture of the pattern of life he has formulated. Birth order is the primary element of the family constellation clarifying an immediate impression of the grouping within the family and the position the individual occupies. His interpretation of his environment will be different if he is the first, second, middle, or youngest child, the only girl among boys, or vice versa. The individual's perception of life depends upon the interpersonal relationship between members of the family and is not exclusively dependent on the birth order. Each becomes different depending upon who among the siblings is the competitor, who is the most different in character, temperament, and interest. The individual will withdraw in the area in which the competitor succeeds. He moves in to fill the vacuum where another fails. The character traits of each child express the action he takes to find a place in the family, the interactions that take place, and the manner in which they influence each other.

The oldest, for example, generally strives to stay in first place and to push the other siblings down, especially the second born. This appears to be verified by research. Galton (1874) pointed out that first born children were over-represented among eminent men of science. Others have found a larger number of first-borns attaining better grades in high school (Schachter, 1963). Smelser and Steward (1968) concluded from their study that the finding of researchers that more first-borns attending college was not a phenomenon of birth order as such, "but instead an effect, first of all, of some interaction of birth order, sex of child, and sex of siblings." The

Manford Sonstegard, Life Style Identification and Assessment, *Individual Psychologist*, 10(2), 1973, 1–4. Reprinted from the *Individual Psychologist* by permission of the publisher.

findings of Bragg (1970) support other findings in showing that an elder sibling acts as an intellectual depressant on the later born, especially if he is of the opposite sex. Bragg postulates on the basis of his data that "if the older sibling is of the opposite sex, the second born will label academic behavior sex-role inappropriate for himself." For example, a second born male seeing his older sister studying will come to label studying as "feminine" behavior. In consequence he will attempt to select a "masculine" role which excludes or reduces such "feminine" behavior as study.

"Thus, it appears that from the moment of birth the child acts, thinks, and feels in accordance with how he experiences or perceives his world, and the way in which he perceives his world is to him reality. We must remember that it is not the position in the family sequence that is the decisive factor but how the individual interprets his position" (Pepper, 1971).

The early recollections can provide an immediate insight into the individual's life style. They indicate the convictions toward life which he has developed and maintained since childhood. The individual remembers only the incidents that are consistent with his idea of life (Mosak, 1971; Nikelly and Verger, 1971).

"Thus his memories," wrote Adler (1931), "represent his 'Story of My Life,' a story he repeats to himself to warn him or comfort him, to keep him concentrated on his goal, to prepare him by means of past experiences, to meet the future with an already tested style of action."

Early recollections have the advantage, as a projective technique, of being completely unstructured. The individual is asked, "How far back can you remember? Think as far back as you can and tell your earliest memory when you were a child."

Early recollections have been a subject of interest since 1899 when G. Stanley Hall wrote a paper entitled "Notes on Early Memories." Research to support life style formulations based on early recollections as reliably communicable to professional workers is comparatively recent. Purcell (1952), from his experimental study, concluded that there was a general support for Adler's views on early memories. Ferguson (1964) concluded from her investigation that it was clear "that life style formulation derived from early recollections are not just spurious idiosyncratic products of the clinician but are reliably communicable to a wide range of other professional workers, even to those whose own frame of reference is not Adlerian."

The psychologist has at his disposal three techniques for the identification and assessment of the individual's life style. Through the observation of behavior, analysis of family constellation and examination of early recollections, the clinician gains insight into the individual's intentions and can disclose his mistaken goals.

Summary

The life style is identified and assessed by investigating the individual's family constellation and by interpreting his early recollections. Birth order is the primary element of the family constellation. It presents an immediate impression of the grouping within the family and the position the individual occupies within it. His interpretation of his environment will be different if he is the first, second, middle, or youngest child, the only girl among boys, or vice versa. The individual's perception of life depends upon the interpersonal relationships between members of the family and is not exclusively dependent on birth order. Each varies depending upon whom among the siblings is the competitor, who is the most different in character, temperament, and interest. The individual will withdraw in the area in which the competitor succeeds. He moves in to fill the vacuum where another fails. The character traits of each child express the action he takes to find a place in the family, the interactions that take place, and the manner in which they influence each other.

Early recollections provide an immediate insight into the individual's life style. Another advantage is that it is the only projective technique which is completely unstructured. From the individual's early recollections one can determine the conclusions which he draws concerning his present situation. He draws from the innumerable experiences of his early childhood only those that are in harmony with his present outlook on life.

Bibliography

Adler, A. Prevention of neurosis. *International Journal of Individual Psychology.* 1935, 1.

Adler, A. The Individual Psychology of Alfred Adler. Edited by H. L. and Rowena R. Ansbacher. New York: Plastic Books, 1956.

Adler, A. *What Life Should Mean to You.* New York: Grosset and Dunlap, 1931.

Bragg, B. W. Academic primogeniture and sex-role contrast. *Journal of Individual Psychology.* 1971, 26, 106–196.

Dreikurs, R. *Fundamentals of Adlerian Psychology.* Chicago: Alfred Adler Institute, 1935.

Dreikurs, A. Group psychotherapy from the point of view of Adlerian Psychology. *The International Journal of Group Psychotherapy.* 1957, 7.

Ferguson, E. D. The use of early recollections for assessing life styles and diagnosing psychopathology. *Journal of Projective Techniques and Personality Assessment.* 1964, 28, 403–412.

Galton, F. *English Men of Science: Their Nature and Nurture.* London: MacMillian, 1974.

Grunwald, B. How the group helped a discouraged boy. *Individual Psychologist.* 1970, 7, 14–26.

Hall, G. S. Notes on early memories. Pedagogical Seminar. 1899, 6, 485–512.

Mosak, H. Life style. *In* Nikelly, A. (Ed.) *Techniques for Behavior Change.* Springfield, Illinois; Charles C. Thomas, 1971.

Nikelly, A. and D. Verger. *In* Nikelly, A. (Ed.) *Techniques for Behavior Change.* Springfield, Illinois; Charles C. Thomas, 1971.

Pepper, F. C. Birth order. *In* Nikelly, A. (Ed.) *Techniques for Behavior Change.* Springfield, Illinois; Charles C. Thomas, 1971.

Purcell, K. Memory and psychological security. *Journal of Abnormal Social Psychology.* 1952, 47, 440–443.

Schachter, S. Birth order, eminence and higher education. *American Sociological Review.* 1963, 28, 756–757.

Smelser, W. T. and L. H. Stewart. Where are the siblings: A re-evaluation of the relationship between birth order and college attendance. *Sociometry.* 1968, 31, 294–303.

Position in Family Constellation Influences Life Style

Alfred Adler

It is a common fallacy to imagine that children of the same family are formed in the same environment. Of course there is much which is the same for all children in the same home, but the psychic situation of each child is individual and differs from that of others, because of the order of their succession.

There has been some misunderstanding of my custom of classification according to position in the family. It is not, of course, the child's number in the order of successive births which influences his character, but the *situation* into which he is born and the way in which he *interprets* it. Thus, if the eldest child is feeble-minded or suppressed, the second child may acquire a style of life similar to that of an eldest child; and in a large family, if two are born much later than the rest, and grow up together separated from the older children, the elder of these may develop like a first child. This also happens sometimes in the case of twins.

Position of the First Child

The first child has the unique position of having been the only one at the beginning of his life. Being thus the central interest he is generally spoiled. In this he resembles the only child, and spoiling is almost inevitable in both cases. The first child, however, usually suffers an important change of situation being dethroned when the second baby is born. The child is generally quite unprepared for this change, and feels that he has lost his position as the center of love and attention. He then comes into great tension for he is far from his goal and there begins a striving to regain favor. He uses all the means by which he has hitherto attracted notice. Of course he would like to go the best way about it, to be beloved for his goodness; but good behavior is apt to pass unnoticed when everyone is busied with the new-comer. He is then likely to change his tactics and to resort to old activities which have previously attracted attention—even if it was unfavorable attention.

If intelligent, he acts intelligently, but not necessarily in harmony with the family's demands. Antagonism, disobedience, attacks on the baby, or even attempts to play the part of a baby, compel the parents to give renewed attention to his existence. A spoiled child must have the spotlight upon himself, even at the cost of expressing weakness or imitating a return to babyhood. Thus, under the influence of the past, he attains his goal in the present by unsuitable means; suddenly showing inability to function alone, needing assistance in eating and excretion and requiring constant watching, or compelling solicitude by getting into danger and terrifying the parents. The appearance of such characteristics as jealousy, envy, or egotism has an obvious relation to the outside circumstances, but he may also indulge in—or prolong—illnesses such as asthma and whooping cough. The tension in certain types (depending upon the bodily organization) may produce headache, migraine, stomach trouble, petit mal, or hysterical chorea. Slighter symptoms are evidenced in a tired appearance and a general change of behavior for the worse, with which the child impresses his parents. Naturally, the later the rival baby is born, the more intelligible and understandable will the methods appear which the first child uses in his change of behavior. If dethroned very early, the eldest child's efforts are largely "instinctive" in character. The style of his striving will in any case be conditioned by the reaction of others in the environment and his evaluation of it. If, for instance, the dethroned child finds that fighting does not pay, he may lose hope, become depressed, and score a success by worrying and frightening the parents. After learning that such ways are successful for him he will resort to ever more subtle uses of misfortune to gain his end.

Alfred Adler, Position in Family Constellation Influences Life Style, *International Journal of Individual Psychology*, 3(3), 1937, 211-227. By permission of Sydney M. Roth, publisher.

The type of activity which in later life will be based on the prototype was shown in the case of a man who became afraid to swallow for fear of choking. Why did he select this symptom instead of another? The patient had an immediate social difficulty in the behavior of an intimate friend, who attacked him violently. Both the patient and his wife had come to the conclusion that he must put up with it no longer, but he did not feel strong enough to face the struggle. Upon inquiry into his childhood, it appeared that he had had such a difficulty in connection with swallowing before. He was the eldest child, and had been surpassed by his younger brother, but he had at that time been able, by means of difficulty in eating, to make his father and mother watch over him. Now faced with a personal defeat in later life, and not knowing what to do about it, he fell back upon this old line of defense, as though it might make someone watch over him and help him.

Effects of Dethronement

The dethronement of the first child by another may make it turn away from the mother towards the father, and a very critical attitude towards the mother will then persist ever after. A person of this type is always afraid of being "pushed back" all through life; and we notice that in all his affairs he likes to make one step forward and then one backward, so that nothing decisive can happen. He always feels justified in fearing that a favorable situation will change. Towards all the three life-questions he will take up a hesitative attitude, with certain problem behavior and neurotic tendencies. Problem behavior and symptoms will be felt by him to be a help and a security. He will approach society, for example, with a hostile attitude; he may constantly be changing his occupation; and in his erotic life he may experience failure in functioning, and may show polygamous tendencies—if he falls in love with one person he very quickly falls in love with another. Dubious and unwilling to decide anything, he becomes a great procrastinator. I met a very perfect example of this type once, and his earliest remembrance was this: "At three years of age I caught scarlet fever. By mistake my mother gave me carbolic acid for a gargle, and I nearly died." He had a younger sister who was the favorite of his mother. Later in life this patient developed a curious fantasy of a young girl ruling and bullying an older one. Sometimes he imagined her riding the old woman like a horse.

First Child May Keep Position

The eldest child may, however, be so firmly fixed in the parents' favor that he cannot be supplanted. This may be either by virtue of his own good native endowment and development, or because of the second child's inferiority, if the latter is ugly, organically handicapped, or badly brought up. In such a case it is the second child who becomes the problem, and the eldest may have a very satisfactory development, as in the following case:

Of two brothers, differing four years in age, the elder had been much attached to the mother, and when the younger was born the father had been ill for some time. Caring for the father took the entire time and most of the attention of the mother. The elder boy, trained in friendship and obedience to her, tried to help and relieve her, and the younger boy was put into the care of a nurse, who spoiled him. This situation lasted for some years, so that the younger child had no reasonable chance to compete with the elder for the love of the mother; and he soon abandoned the useful side of life, and became wild and disobedient. His behavior became still worse four years later, when a little sister was born, to whom the mother was able to devote herself owing to the death of the father. Thus twice excluded from the mother's attention and spoiled by the nurse, this second child turned out to be the worst pupil in his class, while the elder boy was always the best. Feeling hopelessly handicapped in competition with his brother, unloved at home, and reproached at the school (from which he was finally expelled), this second son could find no goal in life but to dominate his mother by worrying her. Being physically stronger than either the brother or sister, he took to tyrannizing over them. He trifled away his time, and at puberty he began to waste money and to incur debts. His honest and well-meaning parent, provided a very strict tutor for him who did not, of course, grasp the situation, and dealt with it superficially by punishments. The boy grew into a man who strove to get rich quickly and easily. He fell an easy prey to unscrupulous advisers, followed them into fruitless enterprises, and not only lost his money but involved his mother in his dishonorable debts.

The facts of the case clearly showed that all the courage this man ever displayed resulted from his unsatisfied desire to conquer. He played a queer game from time to time, espeically when things went against him. His nurse was now an old woman, earning her living in the family as a superior servant; she still worshipped the second boy and always interceded for him in his numerous scrapes. The odd sport in which he indulged was to lock her in a room with him and make her play at soldiers with him, commanding her to march, to fall and to jump up again at his orders; and sometimes he quickened her obedience by beating her with a stick. She always obeyed although she screamed and resisted.

This singular sport revealed what he really wanted, the completest domination in the easiest way. Some writers would describe this as sadistic conduct, but I demur at the use of a word which implies a sexual interest, for I could discover nothing of the kind in it. In sexual matters the man was practically normal, except that he changed his mates too frequently and always chose inferiors. Genuine sadism itself is a domineering tendency availing itself of the sexual urge for its expression, owing to the discouragement of the individual in other spheres.

In the end this man brought himself into very bad circumstances, while the elder brother became very successful and highly respected.

Attitude of Eldest Toward Authority

The eldest child, partly because he often finds himself acting as representative of the parental authority, is usually a great believer in power and the laws. The intuitive perception of this fact is shown in the ancient and persistent custom of primogeniture. It is often observable in literature. Thus Theodore Fontane wrote of his perplexity at his father's pleasure in hearing that ten thousand Poles had defeated twenty thousand Russians. His father was a French emigrant who had sided with the Poles, but to the writer it was an inconceivable idea that the stronger could be beaten; he felt that the status quo should be preserved and that might must, and ought to, succeed. This was because Theodore Fontane was a first child. In any case the eldest child is readier than others to recognize power, and likes to support it. This is shown in the lives of scientists, politicians, and artists, as well as in those of simpler people. Even if the person is a revolutionary we find him harboring a conservative tendency, as in the case of Robespierre.

Position of Second Child

The second child is in a very different situation, never having had the experience of being the only one. Though he is also petted at first, he is never the sole center of attention. From the first, life is for him more or less of a race; the first child sets the pace, and the second tries to surpass him. What results from competition between two such children depends on their courage and self-confidence. If the elder becomes discouraged he will be in a serious situation, especially if the younger is really strong and outstrips him.

If the second child loses hope of equality he will try to *shine* more rather than to *be* more. That is, if the elder is too strong for him, the younger will tend to escape to the useless side of life. This is shown in many cases of problem behavior in children where laziness, lying or stealing begins to pave the way towards neurosis, crime, and self-destruction.

As a rule, however, the second child is in a better position than the first. His pacemaker stimulates him to effort. Also, it is a common thing for the first child to hasten his own dethronement by fighting against it with envy, jealousy and truculence, which lower him in the parental favor. It is when the first child is brilliant that the second child is in the worst situation.

But the elder child is not always the worst sufferer, even when dethroned. I saw this in the case of a girl who had been the center of attention and extremely spoiled until she reached the age of three, when a sister was born. After the birth of her sister she became very jealous and developed into a problem-child. The younger sister grew up with sweet and charming manners, and was much the more beloved of the two. But when this younger sister came to school the situation was not to her taste; she was no longer spoiled and, being unprepared to encounter difficulties, was frightened and tried to withdraw. To escape defeat both in fact and in appearance, she adopted a device very common among the discouraged—she never finished anything she was doing, so that it always escaped final judgment, and she wasted as much time as possible. We find that time is the great enemy of such discouraged people for, under the pressure of the requirements made on them by social living, they feel as if time were persecuting them continually with the question, "How will you use me?" Hence their strange efforts to "kill time" with silly activities. This girl always came late and postponed every action. She did not antagonize anyone, even if reproved, but her charm and sweetness, which were maintained as before, did not prevent her from being a greater worry and burden than her fighting sister.

When the elder sister became engaged to be married the younger sister was desperately unhappy. Though she had won the first stage of the race with her rival by gentleness and obedience, she had given up in the later stages of school and social life. She felt her sister's marriage as a defeat, and that her only hope of regaining ground would be to marry also. However, she had not courage enough to choose a suitable partner, and automatically sought a second-best. First she fell in love with a man suffering seriously from tuberculosis. Can we regard this as a step forward? Does it contradict her preestablished custom of leaving every task unfinished? Not at all. The poor health of her lover and her parents' natural resistance to the match were sure causes of delay and frustration. She preferred an element of impossibility in her choice. Another scarcely eligible partner appeared later in her life, in a man thirty years older than herself. He was senile, but did not die as the previous one had done, and the marriage took place. However, it was not a great success for her, as the attitude of hopelessness in which she had trained herself did not allow her to undertake any useful activity. It also inhibited her sexual life, which she considered disgusting, feeling humiliated and soiled by it. She used her usual methods to evade love and postpone relations at the appropriate times. She did not quite succeed in this, however, and became pregnant, which she regarded as another hopeless state, and from that time onward not only rejected caresses but complained that she felt soiled, and began to wash and clean all day long. She not only washed herself, but cleaned everything that had been touched by her husband, by the maid servant or the visitors, including furniture, linen, and shoes. Soon she allowed no one to touch any of the objects in her room, and lived under the stress of a neurosis—in this case, a washing-compulsion. Thus she was excused from the solution of her problems, and attained a very lofty goal of superiority—she felt more fastidiously clean than anyone else.

Exaggerated striving for a lofty goal of high distinctiveness is well expressed in the neurosis of "washing-compulsion." As far as I have been able to ascertain, this illness is always used as a means of avoiding sexual relations by a person who feels that sex is "dirty." Invariably it gives the fantastic compensation of feeling cleaner than everybody else.

However, due to his feeling life to be a race, the second child usually trains himself more stiffly and, if his courage holds, is well on the way to overcome the eldest on his own ground. If he has a little less courage he will choose to surpass the eldest in another field, and if still less, he will become more critical and antagonistic than usual, not in an objective but in a personal manner. In childhood this attitude appears in relation to trifles: he will want the window shut when the elder opens it, turn on the light when the other wants it extinguished, and be consistently contrary and opposite.

This situation is well described in the Bible story of Esau and Jacob, where Jacob succeeds in usurping the privileges of the eldest. The second child lives in a condition like that of an engine under a constantly excessive head of steam. It was well expressed by a little boy of four, who cried out, weeping, "I am so unhappy because I can *never* be as old as my brother."

The fact that children repeat the psychic behavior of older brothers and sisters and of parents is, by some writers, attributed to an "instinct" of imitation or to "identification" of the self with another; but it is explained better when we see that a child imitates only that kind of behavior which he finds to be a successful way of asserting an equality which is denied to him on other grounds. Psychic resemblances to the conduct of ancestors or even of savages do not signify that the pattern of psychic reaction is hereditary, but that many individuals use the same means of offense and defense in similar situations. When we find so much resemblance between all first children, all second, and all youngest children, we may well ask what part is left for heredity to play in determining those resemblances. Thus, as psychologists we have also not sufficient evidence to accept the theory that the mental development of the individual ought to repeat the development of the race of mankind in successive stages.

In his later life, the second child is rarely able to endure the strict leadership of others or to accept the idea of "eternal laws." He will be much more inclined to believe, rightly or wrongly, that there is no power in the world which cannot be overthrown. Beware of his revolutionary subtleties! I have known quite a few cases in which the second child has availed himself of the strangest means to undermine the power of ruling persons or traditions. Not everybody, certainly not these rebels themselves, would easily agree with my view of their behavior. For though it is possible to endanger a ruling power with slander, there are more insidious ways. For example, by means of excessive praise one may idealize and glorify a man or a method until the reality cannot stand up to it. Both methods are employed in Mark Antony's oration in "Julius Caesar." I have shown elsewhere how Dostoievsky made masterly use of the latter means, perhaps unconsciously, to undermine the pillars of old Russia. Those who remember his representation of Father Zosima in "The Brothers Karamazov," and who also recall the fact that he was a second son, will have little difficulty agreeing with my suggestion regarding the influence played by position in the family.

I need hardly say that the style of life of a second child, like that of the first, may also appear in another child—one in a different chronological position in the family—if the *situation* is of a similar pattern.

Situation of Youngest Child

The youngest child is also a distinct type, exhibiting certain characteristics of style which we seldom fail to find. He has always been the baby of the family, and has never known the tragedy of being dispossessed by a younger, which is more or less the fate of all other children. In this respect his situation is a favored one, and his education is often relatively better, as the economic position of the family is likely to be more secure in its later years. The grown-up children not infrequently join with the parents in spoiling the youngest child, who is thus likely to be too much indulged. On the other hand, the youngest may also be too much stimulated by elders—both mistakes are well known to our educationists. In the former case (of over-indulgence) the child will strive throughout life to be supported by others. In the latter case the child will rather resemble a second child, proceeding competitively, striving to overtake all those who set the pace for him, and in many cases failing to do so. Often, therefore, he looks for a field of activity remote from that of the other members of the family—in which case, I believe, he gives a sign of hidden cowardice. If the family is commercial, for instance, the youngest often inclines to art or poetry; if scientific, he wants to be a salesman. I have remarked elsewhere that many of the most successful men of our time were youngest children, and I am convinced this is also the case in any other age. In biblical history we find a remarkable number of youngest children among the leading characters, such as David, Saul, and Joseph. The story of Joseph is a particularly good example, and illustrates many of the views we have advanced. His younger brother Benjamin was seventeen years his junior and, therefore, played little part in Joseph's development. Joseph's psychological position, therefore, was that of a youngest child.

It is interesting to note how well Joseph's brethren understood his dreams. More precisely, I should say that they understood the feeling and emotion of the dreamer, a point to which I shall return later. The purpose of a dream is not to be understood but to create a mood and a tension of feeling.

In the fairy tales of all ages and peoples the youngest child plays the role of a conqueror. I infer that in earlier times, when both circumstances and men's apprehension of them were simpler, it was easier to collect experiences and to understand the coherent current of the life of the latest-born. This traditional grasp of character survives in folk-lore when the actual experiences are forgotten.

A strange case of the type of youngest child who is spoiled, which I have already given elsewhere, is that of a man with a "begging" style of life. I found another such case in that of a physician who was having difficulties with his mouth and was fearful of cancer. For twenty years he had been unable to swallow normally and could take only liquid food. He had recently had a dental plate made for him, which he was continually pushing up and down with his tongue, a habit which caused pain and soreness of the tongue, so that he feared he was developing cancer.

He was the youngest of a family of three, with two older sisters, and had been weakly and much indulged. At the age of forty he could eat only alone or with his sisters. This is a clear indication that he was comfortable only in his favorite situation—of being spoiled by the sisters. Every approach to society had been difficult for him. He had no friends, and only a few associates whom he met weekly in a restaurant. His attitude towards the three questions of life being one of fear and trembling, we can understand that his tension when with other people made him unable to swallow food. He lived in a kind of stage fright, fearful that he was not making a sufficiently good impression.

This man answered the second life-question (that of occupation) with tolerable competence, because his parents had been poor and he could not live without earning, but he suffered exceedingly in his profession, and nearly fainted when he had to take his examinations. His ambition, as a general practitioner, was to obtain a position with a fixed salary, and, later on, a pension. This great attraction to a safe official position is a sign of a feeling of insecurity. People with a deep sense of inadequacy commonly aspire to the "safe job." For years he gave himself up to his symptoms. When he became older he lost some of his teeth, and decided to have a plate made, which became the occasion of the development of his latest symptom.

When he came to me, the patient was sixty years of age, and was still living in the care of his two sisters. Both were suffering from their age, and it was clear to me that this man, aging, and spoiled by two unmarried and much older women, was facing a new situation. He was very much afraid his sisters would die. What should he do in that case—he who needed to be continually noticed and watched over? He had never been in love, for he could never find a woman whom he could trust with his fragile happiness! How could he believe that anyone would spoil him as his mother and older sisters had done. It was easy to guess the form of his sexuality—masturbation, and some petting affairs with girls. But recently an older woman had wanted to marry him; and he wished to appear more pleasant and attractive in behavior. The beginning of a struggle seemed imminent, but his new dental plate came to the rescue. In the nick of time he became anxious about contracting cancer of the tongue.

He himself, as a doctor, was very much in doubt about the reality of this cancer. The many surgeons and physicians he consulted all tried to dissuade him from belief in it; but he persisted in his uncertainty, continued to press his tongue against the plate until it hurt; then he consulted another doctor.

Such preoccupations—"overvalued ideas," as Wernicke calls them—are carefully cherished in the arrangement of a neurosis. The patient shies away from the right objective by fixing his glances more and more firmly upon a point somewhere off a good, productive course. He does this in order to swerve out of a direction which is beginning to be indicated by logical necessity. The logical solution of his problem would be antagonistic to his style of life, and as the style of life rules (since it is the only way of approach to life the individual has learned), he has to establish emotions and feelings which will support his life-style and will insure his escape.

In spite of the fact that this man was sixty years old, the only logical solution was to find a trustworthy substitute for his spoiling sisters before their departure. His distrustful mind could not rise to the hope of achieving this possibility; nor could his doubts be dissipated by logic, because he had built up throughout his life a definite resistance to marriage. Because it improved his appearance, the dental plate should have been a help towards marriage but he made it into an insuperable impediment.

In the treatment of this case it was useless to attack the belief in the cancer. When he understood the coherence of his behavior the patient's symptoms were very much alleviated. The next day he told me of a dream: "I was sitting in the house of a third sister at a birthday celebration of her thirteen-year-old son. I was entirely healthy, felt no pain, and could swallow anything." But this dream was related to an episode in his life which took place fifteen years before. Its meaning is very obvious: "If only I were fifteen years younger." Thus is the style maintained.

Difficulties of Only Child

The only child also has his typical difficulties. Retaining the center of the stage without effort, and generally pampered, he forms a style of life that calls for his being supported by others and at the same time ruling them. Very often he grows up in an intimate environment. The parents may be fearful people and afraid to have more children. Sometimes the mother, neurotic before this advent, does not feel equal to rearing more children, and develops such behavior that everyone must feel, "It is a blessing that this woman has no more children." Birth control may absorb much of the attention of the family, in which case we may infer tension, and that the two parents are united to carry on their life in anxiety. The care then devoted to the only child never ceases by day or night, and often impresses the child with a belief that it is an almost mortal danger not to be watched and guarded. Such children often grow up cautious, and sooner or later they may often become successful and gain the esteem and attention they desire. But if they come into wholly different conditions where life is difficult for them, they may show striking insufficiency.

Only children are often sweet and affectionate, and later in life they may develop charming manners in order to appeal to others, because they have trained themselves this way both in early life and later. They are usually closer to the more indulgent parent, which is generally the mother; and in some cases develop a hostile attitude towards the other parent.

The proper upbringing of an only child is not easy, but it is possible for parents to understand the problem and to solve it correctly. We do not regard the only child's situation as dangerous, but we find that, in the absence of the best educational methods, very bad results frequently occur which would have been avoided if there had been brothers and sisters.

Case of Homosexual Development

I will give a case of the development of an only child, a boy whose attachment was entirely to the mother. The father was of no importance in the family; he contributed materially but was obviously without interest in the child. The mother was a dressmaker who worked at home, and the little boy spent all his time with her, sitting or playing beside her. He played at sewing, imitating his mother's activity, and ultimately became very very proficient in it, but he never took any part in boys' games. The mother left the house each day at five P.M. to deliver her work, and returned punctually at six. During that time the boy was left alone with an older girl cousin, and played with sewing materials. He became interested in timepieces, because he was always looking for his mother's return. He could tell the time when he was only three years old.

The cousin played games with him in which she was the bridegroom and he was the bride, and it is noteworthy that he looked more like a girl than she did. When he came to school he was quite unprepared to associate with boys, but he was able to establish himself as a favored exception, for others liked his mild and courteous disposition. He began to approach his goal of superiority by being attractive, especially so to boys and men. At fourteen years of age he acted the part of a girl in a school play. The audience had not the slightest doubt that he was a girl; a young fellow began to flirt with him and he was much pleased to have excited such admiration.

He had worn girlish dress during his first four years, and until the age of ten he did not know whether he was a boy or a girl. When his sex was explained to him he began to masturbate, and in his fantasy he soon connected sexual desire with what he had felt when boys touched him or kissed him. To be admired and wooed was his goal in life; to this end he accommodated all his characteristics in such a way that he might be admired especially by boys. His older cousin was the only girl he had known, and she was gentle and sweet, but she had played the man's role in their games and otherwise she had ruled him like his mother. A great feeling of inferiority was his legacy from his mother's overindulgent and excessive care. She had married late, at the age of thirty-eight, and she did not wish to have more children by the husband she disliked. Her anxiety, then was doubtless of earlier origin, and her late marriage indicative of a hesitant attitude to life. Very strict in sexual matters, she wanted her child to be educated in ignorance of sex.

At the age of sixteen this patient looked and walked like a flirtatious girl, and he soon fell into the snare of homosexuality. In order to comprehend this development we must remember that he had had, in a psychological sense, the education of a girl, and that the difference between the sexes had been made clear to him much too late in his development. Also he had experienced his triumphs in the feminine role, and had no certainty of gaining as much by playing the man. In the imitation of girlish behavior he could not but see an open road to his goal of superiority.

It is my experience that boys who have this type of upbringing always look like girls. The growth of the organs and probably also of the glands is partially ruled by the environment and the child's attitude toward it; and they are adapted to them. Thus if such an early environmental training towards femininity is succeeded by a personal goal of the same tendency, the wish to be a favored girl will influence not only the mind, but also the carriage and even the body.

This case illustrates very clearly how a pervert trains himself mentally into his abnormal attitude towards sex. There is no necessity to postulate an inborn or hereditary organic deviation.

When the boy in question came to me he was involved in a relationship with another boy who was the neglected second child of a very domineering mother; this boy's striving was to overcome men by his personal charm. It was by his charm that he had succeeded early in ruling his weak father. When he reached the age of sexual expression he was shocked. His notion of women was founded upon experience of his domineering mother, who had neglected him. He felt the need to dominate but he entertained no hope of dominating women for, in accordance with the generalization he had made of his early experiences connected with a strong and ruling mother, he had come to feel that a woman was too powerful to control. His only chance to be the victor, he felt, was in relationship with men; so he turned homosexual. Consider then the hopeless situation of my patient! He wanted to conquer by female means—by having the charm of a girl—but his friend wanted to be a conqueror of men.

I was able to make my patient realize that, whatever he himself thought or felt in this liaison, his friend felt himself to be a conquering man-charmer. My patient, therefore, could not be sure that his was the real conquest, and his homosexuality was accordingly checked. By this means I was able to break off the relationship, for he saw that it was stupid to enter into such a fruitless competition. This also made it easier for him to understand that his abnormality was due to a lack of interest in others, and that his feeling of inadequacy, as the result of being pampered, had led him to measure everything in terms of personal triumph. He then left me for some months; when he visited me again he had had sexual relations with a girl, but had tried to play a masochistic part towards her. He obviously wished, in order to prove to himself that his original view of the world was correct, to experience with her the same inferiority that he had felt with his mother and cousin. This masochistic attitude was shown in the fact that his goal of superiority required that the girl should do to him what he commanded, and he wished to complete the act at this point, without achieving sexual intercourse, so that the normal was still excluded.

The great difficulty of changing a homosexual lies not only in his lack of general social adjustment, but also in the invariable absence of right training toward the sexual role, which ought to begin in early childhood. The attitude towards the other sex is strained in a mistaken direction almost from the beginning of life. In order to realize this fact one must note the kind of intelligence, of behavior, and of expectations which such a case exhibits. Compare normal persons walking in the street or mixing in society with a homosexual in the same situations! Those who are normal are chiefly interested in the opposite sex, the homosexuals only in their own. The latter evade normal sexuality not only in behavior but even in dreams. The patient I have just described used frequently to dream that he was climbing a mountain, and ascending it by a serpentine road. The dream expresses his discouraged and circuitous approach to life. He moved rather like a snake, bending his head and shoulders at every step.

In conclusion I will recall some of the most disastrous cases I have known among only children. A woman asked me to help her and her husband in the case of their only boy, who tyrannized over them terribly. He was then sixteen, a very good pupil at school, but quarrelsome and insulting in behavior. He was specially combative toward his father, who had been stricter with him than had the mother. He antagonized both parents continually, and if he could not get what he wanted he made open attack, sometimes wrestling with his father, spitting at him, and using bad language. Such a development is possible in the case of a pampered and only child who is trained to give nothing but to expect everything— and gets it, until the time comes when indulgence can go on no longer. In such cases it is difficult to treat the patient in his old environment, because too many old recollections are revived, which disturb the harmony of the family.

Another case was brought to me, a boy of eighteen, who had been accused of murdering his father. He was an only child, and a spoiled one, who had stopped his education and was wasting, in bad company, all the money he could extort from his parents. One day when his father refused to give him money, the boy killed him by hitting him on the head with a hammer. No one but the lawyer who was defending him knew that he had killed another person several months before. It was obvious that he felt perfectly sure of escaping discovery this second time.

In yet another case of criminal development, an only boy was brought up by a very well-educated woman who wanted him to be a genius. At her death another experienced woman continued his nurture in the same way, until she became aware of his tyrannical tendencies. She believed it to be due to sexual repression, and had him analyzed. His tyrannical attitude did not cease, however, and she then wished to be rid of him. But he broke into her house one night intending to rob her, and strangled her.

All the characteristics which I have described as typical of certain positions in the family can, of course, be modified by other circumstances. With all their possibilities of variation, however, the outlines of these patterns of behavior will be found to be substantially correct. Among other possibilities, one may mention the position of a boy growing up among girls. If he is older than they are he develops very much the same as an elder brother close to a younger sister. Differences in age, in the affection of the parents, and in the preparation for life, are all reflected in the individual pattern of behavior.

Where a female majority and feminine influence dominates the whole environment, a single boy is likely to have a goal of superiority and a style of life which are directed towards feminity. This occurs in various degrees and various ways: in a humble devotion to women and worship of them, in an imitative attitude, tending towards homosexuality, or in a tyrannical attitude towards women. People usually avoid educating boys in a too feminine environment; for it seems to be a matter of general experience that such children develop towards one of two extremes— either exaggerated vanity or audacity. In the story of Achilles there are many points from which we may assume that the latter case was well understood in antiquity.

Importance of Evaluation of Women and Men

We find the same contradictory posibilities in the cases of only girls who grow up among boys or in a wholly masculine environment. In such circumstances a girl may, of course, be spoiled with too much attention and affection; but she may also adopt boys' attitudes and wish to avoid looking like a girl. In any case, what happens is largely dependent upon how men and women are *valued* in the environment. In every environment there is always a prevailing attitude of mind in regard to this question; and it is largely in accordance with the relative value given to men and women in that attitude that the child will wish to assume the role of a man or of a woman.

Other views of life which prevail in the family may also influence the pattern of a child's behavior, or bring it into difficulties, as for example the superstition about character being inherited, and the belief in fancy methods of education. Any exaggerated method of education is likely to cause injury to the child, a fact we can often trace in the children of teachers, psychologists, doctors, and people engaged in the administration of laws—policemen, lawyers, officers, and clergymen. Such educational exaggerations often come to light in the life-histories of problem-children, delinquents, and neurotics. The influence of both factors—the superstition regarding heredity and a fanatical mode of training—appear in the following case:

A woman came to me with a daughter of nine, both of them in tears and desperation. The mother told me that the girl had only recently come to live with her, after having spent years under the care of foster parents in the country. There she had completed the third grade of her schooling, and she had entered the fourth grade in the city school, but her work became so bad that her teacher had her put back into the third grade. Soon afterwards her work had become still worse, and she was graded still lower and put in the second. The mother was thoroughly upset at this and obsessed with the idea that her daughter's deficiency was inherited from the father.

At first sight it was evident to me that the mother was treating the child with exaggerated educational insistence, which in this case was particularly unfortunate, because the girl had been brought up in a congenial, easy environment and expected still greater kindness from the mother. But in her eagerness that her child should not be a failure the mother was overstrict, and this gave the child the keenest disappointment. She developed a great emotional tension which effectually blocked her progress both at school and at home. Exhortation, reproaches, criticism, and spanking only intensified the emotion, with consequent hopelessness on both sides. To confirm my impression, I spoke with the girl alone about her foster parents. She told me how happy her life with them had been; and then, bursting into tears, told me also how she had at first enjoyed being with her mother.

I had to make the mother understand the mistakes in which she had become involved. The girl could not be expected to put up with such a hard training. Putting myself in her place I could perfectly understand her conduct as an intelligent reaction—that is, as a form of accusation and revenge. In a situation of this type, but where there is less social feeling, it is perfectly possible for a child to turn delinquent, neurotic, or even to attempt suicide. But in this case I was sure it would not be difficult for the girl to improve if the mother could be convinced of the truth, and could impress the child with a sufficiently definite change of attitude. I therefore took the mother in hand, and explained to her that the belief in inheritance was nothing but a nuisance, after which I helped her to realize what her daughter had not unreasonably expected when she came to live with her, and how she must have been disappointed and shaken by such disciplinary treatment, to the point of utter inability to do what was expected of her. I wanted the mother to confess to the child that she had been mistaken and would like to reform her method, so I told her I did not really believe she could bring herself to do it, but that it was what I would do in the circumstances. She answered decidedly, "I will do it." In my presence and with my help, she explained her mistake to the child, and they kissed and embraced and cried together. Two weeks later they both visited me, gay and smiling and very well satisfied. The mother brought me a message from the third-grade teacher: "a miracle must have happened. The girl is the best pupil in the class."

Life Style and Dreams
Leo Gold

In developing a structure for the understanding of dream process and interpretation, it is necessary to establish working postulates about its nature. Dream research has clearly defined the physiology and cyclic process of the dream during sleep. Our purpose is to explore its function as a cogent part of the thought process and explore its relationship to the concept of life style.

The most basic postulate we can make about the dream, in keeping with Adler's construct of the uniqueness of the individual, is that all dreams are consistent with the life style of the dreamer. Therefore, each dream reflects the private logic of the dreamer and reflects that person's approach and interpretation of his life situation. It can also be postulated that dreams are teleologically purposive and are geared to goal directedness. The dream in this sense gives us a fairly direct access to the unique thought processes of the individual and shows us how that person characteristically moves through life.

If we define life style as a kind of life plan then the dream serves the purpose, as does thought in general, of clarifying the possible directions and understandings necessary in order to create movements and choices conducive to either achieving or modifying that plan. In this sense the dream is not seen as an isolated aspect of the individual's experience but rather holistically as an integral part of the total thought process. It is an inner process of thought derived from the ongoing experiences of the day that continues the analysis and synthesis of these experiences throughout the night.

Human experience thus rarely achieves a so-called perfect state of rest, but rather must be understood as functioning continuously through various levels of wakefulness and sleeping. The kind of reasoning that occurs during these states is consistent and in keeping with the unique style of the dreamer. No matter how fanciful the content of the dream it is never alien to the nature of the dreamer but always reflects his unique process of thought and experiencing. There is, in a sense, only one significant way in which the dream process is different from thought during waking life: the individual is freed from external reality and the need to communicate or interreact with others. Since there is only the barest awareness of the external environment during sleep, the level of introspection is at its greatest and the individual is more directly focused on his inner ideation with minimal external distraction. Whereas in waking life one is minimally aware of how one thinks, in sleep—particularly during REM sleep—one is more fully aware of one's introspective ideation.

Without the external distractions it becomes possible to more fully apply our private systems of logic to the experiences that preoccupy us and explore the possibilities of understanding or problem solving. In this process we apply our ideosyncratic modes of functioning and reasoning to the events of the day not only to clarify their meanings but to lay the foundations of continuity into the activities of the next day. The dream, in this sense, serves to prepare the individual for the future by dealing with the here and now and seeking to establish syntheses that permit the individual to continue to move actively into the next day. It permits the continuity of thought, feeling and understanding from one period of wakefulness to the next without serious interruption.

Dreaming in this sense, like every other somatic process, is purposive in that it contributes to the furthering of the individual's survival by creating tools of awareness that enable that person to assess his environment and calculate how to move through it. The concept of movement is most important in dream interpretation in that it requires a teleological structure and a dynamic configuration if it is to make any sense. This does not happen haphazardly but is based on the individuals inner construct of logic. It is also important to be clear that inner logic as it appears in the dream process does not have to observe the rules established by waking systems based on the need to communicate with others. The logic of communication with others is much more strictly limited because of the need for consensual understanding when compared to the logic of dreams or thought which are geared to the private logic of the individual. The fancifulness that can exist within the

Reprinted by permission of the author.

dream is not illogical but rather follows a freer mode of thinking. It is the juxtaposition of various ideas and experiences that might not make sense to another which facilitates the understanding and judgement of the dreamer or thinker.

Logic can, in a sense, be defined as a sequential structure of ideas and experiences which lead to understanding and awareness. It is a process of ordering in order to achieve clarification in order to facilitate movement in life at various ideational and physical levels. This is true both in waking life in the inter-personal process and in sleep in the dream process. Since there is a difference as previously postulated regarding the demands of communication with others and private logic, the structure of creating logic is significantly different in the dream process in terms of conscious awareness than in waking life. One can further postulate that the type of imagery and experience which exists in the dream life is not significantly different than thought in waking life but that we are simply less aware of it because of our shift of focus to the external world. Awareness is externalized rather than focussed inwardly so that while we may be utilizing the same admixtures that exist in the dream we are not aware of them but rather of the final syntheses which we utilize to mediate with our immediate and future reality.

Logic consists of the ordering of all kinds of stimuli, internal and external, in order to make sense of both our inner total experience and our external total experiences. Logic draws from sensations, feelings, body response, sensual reactions, visual imagery, interreaction process, judgments, doubts, certainties, etc.—the totality of the individual experience. Logic is thus a functional process and, dependent upon how it is utilized, requires language. Language can be defined at two different levels. That which is used to communicate with others in a logical fashion and that which is used to communicate with self in a logical fashion. Language is basically a symbolic process which enables us through symbols to condense large quantities of data into workable units that enables us to make, through synthesis, fairly complex inductive leaps toward judgments, awarenesses and movements.

The beauty of symbols in dreams is that they provide a richness of ideas condensed for a high level of activity. As we do a lot of things automatically in waking life, we do a lot of things automatically in the dream life. I would postulate that in the dream process, where one is free from the demands of external reality, this process is much richer in that it gives the imagination full play in terms of where it wants to go. Even in full play of what one is capable, it is

necessary to have short cuts. Therefore, as we need a language to communicate with others which is based on consensual validation of symbols, we must have a language within ourselves to communicate and define our thinking to ourselves. We thus speak two languages: the language of communication with others (speech), and the language of communication with self (thought).

The language of communication with self, therefore, will have a range of condensations, symbolic interpretations, and richness that will enable us to make a whole series of inductive leaps much more freely than when we are trying to do it with someone else. I would postulate that peculiarly the language of dreams also carries into waking life, that the process of our private language goes on simultaneously with our language of communication with others.

Important in the technique of dream interpretation is the recognition and the understanding of the basic use of symbols utilized by the dreamer. The mastery of his inner symbol structure gives us direct understanding of the meaning and intent of his dream and therefore clarifies the nature of his private logic and clarifies the nature of the life style. Within this structure there is no such thing as a universal symbol. Rather we look essentially for the unique way in which the individual utilizes symbols in keeping with his life style. All symbols are idiosyncratic and have special meanings which serve to facilitate the purposes and understandings of the dreamer.

Symbol formation, at its base, is internalized from the environment. This deivation is what makes it possible to carry out the process of interpretation. In terms of private logic, it is not the symbol which is unique but rather its use which is consistent with the life style of the individual. All symbolic ideation that the dreamer uses is internalized from the outside, and is done so on a functional base since the human being is constantly geared to seeking greater understanding and meaning in the world. In a sense, all thinking is geared to clarification and understanding in order to facilitate the individual's achieving of goals. The symbols reflect, in the way they are utilized, the characteristic movement of the individual through life in his relationship to others. By observing how an individual utilizes symbols in the dream, it becomes possible to make a series of relatively accurate guesses about how he perceives the here and now and the kinds of anticipations he may have about the future. The dream, like thought, suggests possible solutions which, in the end, must be experimented with in life. No solution imagined is ever truly a solution until it has been verified by direct life experience. The dream serves, in part, as a vicarious experimental stage on which the dreamer can try on a range of possibilities in order to project the possible consequences or solutions available to him.

It should be noted that the thought process deals with a number of ideas simultaneously. Hence, a dream does not have a single meaning, but because it is multidetermined, it can be interpreted at several levels of meaning which may be congruent, disparate, or somewhere in-between. This is in keeping with the holistic base of interpretation which requires our examining the total process rather than focussing on isolated phenomena. In the art of interpretation we look for a range of meanings that deal with the different aspects of what is going on in the dreamer's current life situation. An overly simplistic approach will miss the richness of the dream material. In the arrangement and flow of dream imagery the interpreter looks for the dreamer's unique usage of the usual. There is, in fact, nothing in the dream that violates reality. Rather, the dreamer creatively moves these symbols about consistent with his life style and in broader parameters than is permissible in external reality in order to achieve his purpose. The imagery of imagination, like play, creates more than actually exists in everyday life in order to create a greater availability of possibilities through unorthodox juxtapositions in order to open up new solutions, either correctly or incorrectly.

If we postulate that all dream symbols are internalized from the social milieu, then, as we share common learned symbols in waking life, these symbols are absorbed to form the language of the dream. It is because in a given sub-culture or society there is this commonality, making relatively valid interpretations possible because there is consensual validation as to their meaning. In this sense no symbol is universal but is directly learned by the individual from his immediate life space as he develops. In a society, for example, where hot and cold are concepts attributed to the passions, the affective meaning of someone dreaming either of fire or ice can be clearly understood. The converse is true of a society where such a construct does not exist and to interpret in this direction would be misleading.

To go a step further, while a particular symbol may have a culturally determined meaning, its use by a given dreamer is always idiosyncratic and can be effectively understood when we know the dreamer's life style and the functioning of his private logic. In this sense, two people viewing a fire burning in the distance in a dream may have quite different interpretations. The individual with an essentially optimistic view of life may give it the meaning of possessing the possibility of warmth and comfort, while one negatively oriented may perceive it as the anticipation of danger in the distance. The difference between the two reflects how they perceive what lies in their path as they move toward life goals.

All dreams are geared to some concept of goals. All dreams are constantly moving in a direction. To move in any ideational direction or, in fact, to create a road map to follow into the future, the dreamer requires a range of symbols to interpret and explain both to himself and others where he is going, the kinds of certainties and uncertainties which affect him in the process and what he can anticipate upon arrival. Specific symbols, such as fire and water, have been interpreted in dreams from time immemorial and appear with great regularity. Jung, in keeping with the construct of the racial unconscious, would see these as genetically determined and inherent as memory traces within the gene structure of the individual which subtly recapitulates the history of the human race. The truth of the matter is that these are simply learned. We maintain certain traditions which go on for centuries because there are human beings who are thinking. They are not passed on genetically, but are simply factors which operated continuously in human culture. These are elements which we perceive as basic to human existence. We walk on earth, breathe air, cook our food and warm our homes with fire, and drink and wash with water. These elements appear commonly in dreams because they appear continuously and play significant roles in human existence. The unusual symbol also exists because it has specific relevance for the given dreamer.

Each symbol has a range of associative ideas attached to it that gives the dreamer play in applying it to life situations. The ideas in the dream are played off against each other in varying orthodox and unorthodox ways as the dreamer creates movement in order to find a relatively workable base of understanding. All ideas, in this sense, within dream symbolism, are relative because in the dream symbol one is playing a range of associative things against each other in order to assess a location in terms of where the individual finds himself in his current life situation in regard to what he is experiencing and where he is going. The part that thinking does in the dream process is to see if it can achieve a degree of precision terms of clarifying ideas, feelings, and emotions that we have. Complex thought is a continuous play of this type of ideation which carries on an interpretive process that is translatable first into our private language which is richer, and then, if we are going to talk about it with somebody else, into the more simplistic language of communication deriving from consensual validation. In speech there is the requirement that we synthesize ideas into communal patterns of understanding rather than within the structure of private logic.

It is generally safe to assume that the meaning of all symbols are general. Only in how the symbol is used in relation to a given situation does it become specific. The combination of symbols forms the general pattern of meaning that the individual is seeking. We do not seek for the specific meaning of the symbol, but rather to find the thrust of ideation in a range of symbols that are used within the holistic pattern of the dream.

Let us look at the following fragment of a dream and see how this works. The dreamer states: "I am alone on an island. It is surrounded by a ring of fire. Surprisingly, I am not afraid. I dive into the water and swim under the flames and strike out for the mainland."

The first thing we look for in this dream is the overall thrust and purpose of the dream. The basic theme seems clear: if one is not afraid of seeming difficulties or dangers, one can readily find a solution. Here the dreamer is a person who generally would appear to seek active rather than passive solutions to life problems. We could further guess that he is relatively flexible and direct in his approach since he appears to know how to get around things or obstacles in life, reflected in the diving under the flames.

The dream also indicates something of the nature of the individual since he is alone on an island. Here we can postulate that he experiences himself in a relatively alone position in life and, at times, is relatively detached from others. The flames might indicate some basic fear in moving toward life directly since there is the risk of being burned or, in essence, hurt when one risks going outside one's "magic circle." There is also an awareness that to maintain or sustain this view inhibits or prevents him from effectively moving in life and indicates that the problem he is experiencing is based on his wish to transcend his fears (ring of fire) in order to overcome his sense of aloneness and, in fact, to get into the swim of things. Here the water symbolizes life for him. Life is seen as a sustaining medium through which he moves that contains risk.

The island, at the same time, represents a mistaken concept of safety that he must confront in his private logic. In the dream he recognizes the basic mistake inherent in the concept of the island and the fears that bind him there and seeks to find the means to correct this. Involved here is a beginning reinterpretation on the part of the dreamer as to what safety really means. There is a confrontation of this mistake and a

concept that he has to take on a positive and creative new approach which involves increased activity on his part in order to achieve change. The goal is clear in the movement from a tight place, the island, to a broader concept of the shore or a large land mass. He wishes to achieve a greater sense of freedom and a broader range of life experiences than he has heretofore permitted himself. He states that there is the element of danger but that this is no longer so inhibiting that he cannot venture beyond. If we see the dream as preparation for the future, we see the statement clearly, that despite the risks, the dreamer is prepared to make changes in his movements toward life. In fact, he now has sufficient belief in himself and his abilities so that he has the courage to jump into life.

Let us specifically summarize the language of symbol that appears in the private logic of the dreamer:

Island—symbolizes a concept of aloneness with a mistaken concept of security.

Fire—fears, imaginary or real, that exist in himself which interfere with his ability to relate to the external world. Danger!

Water—the medium through which he has to move; his current life situation.

Diving or swimming—a concept of action or how to move. The concept is active rather than passive.

Mainland—concept of goals. The place where life can be more fully lived in contrast to his construct of island.

The dream is interpreted teleologically in that it describes where he has been, what he must deal with in the present, and what he has in mind. It defines a course of action and indicates the kind of affective state that is necessary in order to make this possible. The dream, if we were to apply it to the practical life situations of the dreamer, would relate to more than one aspect of the dreamer's life situation. In fact, it would have relevance to role in relationship to others, to the area of work, and to his ability to risk intimacy in relationship to significant others. Our application of the interpretation must be richly applied to various aspects of the individual's life situation rather than a sole, overly delimited specialized event. The dream makes clear that, if he is to effectively achieve a broader approach to life, he must initiate the activity on his own rather than wait for others to come and bring him out. This will be true for him in each of the life tasks that he must confront.

In our interpretation, we note that there is no violation of common sense. The imagery is certainly fanciful because the need is to create a heightened state of awareness that also contains the dramatic power needed to promote new actions toward change. The ring of fire certainly has its antecendent in Wagner's Ring Cycle where it also serves to block Brünnehilde from life. As used in the above dream it contains much of the same quality of effect as one finds in "Die Walküre" but is, at the same time, significantly different since our dreamer, unlike Brünnehilde, is not asleep and clearly perceives that he can overcome the situation without the help of others. He doesn't require a Siegfried to rescue him from a fate beyond his control. Like Wagner, the dreamer has created a scenario utilizing a common element and then found his unique solution. In each, the human condition is expanded in a fanciful fashion in order to assess the possibilities, and each finds a solution in keeping with his life style. The ring of fire in both cases encloses a victim. Certainly, as long as the dreamer maintains his position on the island, he subtly perceives himself as a victim trapped by fate. The dream indicates an awareness of how this self-concept can be overcome through belief in one's own inner resources. The overall classification of the dream is one belonging to transition. It is the dream of someone who has come to the point of change and has agreed with himself that he is able to do so.

Since the dream occurs at the point of change, we might look at the symbol structure for an additional theoretical postulate. In dream symbol interpretation it is necessary to consider the law of opposites as one of the ways of seeking understanding and the resolution of the dreamer's problematic ideas. If we perceive the meaning of symbols as general and relative, even the negative can be interpreted as positive depending upon how the symbol is used. We might also state that every negative has an implied positive, following Adler's construct of moving from a minus to a plus. A person who hates may imply love. A person who dreams of war may desire peace. A person preoccupied with excitement may have an underlying preoccupation with serenity. Thus, when we deal with the convents of a dream, we play it two ways: in terms of its manifest meaning, and the seeking for implications which lie in either opposite or other directions. Here we move away from Freud's latent concept and holistically view the dream as multi-determined.

If we go back to the dream illustration we can now begin to draw additional conclusions about how the dreamer moves through life. Though he perceives how to act, we note that in the past he rarely had great confidence in himself. Fear had been a dominant force in his life and, in part, still operates in the dream as symbolized by the element of fire. What is interesting in the dream is the word "surprisingly." At this point his capacity for change is unexpected;

thus, he is in an ambivalent state where his more conservative, neurotic status quo orientation, while still functioning in part, is being questioned or undercut (swimming under the ring of fire) by his new concept of courage.

Essentially, he is equipping himself with new methods of compensation for a felt sense of inferiority which is no longer relevent to where he is in the present. The vulnerability still operates, but is being acted against. While he still, in part, continues to see the world as dangerous, he is reaching out actively for the concept of risk as a means of achieving change. He says in his dream that life is an unknown quantity (the mainland is at a distance), and that this not knowing feeds his fears and, in the past, immobilized him. A considered rule of his life up to this point is that no change may be the safest way of living. The implication is that even if it is not good, the familiarity of the situation is to be preferred as safe rather than risk the unknown.

Another concept for such a dreamer would be that, since his idealized fictional goals cannot be readily realized, it is better to remain inactive or relatively isolated until somewhere in the future some magical solution will present itself. He puts off goals for fear of being "burned" by life. The implied opposite of swimming suggests a belief that he lacks the ability or strength to control the events of everyday life, and that passivity in the interpersonal process is the most effective way to survive. In the interpretation, we see the play of opposites in terms of certainty vs. uncertainty, passivity vs. assertiveness, safety vs. risk, and negative compensation vs. positive compensation.

As we look to understand the play of these elements in the dream, we, in fact, reason through analogy. Through utilizing the law of opposites, we seek to achieve a sense of precision. In the above dream, between his concept of danger and safety, he has discovered the willingness to risk. As we balance the opposites, looking for the relative state where the dreamer finds himself, what we get is a blend of percepts and feelings that form an understandable structure of how the dreamer experiences himself in the here and now.

Let us go back again to the symbol of the island and question the dreamer about its nature. Suppose he states that it is a dull, beautiful place where nothing happens, and though he feels serene, he, in fact, feels vaguely uncomfortable. We now begin to understand in part what he is reacting against. Here is a person moving out of a state of little activity because, despite his fear, the element of boredom has become stronger. He might be saying: "I seek change because, despite the fact that life as I have lived it has its own kind of comfort and might be all right, it has no flavor. I want that which will make life more live-able, more stimulating, and even more dangerous. Maybe I had better dive in and get out in order to achieve something. It is better to risk drowning or burning than dying of boredom." He is saying that, surprisingly the movement might make him feel better.

Each person has something in mind (fictional goal) and sets up a range of alternatives as to where he is, makes an assessment of these and then determines the kind of actions he might take toward achieving that goal, or even how to modify the goal if it is perceived as mistaken. Generally, since humankind is always geared to a concept of becoming, one is seldom satisfied with where one is. What prevents change is fear or self doubt, but the pre-occupation with change always remains. Humans, as long as they are alive, are restless types who are constantly looking to move on, to transcend the past through achieving the future. Each individual seems continuously preoccupied with change and his language reflects this process. Therefore, since we talk of the dream process as representing a second type of language, it must always have its own distinctive movement. A dream is never a still photo. In every dream there is, invariably, movement consistent with the life style of the individual. This must be so since movement is the condition of life itself. Life is movement and death is the cessation of movement. Humankind's view of life must always be kinetic.

In the interpretation of the above dream we paid careful attention not only to the imagery and verbal ideas but to how the individual was moving through it. The movement is what clarifies how he perceives his and the manner in which he anticipates confronting the future. In symbolic logic, it is not only the symbol which defines the language of dreams but the movement as well which clarifies how the symbol is used in the service of the goal.

Generally, we look to move away from the stereotypes of the traditional interpretation of symbolism. We are going to translate symbols into the commonsense reality of where the dreamer is in life. The dream must never be interpreted in terms of an abstruse theory. It must be interpreted only in terms of the behavior and life style of the dreamer relevant to the events in his life in the here and now. Within this structure one should keep in mind what one can remember in a dream. One can reach all the way back into the past to childhood to remember and use specific kinds of memories. The reason we do this is not because we have regressed into the past, but because, in some way, it is relevant to the here and now and contributes to the solution of, or the dealing with, present life situations. As in early recollections

the memory may not in fact be accurate, but this is not significant; it is only relative to the immediate situation. It can be assumed that memory is an associative process whereby we recall the past selectively in terms of the stimulation of the here and now. We remember anything because we perceieve within our private logic its relevance to present life situations. Relevancy is the major consideration. While one may, theoretically, have total access to memory, only that comes out which is stimulated by current needs. It makes sense in that from a functional point of view there is no inherent value in remembering everything that happened in one's past. It would be both impossible and absolutely overwhelming. To remember everything is to deal with a monumental amount of nonsense as what is in fact significant. There is always a selective process, in both thought and dream, of input to the memory bank which then sorts out what is relevant to the input that feeds into the structure of the dream to assist our private logic in the carrying out of its function. We use the memory system by constantly playing the relevant images around in relation to current ideas, problems, or goals in order to achieve deeper or richer or more effective insights in terms of the here and now. The memory system serves as a contributing factor to the whole of what the dreamer is experiencing.

It is important to stress again the idea that the dream must be dealt with holistically in keeping with the nature of the life style of the dreamer, and that the dream process is seen as part of the total functional process of everyday living. When we approach the interpretation of the dream holistically, we are really asking fundamental questions about the application of the life style of the individual to the goal that the individual seeks to achieve, and that the dream reflects this process consistently. All dreams reflect the process of movement toward a goal. All dreams are influenced strictly by the life style. All dreams reflect an ongoing process.

In our approach to dream interpretation since evolving the concept of holism we are not looking for a system which is bound by rigid rules, universal symbols, and so on. Rather, we are looking for a flexible mode of grasping the whole intent of the individual within his life style. The transistion we find from Freud to Adler, as I have sought to deal with it in this chapter, is to move from a fixed system of dream interpretation to a more flexible approach based on social behavior. This carries with it the implication of the unique nature of the individual style of the dreamer. In this process we seek to learn the unique language of the dreamer's private logic. Each one of us has his own peculiar way, his own kind of symbolism, his own kind of coloration, his own special mode of synthesis which makes him recognizable to himself and to others. Out of this he shapes his unique language and movement that we seek to understand in the art of dream interpretation.

If you think about it, nothing one creates in dreams, no matter how bizarre or fanciful, is unfamiliar to you. Even in a nightmare you know where you are because you are going into an interior dialogue. The world you visit inside yourself is a world which is there continuously in imagery that you are a part of, you live in, you preoccupy yourself with, you function in and externalize in part. Peculiarly, that world is not seen as separate from the world but rather contiguous to it and flowing constantly back and forth. The dream is simply the clearest picture we have of our interior world. The interior world is a world we invent in terms of our interpretation of external reality, and we use that world continuously as part of our holistic function in life.

Bibliography

Adler, Alfred. *The practice and theory of individual psychology.* Paterson and Littlefield: Adams & Co., 1959.

———. *Superiorty and social interest.* Evanston: Northwestern University Press, 1964.

Ansbacher, Heinz and Rowena. *The individual psychology of Alfred Adler.* New York: Basic Books, 1956.

Bonime, Walter. *The clinical use of dreams.* New York: Basic Books, 1962.

Foulkes, David. *The psychology of sleep.* New York: Charles Scribner & Sons, 1966.

Freud, Sigmund. *The interpretation of dreams.* New York: Basic Books, 1960.

Fromm, Erich. *The forgotten language.* New York: Rhinehart & Co., 1951.

Hartmann, Ernst. *Sleep and Dreaming.* Boston: Little Brown & Co., 1970.

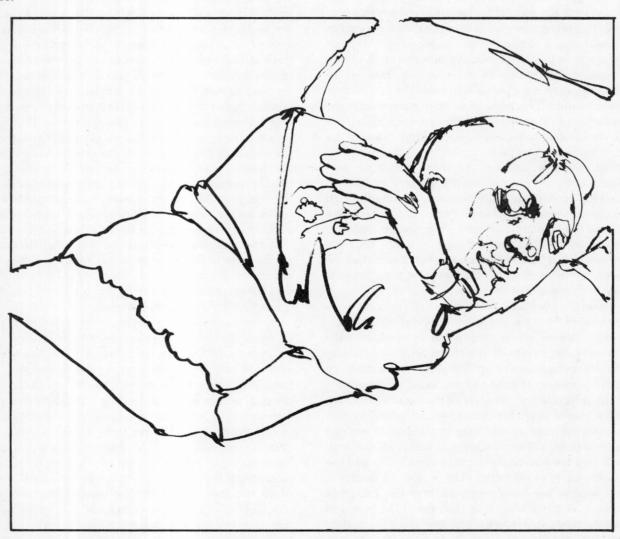

Eight Avenues of Life Style Consistency

Donald N. Lombardi

Three very important developments of modern psychological science have been the lawful and orderly arrangement of factual data, the phenomenon of subjective perception, and the notion of growth motivation in human striving. There are three parallels in Adler's Individual Psychology. There is a unity and consistency in personality which follows the dictum of the lawful and orderly nature of science. The same pattern is found in all regions of the psyche. Adler's contribution here is the concept of life style. Secondly, there is the phenomenon of subjective perception, each of us viewing the world from a particular frame of reference. Psychology tells us how interests, motivations, values, norms and the goals for which we strive affect and influence our perceptual selection and interpretation. Adler's parallel concept is that of private logic which is peculiar to each unique personality. With regard to growth motivation in human striving, there are different conceptions such as "self-actualization" and "competence." Adler's concept is the great upward drive of overcoming felt weakness and going from a minus to a plus position (Ansbacher and Ansbacher, 1956).

Two important bases of Adler's Individual Psychology are goal directed striving for mastery and significance as well as consistency in personality. Each person in his own way and through his subjective perception or private logic is striving for his place and sense of significance. In striving for this self created goal, there is essential consistency in all spheres of the psyche and in all dimensions of personality. This includes the conscious and the unconscious, the sexual and non-sexual areas, as well as thinking (cognitive), feeling (affective), and doing (action) processes. The same consistency is found in all regions of the mind and personality. All parts of the person are basically striving for the same goal of significance according to one's life plan and logic.

A prior approach for understanding human behavior was to look at the past for etiological and casual factors. Another increasingly appreciated approach is based upon teleoanalytic theory, that is, understanding the purposefulness of behavior. To understand a person one must think of his behavior in terms of goal directedness.

Life style is the way the individual sees himself and views life. It gives a distinctiveness to one's strivings and approaches to the problems of life. A person very early in life begins to say I am like this, the world is like that, and this is what I must do to find my place. The mind is a unity and the same style of life runs through all of its expressions. To further clarify I shall explain the rubber stamp analogy. Each person is like a rubber stamp. The essence of personality is reflected in all that he does. If the rubber stamp has the imprint "John Doe" and is pressed on a surface, we see a reflection of the name John Doe. Some of the variables that determine the clearness and legibility of the imprint include the following: amount of ink on the rubber stamp, pressure on the stamp when making the imprint, texture and color of the surface upon which the imprint is made. For instance, a black imprint on a black rough surface will hardly be seen. A heavily inked stamp gives a different impression than a relatively dry one. But no matter where you press the rubber stamp—on a sheet of white paper, on the wall, the blackboard, your arm—there is always a reflection of a part of the imprint John Doe. Each person is like a rubber stamp in that no matter what he does, his life style is reflected in his behavior, feelings, and thoughts. The life style is reflected in much, if not all, of what the person is and does.

Eight Avenues of Life Style Consistency

Eight different avenues or ways to know and learn about the life style are now listed and briefly highlighted. They are as follows:

1. Case history data—knowing about subject.
2. Psychological interviewing—talking to subject.

Donald Lombardi, Eight Avenues of Life Style Consistency, *Individual Psychologist*, 10(2), 1973, 5-9. Reprinted from the *Individual Psychologist* by permission of the publisher.

3. Expressive behavior—observing subject.
4. Psychological testing—measuring subject.
5. Family constellation—social influence on subject.
6. Early recollections—subject's meaning of life.
7. Grouping—interacting with subject.
8. Symptomatic behavior—subject's telltale signs.

The consistent and patterned life style is found in each of the eight categories. All spheres of the psyche and personality reflect this consistency. All partial functions are entities of the same organized, unified whole person. The eight different avenues can be utilized to help find the uniqueness and consistency of life style. The best procedure is to elicit data from all of the avenues.

With **case history information** we simply find out about the person whose life style we are trying to diagnose and understand. There is no need for observing or talking to the subject. Case notes from parents, a social worker, teacher, peers, and the like can often facilitate making significant inferences about life style organization and consistency. An excellent demonstration by Adler (1931) of understanding a life style from reading a case history prepared by a physician is presented in the case of Mrs. A. The case was presented to him before a professional group for his extemporary consideration and impromptu interpretation. The coherence of life style that Adler finds is quite apparent.

In **psychological interviewing** we talk to the client. The special significance of interviewing, however, is in trying to find consistency in personality. Numerous questions are available to help tap this consistency. With any given question it is important to ask why the response is given. It is well known in psychology that two people may do the same thing for different reasons. In response to the question, "Who is the most famous person who ever lived?" person number one says Christ because he founded Christianity and preached love. Person number two says Christ because he was known by so many. A third person says Christ because he could walk on the water and do other miracles.

Expressive behavior is the third way to help find and understand life style. The intention here is to see, hear, and observe the client. Posture, dress, nonverbal communicative signs can be organized into a meaningful and coherent whole. They are going to the same goal-directed striving for mastery and security. For example, Lombardi (1969) shows how the picture that emerges from an analysis of the drug addict's special language is quite compatible with the professional concensus of him as a deviant person.

The next avenue is **psychological testing** considered from an idiographic point of view. The response set of an individual often yields more insight than the normative scores and data themselves. The intention with intelligence testing is to elicit one's best or highest performance. With personality testing the idea is to observe the testee's typical or usual performance, not his best performance. As many psychometricians know, personality is reflected in intelligence testing and the converse is also true. A good testing procedure is to become aware of patterns and styles rather than attending to separate traits and characteristics. A partial function alone cannot be examined because it takes on a different meaning in the total context. Angers (1963) presents guidelines for Minnesota Multiphasic Personality Inventory (MMPI) interpretation that can easily be adapted for life style consistency inquiry.

Of all the means to understand life style, a study of the **family constellation dynamics** is not only the starting point but also the single most important avenue. One's ordinal position in the family leaves an indelible imprint upon one's personality and life style. Rudolf Dreikurs (1968, 1971) has taken the lead in showing, teaching; and demonstrating how the family constellation reveals the life style of an individual. In the family constellation, each sibling develops unique character traits, thus adapting to peculiar circumstances which disclose his style of life (Adler, 1931).

Early recollections of first memories should be obtained and interpreted after the dynamics of the family constellation are understood. In order to obtain these memories the subject is asked to relate the first specific incidents in his life that he remembers. First memories show the life style in its origin and in its simplest form. They represent the person's estimation of his life situation—I am like this, the world is like that, this is what I expect from others and what I must do to find my place. The family constellation is the starting point for understanding life style; however, early recollections help bring it into clearer focus. Adler (1931) shows how both early memories and dreams help recover life style.

The next avenue of insight into one's personality is **grouping** or interacting with the subject. In a group encounter the opportunity is afforded to witness one's life style. The concern with behavior in the group is not with the past and casual factors; rather, emphasis is based upon the here and now and the purposive and goal directed nature of behavior. Malamud (1959) suggests how a person's understanding of himself and of the formative influences in his life can be explored in a group setting. Many situations and techniques in a group lend themselves to conscious exploration and show how differing reactions reflect varying orientations in life.

The last avenue for understanding life style is an understanding of **symptomatic behavior.** Symptoms are especially conspicuous in the care of persons with psychopathology. In such cases the symptoms help provide dramatic insights. Symptoms are also looked at from the teleological point of view. In other words, what is the purpose of the symptom and what does it accomplish? Symptoms like all of the preceeding avenues are always in accord with life style. Shulman and Mosak (1967) stress the purposive nature of the symptom in accordance with the point of view that behavior is goal-directed, and that the functional mental illnesses represent inadequate or socially useless ways of dealing with the demands of life.

Case Study Clarification of
Life Style Consistency and Identification

At this point let me briefly present a clinical case to demonstrate life style consistency and its identification. Sue is the youngest of three children. There are two older brothers. An older sister has died at the age of four. All of the children were petrified of the father, but Sue showed it least. The mother was perceived as clean and neat and the father as a nag. As a child Sue was active rebellious, and somewhat tomboyish. And at other times she was the good child who did things for others. Of all the siblings she felt she was the least intelligent and had the most friends. Her earliest recollections indicate she never did anything right. She recalls her mother telling her, "You are cute but not beautiful like your sister who died," and her father saying, "If your sister had not died you would not be here." In expressive behavior, Sue is a life-of-the-party character, liking people to think of her as witty and the center of attraction. She is looking for love and respect in an extraordinary way. In sex behavior fellatio is desired above all other sexual expressions. Only after this will she move toward heterosexual intercourse and perhaps cunnilingus. In sexual intercourse, climax is reached when she is in the upper active position. It is interesting that her choice of a most famous person is Leonardo da Vinvi and Michelangelo because of what they could do and produce not for themselves but for others. As both a child and an adult Sue was quite fearful and could become attended to and recognized by being active, rebellious, sociable and going above and beyond the call of duty. The refrain of "she's amazing" and "look what she can do" is found throughout her personality and life style. Sue's situation improved when she began to understand and appreciate the purpose of her maladaptive behavior. "Look and see what she could do" was no longer the yardstick to measure her worth as a person. She understood why she behaved as she did in the past. Now, with increased courage, self confidence and social competence, and with lots of encouragement from the therapist she began to act independent of her past conditioning.

References

Adler, A. *The Case of Mrs. A.* Chicago, Ill.: Alfred Adler Institute, 1931. (Reprinted 1969?)

Adler, A. *What Life Should Mean to You.* New York: Capicorn Books, 1931.

Angers, W. P. Guidelines for counsellors for MMPI interpretation. *The Catholic Counselor.* 1963, Spring, 120–124.

Ansbacher, H. & Ansbacher, Rowena. *The Individual Psychology of Alfred Adler.* New York: Harper and Row, 1956.

Dreikurs, R. *Psychology in the Classroom.* Second Edition. New York: Harper and Row. 1968.

Dreikurs, R. *Social Equality: The Challenge of Today.* Chicago: Henry Regnery Company, 1971.

Lombardi, D. N. The special language of the addict. *Pastoral Psychology,* 1969, *20,* 51–52.

Malamud, D. A. Toward self-understanding: A new approach in mental health education. *In Essays in Individual Psychology* edited by Kurt A. Adler and Danico Deutsch. New York: Grove Press, 1959.

Shulman, B. H. & Mosak, H. H. Various purposes of symptoms. *Journal of Individual Psychology.* 1967, *23,* 79–87.

The Three Life Tasks

Rudolf Dreikurs, M.D.

I. Work

The three life tasks, Work, Love, and Friendship, may be regarded as representing all the claims of the human community. Ultimately right fulfillment depends on the development of social interest and readiness to co-operate. Consequently if one of the tasks is evaded difficulties will sooner or later be experienced in fulfilling the others also. Occasionally it may seem as if one of the tasks is completely fulfilled, while no real effort is made to fulfill the others. The most striking examples of this apparent inconsistency are found in the different ways in which the same individual seems to regard the tasks of work and love, but closer examination reveals conflict and uncertainty and a very superficial and insecure feeling of happiness beneath all the apparent harmony. In the end the apparent success and evasion can always be reduced to a common denominator. The consistent life plan invariably decides whether and how any achievement is to be attempted or evaded.

Any apparent inconsistency in fulfilling the three life tasks results partly from differences in the demands they make on the courage and social interest which is necessary for their fulfillment. Most people somehow fulfill the occupational task. Only the most discouraged people evade it, which is why inability to work is often regarded as being in itself a symptom of a serious illness. Of the three tasks the occupational task is still the most important for the maintenance of life, and nonfulfillment of it almost imperils existence. Some people devote practically the whole of what capacity for co-operation they have to fulfilling the occupational task. Also, though they could not do their work if other people did not co-operate with them, they are able to maintain a certain distance in their relationships with their fellow workers, for few people devote their whole personality to their work. The more demand the work makes on the whole personality the more plainly every defect of personality is betrayed.

Occupational work may be defined as any kind of work which is useful to the community. It is by no means restricted to work which is remunerated by a wage or its monetary equivalent, but includes the work of the housewife and voluntary worker at welfare centres, provided that such work is not done at irregular intervals as the individual alone sees fit, but as a regular responsibility and obligation. The ultimate test is whether or not useful work is done for the commonweal. Under our present social system recognition of work most often takes the form of monetary remuneration. On the other hand the money paid to a shareholder corresponds to no kind of occupational work. But we shall be justified if we include preparation for a trade or profession in our definition of occupational work.

As occupational work is characterized by the value it has for other people, it seems to be connected with the idea of duty. It certainly deprives the worker of some opportunities to indulge his whims and inclinations which he had when he was not a worker. Apart from quite small children and old and infirm people there are few human beings whom special circumstances exempt from all occupational duties. All other people have some kind of work to do in the interest of their fellow beings, or have a certain necessary function to perform for the human community.

There are differences in the age at which different people begin to have work to do. Girls are usually given some duties to carry out for the family much earlier than their brothers. The more the child evades useful work the more difficult the occupational task appears. This applies to spoiled children whose duties the parents try to shoulder. On the other hand it applies with equal or even greater force to wilful and stubborn children who

Rudolf Dreikurs, M.D., "The Three Life Tasks," *Fundamentals of Adlerian Psychology.* By permission of Mrs. Rudolf Dreikurs and the publisher.

succeed in evading the duties allotted to them by their parents. However, every child is compelled to face the occupational task as soon as he becomes of school age.

The fact that we all have to take over duties does not mean that duty is necessarily characterized by being disagreeable, as many people think. Duties should not supersede the child's games, but grow out of them in fulfillment of the laws of organic development. After all, games constitute a necessary preparation for practical life and in this way they are also connected with preparation for an occupation. Unless wrong approaches are used, it is easy to get the child to undertake duties which are harnessed to games. The apparent contradiction between games and duties exists only for adults, for the child takes his games at least as seriously as the adult his duties. It seems as if this contradiction must have been suggested by mistakes in upbringing. The child sensed that strong pressure was being brought to bear on him and resisted it, and finally allowed himself to be betrayed into a hostile attitude.

If hostility to duty develops during childhood, it generally persists in some form throughout the remainder of life. But it is not in the least necessary to feel resentful about duty. There are many people who derive a feeling of genuine satisfaction and happiness from the fulfillment of obligations in any form, including even the fulfilment of occupational tasks under difficulties, while other people cannot be induced to undertake any occupational tasks no matter how pleasant the conditions of work may be. Ultimately readiness to take over occupational tasks depends on the individual's attitude to society. Only a positive attitude to society permits any satisfaction in making useful contributions to the commonweal.

Difficulties in fulfilling the occupational task arise out of difficulties connected with the problem of personal prestige. We have seen how strongly a feeling of inferiority can affect the individual's attitude to society. The more he is oppressed by a feeling of being lower or less adequate than the others, the more he will try in all he does to overcome it. He will do his utmost to influence events in a way which he thinks will help him to win greater significance. He will tend to think of his work less as a useful contribution to the community than as a circumstance which helps or hinders him in his struggle for prestige. The feeling of inferiority may be aggravated in occupations which are regarded as menial and in subordinate positions where one depends on the arbitrary authority and "prestige-hunger" of a capricious superior.

Many people are ready to put their hearts into their work only on one condition—that is to say, only when they feel that it involves no danger to their prestige but satisfaction of their ambition. They dislike their work as soon as they feel that their personal prestige is threatened, whether by humiliations and slights of the most various kinds, or by possible failures which will prove that they are unfitted to do the work. Nor can one who feels that he is being undervalued or exploited feel happy in his work.

If one begins to evade the occupational task he does so either by skillfully and more or less "unconsciously" accumulating difficulties which make it impossible for him to go on working, or he will suddenly become quarrelsome and irritable and develop nervous symptoms which interfere with his work. These nervous symptoms are generally disturbance of thinking, lack of concentration, deficiencies of memory which often are attributed to insomnia; or we find functional disturbances of the motor activity, cramps which interfere with certain occupations such as writer's cramp.

As a rule these methods of evading the occupational task are employed when failures threaten or have already occurred. Occasionally, however, we find an individual resorting to the same methods immediately after he has achieved an outstanding success as he thinks that people will now expect him to go on achieving successes on the same level and does not feel able to do so.

Even the crucial moments at which various types of people evade the occupational task may be characteristic. Some break down just before they reach their desired goal, others just after reaching it. This behavior, which is typical of some individuals and constantly recurs, can always be traced back to an expectation that personal prestige is at stake. Many people content themselves with insinuating that they could achieve special successes in some occupation but never attempt to achieve them because they are afraid that if they do their best their want of capacity will be revealed. It depends on how much courage they have whether they turn away from the path to achievement at the very beginning, perhaps by constantly chopping and changing from one kind of occupational training to another, i.e., by hesitating between several occupations, or whether they face about just before they reach the goal of achievement. The worker who breaks down when he reaches the goal or after he has reached it is afraid of not being able to hold the position he has gained.

If any nervous or characterological disturbance interferes with an individual's work, he will not feel completely fit to work again until his life plan has been explained to him and his over-weening ambition corrected by psychotherapy. Naturally, any ambition which he can satisfy without trespassing beyond the boundaries of useful achievement will not cause any disturbance in his life, but on the contrary will provide a special impulse for doing extremely valuable work.

While nonfulfillment of any of the life tasks is at once the expression of undeveloped social interest and an experience which aggravates the feeling of inferiority, failure to fulfill the occupational task—that is to say, unemployment is the heaviest burden any human being can have to bear. The burden of unemployment weighs most heavily on people who have met with failures in their love life and in their friendships. These people have no other effective way of keeping in touch with the community. They do not know how to feel useful except in their work. Some of them may have utilized excessive professional ambition as an excuse for evading the love task or for failing to form friendships. It is very understandable that they should feel that the involuntary termination of occupational employment owing to illness, reduction of staff or superannuation spells complete expulsion from the human community. Sundays and holidays have a similar deadening effect on such people. For when work no longer provides them with an outlet, their failures in love and friendship become all the more conspicuous.

II. Love

In contrast to the occupational task the love task is fulfilled comparatively rarely at the present time. On the one hand defective social interest can more readily reveal itself in evasion of this task, because the consequences of evasion do not seriously limit the chances of maintaining life. On the other hand right fulfillment of the love task demands a maximum of social interest, because it involves the closest of all contacts between two human beings, tests their capacity for co-operation to the utmost and destroys the distance which can always be preserved in occupational and social relationships. Further, fulfilment of the love task is bound up with special difficulties at the present time.

By right fulfilment of the love task is meant close union of mind and body and utmost possible co-operation with a partner of the other sex. Such a solution of the problem can be reached only if each partner fully accepts the other and a feeling of mutual obligation grows up between them.

There are several reasons why this task appears to offer more difficulties nowadays than in the past and is fulfilled by only a small number of people. It is obvious that people are less courageous today than they were in the past. Their want of courage is due not merely to economic and social insecurity but also to the smallness of most present day families, for when there are only a few children the danger of spoiling is much greater. We have seen that the more discouraged people are the more value they set on what they regard as their prestige and the more desperately they fight for it. Today the struggle between the sexes for prestige is more bitter than it was in the past. The reason is that the already precarious balance between man and woman has been violently upset of recent years. Formerly one sex was subordinate to the other. This inequality was always a source of sufficiently serious disturbances to make the scales waver, for repression always evokes resistance. Nevertheless, the supremacy of man was so secure, owing to the solidarity of the male sex, that woman had to resign herself to her fate of playing second fiddle. During the last decades, however, as a result of changes in the economic, social and political institutions of human society, masculine supremacy, which had existed since civilization began, was undermined. This gave woman an opportunity for rejecting her subordinate rôle. All men and women individually were then obliged to win a position for themselves in relation to the other sex instead of having their position allotted to them by a hard and fast system. Woman now seeks to obtain equal rights with man, if she does not strive for superiority as over-compensation for her past subjection. Man fears to lose the superiority which was assumed to belong to his sex.

So men and women are now running after a masculine ideal, which no longer corresponds to anything that exists in reality. They measure their own value, expressed in what they are and do, by a standard of masculine superiority, which, as we have seen, they set up for themselves in childhood. This standard can only have corresponded to facts as they were in the time of the absolute autocracy of man. It does not in the least correspond to facts as they are now. Most people have a strong "masculine protest" because their idea of their own value compares so unfavorably with their masculine ideal.

This masculine protest seriously hinders co-operation between sexual partners. Women now revolt much more frequently and violently against the rôle of their sex than they did in the days when they had fewer rights and were kept in greater subjection. Men, too, are troubled more than ever before by doubts as to their own manhood, doubts which sufficiently explain not only their horror of marriage, but also the fear of any deep love relationship which they so frequently betray.

Together with this difficulty in fulfilling the love task, which arises out of the struggle between men and women for prestige, we find the problem of sexuality. Apparently, however, this second difficulty is quite independent of the first. Very few people are just as natural in their attitude toward sex as they are toward any other biological problem of natural science. A very widespread fear of sexuality weakens the comradeship—already so deficient—which should exist between man and woman.

Is there any natural foundation in human modes of thought and feeling for this special attitude to sex? Freud things that the fact of people living together under civilized conditions, which involves the necessity for guarding against incest, is responsible. It is at least true that the human attitude toward sexuality is characterized by shame. Shame alone gives certain natural processes a meaning which they would not otherwise have, and shame is undoubtedly a product of social conventions. There is no natural shame. Otherwise the motives for shame would not differ in different ages and among different peoples. Shame presupposes the existence of certain laws and rules, the observance of which it guarantees. The educators try to train the child to obey the laws which are changing gradually.

The purpose and origin of shame are plainly recognizable in the view people take of the act of defecation. The child must learn clean habits if he is to be properly adjusted to civilized conditions of life. At first he cannot control his digestive mechanism and naturally at the same time his interest is aroused. The object of upbringing is to change all this. Unfortunately the method generally employed is an unsuitable as most of the methods employed in upbringing. The educators try to suggest to the child that there is something disgusting about metabolic functions and the organs which perform them. This is the method which suggests itself most readily to them since they were familiarized with it through the mistakes of their own upbringing. So they say, "Ugh, how nasty!

How horrible! No, that isn't at all nice! You disgusting child!" The more easily and skilfully the educators can teach the child clean habits, the less emphasis they place on metabolic functions and the more natural the processes of defecation appear.

Children who have ranged themselves against their parents and have some grievance against them are inclined to frustrate the parents' efforts to teach them cleanliness. Educators use terms and expressions of disgust more freely against these children than against any others. It follows that the clean habits which the children do finally learn will be associated in their minds with an unusually keen sense of shame.

Shame is akin to aversion and it is noteworthy that aversion characterizes people who are inclined to resist the laws of the community. Just as shame and aversion indicate that the child is resisting pressure brought to bear on him by upbringing, these feelings are employed in later life as ready excuses for further evasions of certain tasks.

The close similarity between shame and aversion is the origin of the error which associates defecation with the sexual function. Therefore the tendency to regard the excretory organs and the sexual organs with similar feelings of shame and aversion is purely and simply the result of identical educational methods.

The question of why people repudiate their sexual desires by a trick of repression similar to the feeling of shame which distorts their view of the act of defecation now claims our attention. The need for cleanliness certainly complicates the problem of defecation, but why must people subject their sexuality to such a strong external check?

We know that the Mohammedans, for instance, have particularly strict shame laws. At the same time we are bound to notice that their women have been so shorn of their rights that they have been practically enslaved. Masculine domination has never been so barefaced as it was among the Mohammedans until a short time ago. This is not to be regarded as a coincidence. Subjection of one sex is always found side by side with particularly strict sexual laws, which operate chiefly against the subjected sex. So in the time of the matriarchy men were forced into a position of shame and modesty similar to the position allotted to the women by our social code until the end of the last century.

As people did not know the real reasons, they thought that shame belonged to the nature of woman and attributed its existence to the wisdom of a divine law. Only the collapse of masculine autocracy in our time has made it clear that woman's greater feeling of shame has nothing to do with her function as mother, for even in the time of the matriarchy when shame had not yet taught her to be submissive, she had to bear children. So the sense of shame which society requires of woman proves to be a means for keeping her sexually and personally dependent on man. By demanding virginity and forbidding intercourse outside marriage man kept *virgo intacta* completely in his power.

Shame laws were directed exclusively against woman, but of course they could not fail to impose some checks on man also, even though he was little restricted sexually. First of all, he could not get away from the fact that he always needed a woman as his partner. Secondly, he was obliged to mount guard as husband, father and brother over woman's honor, and lastly he was himself the son of a woman, whose feeling of shame had helped to confuse him when he began to acquire sexual knowledge.

It was necessary to go into this somewhat lengthy discussion of shame in order to show that even the social problems of sexuality turn entirely on the rivalry between man and woman. Nowadays when the feeling in favor of equality of rights between man and woman is steadily gaining ground, shame complicates sexual problems relatively less, merely because it is no longer necessary for keeping woman in subjection and depriving her of rights. Already it is possible to write and speak openly about these questions. This in itself shows that shame has nothing whatever to do with a danger of incest, which, of course, is hardly more common in our times than it was in the past. Further, this danger does not really exist. Children do not seek sexual intercourse with their parents; neither do healthy parents have such desires. So the fact that human beings live together in civilized communities is not in the least responsible for the tendency to ban sexuality or regulate it by a system of punishments and sanctions.

Nor can any responsibility for this tendency be attached to culture. Culture is not a sublimation of sexuality, but the fulfilment of man's desire to overcome a feeling of weakness and inadequacy.

The nearer we approach the goal of equality of rights between man and woman, and the less danger there is of subjection of one sex to the other, the easier it will become for human beings to regard their sexuality as naturally and fearlessly as any other problem of natural science.

Humanity is still under the spell of the fear of everything sexual which has been instilled into every child. Above all, girls can easily get the impression from what they observe and hear and from experiences shared with other people that sexuality involves a special danger for woman. It is a source of disgrace and dishonor. It is the cause of pregnancy with all its perils and suffering. On these grounds a prejudice against men is often formed at an early age. Many women regard themselves as mere objects for satisfying man's desires and think that he derives only pleasure and they only harm from sexuality.

Adolescents will always continue to form mistaken ideas and magnify certain dangers they see in sexuality until explanations of sexuality are made as dispassionate and straightforward as the explanations given in all other branches of knowledge which help to fit the child for life.[1]

If the educators themselves have no fear of sexuality they need not regard the presentment of sexuality, on which so much depends, as a difficult task. All they have to do is to reply in language which the child can understand to the questions he asks at a very early age—often when he is only three to four years old. If they adhere strictly to the language of the child's questions their explanations will be given naturally and easily, since the child goes on asking questions only in so far as his understanding permits him to frame them.

In addition to the masculine protest (which arises out of the doubt felt by both man and woman in their ability to play a superior masculine rôle) and fear of sexuality, a third difficulty impedes fulfilment of the love task—namely, the difficulty people have in submitting to a union. Anyone who has resented compulsion and dependence in childhood easily imagines that freedom and independence give a secure and lasting feeling of personal value, and anyone who is conscious of being weak fears a close union which may reveal this weakness. As men think they are expected to play a superior rôle but know how little fitted they are

---

1. Today we witness a fundamental change in prevalent sexual attitudes. Far less people are still afraid of sex, but, on the contrary, exaggerate its significance. The previous cultural emphasis on shame has given way to a tendency to disregard standards of decency and a sense of responsibility in sex. Sex became a tool of easy pleasure, inportance and power, particularly for teen-agers who have too few other avenues to feel important in our society. This development is an expression of the transitional period of our culture, where man no longer accepts the strict regulations of an autocratic society and has not yet found his own self-discipline and an order which is not based on force but on self-reliance and responsibility.

to play it well, they fear union much more now-adays than women do. Women on the other hand require the surrender of the man's whole person-ality, and overestimate the value of such a surren-der, because they regard it as a pledge or token which they ought to receive in recognition of the sacrifice they consider they make by yielding. So the sexes turn the question of union into a dispute about prices, each trying to gain an advantage over the other. In particular, the union which involves the most far reaching consequences, that is to say marriage, often proves to be of greater social and economic advantage to the woman than it is to the man. The wish to gain complete possession of somebody is expressed most plainly by jealousy. Jealousy is never a sign of love. It only indicates fear of not being able to hold another person.

The rôle of virginity nowadays complicates the difficulties connected with sexuality and the real or imaginary sacrifices demanded by union. Al-though society no longer requires women to prac-tice chastity so strictly as in the past, the transition from virginity to womanhood still represents an insoluble problem for many women. They fear the step which makes them complete women. This is, of course, due both to their upbringing and to their attitude to sexuality. The dread of losing virginity is particularly marked in women who regard everything sexual as beastly and degrading and therefore resent the manifestations of their wom-anhood, as for example menstruation. (This re-sentment is the origin of many menstrual and premenstrual disorders.) On the other hand many men no longer regard virginity as an estimable or particularly valuable quality of womanhood. This, of course, is only because he wishes to evade re-sponsibility, because he fears that too close a tie will bind the woman to him, and because—unlike men in the past—he does not want to play the part of the first man in a woman's life. (So he volun-tarily surrenders the most characteristic position of masculine supremacy.)

In view of what has been said it becomes easy to understand why the love task is seldom satis-factorily fulfilled. It requires the exercise of great courage on the part of each individual. For this reason the love life of so many people is based on evasion of the real solution, and so many mistaken experiments and evasive arrangements are made by married and unmarried partners.

People betray their want of courage even in their choice of a love partner. We have only to observe how the feeling of love grows and declines to re-alize over and over again that the human being is not controlled by irresponsible urges, as he likes to think. In reality his intentions control his ap-parently automatic "urges." People are easily de-ceived by an alleged contradiction between emotion and reason. If they cannot justify their intentions by an appeal to reason they say that emotion and reason are irreconcilable and they rely on an emotion, which appears to be inde-pendent of their will, and therefore irresponsible, to execute their intentions. Sexuality is by nature without direction. The direction it eventually takes depends entirely on the individual's choice of a personal goal.

Many people drift into unhappy love affairs, chiefly because they are capable of loving only while real union is impossible. They give the impression that they would like to take steps to fulfil the love task. In reality they have no inten-tion of doing so. Instead of admitting that they are at fault in some way, they pretend that they are the victims of their emotions—victims of a fate which stands between them and fulfilment of their desire. Desire and emotion are strongest when the individual is least prepared to take any step in the direction of a real solution. No love seems so pas-sionate as unrequited love, or the love that can never hope for fulfilment because external circum-stances make a union impossible. The wildest erotic fancies fill the minds of people who are anx-ious to evade every practical possibility of a union. In their day dreams they go on a quest which they never undertake in real life. On the other hand their emotion usually begins to decline as soon as it becomes possible for them to realize their "wishes." In this way they show how skilfully they can use their emotion as a weapon for resisting the demands of a union and for evading reality. Often a love emotion vanishes altogether if the danger of a close union arises. A desire for distance may cause one partner to draw away from the other. This is what happens in marriage when distance, which could be maintained previous to marriage, is inevitably decreased by living together.

A particularly clear example of the way in which emotion can be employed for creating distance is to be found in the tendency to feel an attraction to more than one person at the same time. This is sometimes regarded as an argument in favor of the view that some human beings have dual person-alities. The reason why people so often seem to find their physical ideal in one person and their spiritual ideal in another is that they do not wish to give themselves completely to either, and so are determined to go only halfway in accepting either. The tendency to create distance in a marriage may be expressed by a sudden passion for a third person. The Don Juan type uses every new love emotion to end an old liaison. It may be that the Don Juan and the vamp owe their numerous conquests to the fact that they are the most unsuitable partners to have.

In particular, all perversions show how people choose wrongly in order to evade the love task. A long training prepares the way for these perversions and accustoms the naturally blind sexual urge to objects which make a natural love choice impossible. Likewise, people who say that they are incapable of experiencing love emotions or allege the impossibility of finding a love partner show that they intend to evade the love task.

Even if a successful love choice is made and leads to marriage or a union outside marriage, the subsequent history of the relationship often shows how perverse the choice really was. It is not at all rare for people to choose and assign a value to their partners chiefly on account of their faults (though, of course, they do not admit this) so that later on they can shift the whole blame for disaster on to the partner. So many people have too little self confidence to try to find lasting happiness in love. They feel all the more uncertain of themselves if in childhood they saw how difficult the love task could be. It is natural for children whose parents live unhappily together to overestimate the difficulty of this task. In their caution they choose unwisely and give their love to somebody who fulfills their desire for superiority or defensiveness. We may be sure that the man who accuses his wife of want of independence chose her for the very reason that her need for someone to lean on made his superiority apparent, and that the man who complains that his wife is masterful and tyrannical really chose that kind of wife because she looked after him, took all responsibility off his shoulders and mothered him.

Under cover of illness also people may attempt to evade a union or to create distance after a union has been consummated. Illness as a mode of evading the love task includes perversions, sexual impotence and frigidity, which are not organic in origin and are therefore forms of neurosis.

Courage to accept a partner of the opposite sex is necessary for fulfilment of the love task. This suggests an answer to the question: What is love? Desire and acceptance of the partner are essential. If the partners accept each other desire is awakened, and, unless it is intended to keep open a way of retreat, leads to fulfillment of the love task. The partner is not then regarded as a mere object, but is joyfully accepted as a fellow human being. Love is a task for two. When two people completely want and accept each other the problem is solved.

III. Friendship

No one is ever in touch with the whole human community. Each individual is connected with only a few people, but in his relations with them he expresses his attitude to the whole community. Once we know how a man gets on with the other members of his family and his fellow workers, whether he has many friends and how much trouble he takes in order to enjoy the society of other people we have the key to his personality and know more or less what to expect of him. The human being has to establish social relationships and come into contact with other people in order to satisfy an everyday need. The way he behaves to other people is a most trustworthy indication of the quality of his social interest. Many people whose social interest is comparatively undeveloped fulfil the occupational task relatively well and on the other hand people with the average amount of social interest nowadays encounter special difficulties in fulfilling the love task, but each person's social relationships reflect faithfully his attitude to society. No external pressure compels fulfilment of this task as is the case with the occupational task; on the other hand, it is not complicated like the love task by difficulties which go deeper than ordinary human relationships. Everyone is free to decide whether and to what extent he will form friendships, adapt himself to friends and co-operate with them, or whether he will choose solitude and detachment. He uses his judgment spontaneously in these matters. Therefore the way in which he fulfils the task of friendship is the best measure of the strength of his social interest.

A man who makes a muddle of his social relationships will, of course, try to excuse himself before his own conscience, as he does when he fails in the other life tasks. He will blame the mistakes of others for his own mistakes conduct. He may be inclined to regard all other people as worse than himself—more selfish, more disagreeable, more difficult to get on with. This attitude is adopted by people who are conscious of any kind of deficiency when they compare themselves with others and feel that they cannot quite keep pace with them or compete with them. They can even make a virtue of an inferiority by attributing their failures to their "fineness of feeling," their good-nature, or some other supposed quality. In the end they withdraw into a "splendid isolation" and seem to think it worth their while to break off their friendships with other people, because the other people deserve nothing better.

A hostile attitude to society may be concealed beneath pseudo-ethical or philosophical ideas. It is not at all unusal to find a small clique closing itself against the community. Properly developed social interest is ready to recognize the needs of society beyond and above every small group. The small group is generally actuated by selfish interests and tends to range itself against society just as the neurotic ranges himself against his fellow human beings. Family solidarity frequently helps to strengthen feelings that are hostile to the community. A love union may grow out of the partners' common hostility to other people. It may be a union which seems to offer a complete solution of the love problem, but no attempt is made to solve the problem of wider social relationships. The apparent solidarity of these narrow associations, which are formed from motives of hostility to the great human community, recalls the semblance of solidarity found outside the human community among criminals.

Interest in other people also leads us to make efforts to understand universal problems which unite large groups of people. So the individual's attitude to politics is typical of his attitude to his fellow beings. A man who holds aloof from all political discussions, and does not try to help in any active or positive way to solve the problems of the community, and so does not support any of the existing political movements, betrays his lack of interest in universal problems. He may excuse himself on the ground that all the political programmes are inadequate and that political life is full of absurdities and abuses. If he were really community minded he would be willing to co-operate even when things are not done just as he thinks they should be done. We never find a community, a movement or a system of thought which entirely corresponds to our views. No one who is continually emphasizing how much he differs from other people and regards the differences as all-important will be able to co-operate. The individualist arrives at his intellectual and emotional conclusions by a private logic, which is biased by secret hostility to other people and amounts to hostility to the whole society.

Reserved feelings may be concealed by exaggerations in social relationships just as easily as by any other tricks. Many people who are very active in politics and other spheres are actuated less by social interest than by their prestige-hunger, and many ultra-sociable people are secretly lonely and isolated. Even the hail-fellow-well-met person can make it impossible for other people to get any idea of what he is really like by keeping his inmost thoughts, feelings, conflicts and problems to himself. He takes refuge in sociability in order to evade more significant human relationships, whether in his family or in a circle of friends.

PART II: PRACTICE

Teaching and Learning Life Style Assessment

Charles H. Huber

One major function of counselor training should involve trainees learning to conceptualize "what" they will do in the future counseling sessions, as well as " why" they will do it. Very often, either technique, the "what" or theory, the "why" receive an unequal emphasis. For example, trainees well-versed only in theory can easily identify that direction they would like to take with clients, but are unable to offer the means of facilitating movement there. Conversely, an outstanding repertoire of techniques without theoretical direction can result in attempting technique after technique in helter-skelter fashion accompanied by mounting anxiety for both counselor and client if the "right" formula isn't found.

In Adlerian psychology, the term "life style" refers to a person's basic orientation toward life. The theoretical concept of life style has as its primary premise the belief that all behavior is goal-directed. Life style is also extremely valuable as a counseling technique. Assessing clients' life styles can provide information to help clients label their goals as well as assist them gain insights into the often mistaken means they have developed to move towards their self-determined goals.

Dinkmeyer, Pew, and Dinkmeyer (1979) identify four major objectives for the Adlerian counselor, each of which correspond to one of the four proposed stages in the counseling process. The importance of understanding and utilizing life style assessment date permeates all four objectives and, therefore, the entire counseling experience. A knowledge base and skill repertoire relating to both life style theory and practice would be obviously necessary for any trainee intending to employ an Adlerian approach in working with future clients.

The purpose of this article is to convey to both potential instructors and trainees a suggested outline for undertaking a teaching/learning process relating to life style theory and practice. The present author leads a five week seminar in which he structures an experience whereby theoretical concepts and practical applications are equally emphasized. Trainees are asked to explore life style theory, but also undertake practical applications of skills acquired in the form of exercises, activities, and sessions with a volunteer "client." This content and format has been evaluated as highly meaningful and effective by trainees and later, by practicum supervisors assessing trainees' competencies in actual field placements.

Procedural Issues

The following issues comprise the basic procedures utilized as the foundation for achieving the seminar goals. These guidelines are used in the preparation aspects of the seminar and depending upon the focus of individual members, as well as the group as a whole, are often adapted to address specific needs.

1. The core readings for the seminar are *Life Style: What It Is and How to Do It*, by Eckstein, Baruth, and Mahrer (1975) and *Life Style: Theory, Practice, and Research*, by Baruth and Eckstein (1978). The latter offers an excellent theoretical background for understanding life style and also provides more pragmatic readings and research support. The former is what its title implies, a "how to" resource which step-by-step outlines the manner of doing a life style analysis and then integrating the data it provides into the counseling

Reprinted by permission of the author.

process to achieve client attitudinal and/or behavioral change. In addition to these two books, trainees are encouraged to develop a supplementary reading program.

2. For suggested readings, trainees are referred to those specific references given in the back of *Life Style: What It Is and How to Do It*. One additional source highly recommended is *Adlerian Counseling and Psychotherapy*, by Dinkmeyer, Pew, and Dinkmeyer (1979). Also journals such as the *Journal of Individual Psychology,* and *The Individual Psychologist* are proposed as possible resources.

3. The seminar meets for a two-hour segment once a week for five weeks. The first third of each session is generally devoted to a lecture and/or discussion based on the lecture and readings. The second third stresses applications of the specific concepts being studied such as doing various exercises, discussing evaluation questions in small groups, role-playing based on case simulations, and the like. The final third involves critique/discussion of trainees' meetings with their volunteer "clients."

4. Each trainee is asked to secure a volunteer "client" who will agree to meet for a minimum of five sessions with that trainee. It is suggested that volunteers be approached with the idea that this experience has the potential to provide them with an excellent opportunity for personal growth. Growth, not problem remediation, is the focus although the latter often arises as a consequence. All meetings are tape recorded with the present author giving supervision of same. Most all trainees find that volunteers welcome the opportunity to participate and commit themselves wholeheartedly to the experience. This practical endeavor is of immense value in making the seminar richer and more personally significant. Trainees are able to gain a more realistic basis for understanding the concept of life style and become better prepared to implement the various aspects involved with it in their future counseling careers.

5. Based on their meetings with their "clients," trainees prepare a systematic case study relating their experiences. This case study brings together all of their previous seminar and client work. Utilizing an Adlerian orientation, this primarily involves trainees' development in establishing and maintaining an ongoing therapeutic experience. It includes the process of establishing a "relationship," a "psychological investigation," providing "interpretations," and lastly, some type of "reorientation" or change in client attitude and/or behavior. This hopefully taps more than just factual knowledge. It is expected that trainees in this case study will display their abilities to apply what they have learned during and outside seminar sessions and client meetings, to understand the essence of this approach and critically evaluate its effectiveness, as well as indicate how they synthesize it within their own personal and therapeutic value systems.

The Process

As stated previously, theory and technique must be equally and closely intertwined for effective therapeutic intervention to take place. Trainees have related finding it most illuminating to listen to the tape recorded meetings with their "clients" asking themselves such questions as "Were those methods I employed effective, or what other techniques, procedures, or intervention strategies might have been more appropriate?" and "Why theoretically was, or would a certain strategy be effective?" The integration of theory and practice is crucial for actual counseling and it is proposed here similarly crucial for the teaching/learning process.

For these reasons, life style is presented and studied in the seminar sessions in terms of its role within Adlerian counseling process. Four development phases characterize the practice of Adlerian counseling with individal clients: (1) the relationship, (2) a psychological investigation, (3) interpretation resulting in new insights, and (4) a reorientation culminating in some type of attitudinal and/or behavior change. Each of the first four seminar sessions studies life style within the context of its corresponding developmental counseling phase, with the fifth and final session being devoted to summary, critique, and termination.

Session 1: Relationship

The initial seminar meeting, as is an initial counseling session, is extremely important in creating a positive, facilitative climate that will permeate future meetings. During this initial seminar session the following specific areas are generally covered in a friendly, sharing manner so as to begin a relationship building:

1. trainees and instructor share information relating to professional background, experience, and current interests.
2. an overview of the seminar content.
3. a description of basic seminar requirements, including readings, securing a volunteer "client," the systematic case study, and so on.
4. a schedule of topical issues to be covered.

An introduction to basic Adlerian concepts is then presented with the final portion (third) of the seminar session devoted specifically to amplifying points concerning the Adlerian view of the relationship between client and counselor. Points discussed include the essential elements of mutual trust and respect, the issue of goal alignment, the value of tentative hypotheses and encouragement, and the identification of possible disturbances that may interfere with gaining the client's cooperation.

Session 2: Psychological Investigation

The second seminar session is devoted to a psychological investigation involving a life style analysis and assessment. Two primary purposes are focused on: (1) understanding the client's life style, and (2) seeing how that life style affects the client's functioning in life tasks. The "Life Style Interview Guide" (see Appendix G) offers the focal point for in-seminar discussion and applications as well as outside preparation as trainees formlate their own life style statements. In addition, it also provides the means of preparing to obtain life style information from their volunteer "clients." Family constellation and early recollection data are assessed and then analyzed to determine relevant "Life is—Others are—I am—" themes, as well as personal assets and possible mistaken or self-defeating apperceptions.

Session 3: Interpretation

Having obtained and analyzed life style data concerning family atmosphere and early recollections during and outside the previous seminar session, this meeting is spent in identifying how both client and counselor can become actively involved in an interpretation process. The primary goal sought is to have the client take ultimate responsibility regarding the validity of the life style summation.

Dinkmeyer, Pew, and Dinkmeyer (1979) denote the interpretation process as being foremost concerned with creating awareness of: (1) the life style, (2) current psychological movement and its direction, (3) goals, purposes, and intentions, and (4) the private logic and how it works. Thus, utilizing these four areas as focal points, the thrust of this seminar session is on creating insight through constant reference to the basic premises of one's life style ("Life is—Others are—I am—" themes) and to ways in which personal assets can be utilized and mistaken, self-defeating apperceptions can be overcome to allow one to lead to a more successful and satisfying life.

Various techniques to aid in the interpretation process are also presented and practiced. These comprise the more common intervention techniques and also specialized procedures such as Adler's "spitting in the client's soup," Allen's (1971) "sweetening the pot" and "avoiding the client's tar baby," and Nikelly's (1971) "stroke-and-spit tactics."

Session 4: Reorientation

This fourth seminar session conerns the "reorientation" phase of the Adlerian counseling process. Utilizing the insights obtained during interpretation, the focus turns to specifically selected areas on which to concentrate for goal setting and possible implementation of a plan of action. Trainees are encouraged to look past mere awareness of alternatives as an end goal, but further on to developing in themselves and/or clients the courage to risk and make changes.

Dinkmeyer, Pew, and Dinkmeyer (1979) aptly summarize the thrust of this session:

It is at this point in the process that the counselee is made aware that insight has little value by and of itself. It is only a prelude to action. Outsight—the moving of ideas into action—is the real aim of the process. (p. 99)

Session 5: Summary, Critique, and Termination

Just as in any counseling relationship, a final summary, critique and termination is necessary to reach effective closure for this seminar. This final session is a time for evaluation and future planning. Seminar procedures, life style concepts, the general Adlerian approach, etc., all are open for critique.

The systematic case studies provide an excellent reference point for achieving the above stated goals for this session. As the case study assimilates all previous in- and outside-seminar endeavors and is a summary of the work done with their volunteer "clients," it offers trainees a package of ready-made data to identify perceived attitudes and issues relating to the concepts and use of life style. The following discussion questions have been found to encourage pertinent self-examination for both individual trainees and the seminar group as a whole:

1. What about the concept of life style do I now value most? Why?
2. What life style concepts are least meaningful to me? Why?
3. What are my impressions of myself as a counselor and my volunteer "client" after having worked together employing life style concepts within an Adlerian counseling framework?
4. What kind of additional training and/or supervision would I like to receive to even further excel above my present competency in employing life style theory and techniques?

Concluding Remarks

This seminar outline represents one alternative to teaching and learning about life style theory and practice. The present author feels that it has been an effective one because it enables counselor trainees to integrate the two aspects, theory and practice simultaneously, thereby developing both a cognitive and behavioral knowledge/skill base. By studying life style, applying it to their own lives and facilitating another's (their volunteer client) growth utilizing the concepts, they seem to gain a sense of its actual therapeutic value and increase their own self-esteem and competence at the same time.

These procedures, process, and resources offer an organized, proven means of achieving life style teaching/learning goals. However, individuals and groups differ and this seminar outline must necessarily differ at points depending upon those participating in its existence. It might be relevant to note that one important characteristic of life style is its differentiating property. Although there are similarities, each is unique in itself. This consideration has been found to be a valuable one.

References

Allen, T. Adlerian interview strategies for behavior change. *The Counseling psychologist,* 1971, 3(1), 40–48

Baruth, L., and Eckstein, D. *Life Style: Theory, Practice, and Research.* Dubuque, Iowa: Kendall/Hunt Publishing Company, 1978.

Dinkmeyer, D C., Pew, W. L., and Dinkmeyer, D. C., Jr. *Adlerian Counseling and Psychotherapy.* Monterey, Calif.: Brooks/Cole, 1979.

Eckstein, D., Baruth, L., and Mahrer, D. *Life style: What It Is and How to Do It.* Dubuque, Iowa: Kendall/Hunt Publishing Company, 1975.

Nikelly, A. G. *Techniques for Behavior Change.* Springfield, Ill.: Charles C. Thomas, 1971.

The Triad Approach to Teaching Life Style Assessment

Betty Lowe
Raymond Lowe

In the previous article Dr. Charles Huber outlines a method to teach life style assessment. This article presents another approach in which triads are utilized.

The purpose for participating in the triad experience is to gain some practical knowledge and skills in the analysis process. *The purpose is not to engage in a serious undertaking of an individual's life style.* In fact, it is highly unlikely that the results of an analysis would be productive unless two conditions prevailed: (1) the individual was experiencing stress over a period of time, and (2) the individual approached the counselor seeking professional assistance.

Three triad sessions are required, each session being divided into two one-hour subsessions scheduled approximately one week apart. The division into two subsessions is for (1) the gathering of information, and (2) the interpreting of information. (It should be noted that if a serious undertaking were intended, the initial session might well cover a three to four hour period and further, after you have gained the essential skills, you may find that it is appropriate to speculate and interpret throughout the initial session rather than holding all the information until the second session.)

Each triad consists of a student counselor, student observer, and student "client." Each member of the triad assumes each of the three roles on a rotating basis. Ethical concerns require sessions be scheduled where competent supervision is possible. The specific places and times available will be announced in the workshop. If a triad cannot meet at the place designated, *all* members are required to confer with the instructor to make appropriate arrangements.

The function of each triad member and attending responsibilities and considerations are described as follows:

Counselor

Initial Session

When in the role of the counselor, the student assumes the responsibility for scheduling and reserving space in the area designated. Closed-circuit TV, video recording, audio recording, and one-way mirror arrangements are preferable instruments when available.

In the first session, the counselor gathers data to complete the *Interview Guide for Establishing the Life Style* (Appendix H), and actively hypothesizes and seeks clarification to confirm or reformulate hypotheses. If the counselor is able to identify the mistaken goal, s/he may interpret it to the client during the first session. Typically, however, the novice needs time to sort through the data, consider various interpretations, possibly confer with his/her supervisor, and usually chooses to save the final interpretation until the second session.

Later in the experiential sequence, the student counselor presents his/her findings in a staff meeting with the larger workshop. Information regarding staffing is discussed on the next page.

Subsequent Session

By the time the subsequent session is scheduled, the counselor will have considered the client's life style through reviewing the video tapes, analyzing his/her interviewing style, and drafting of a *Life Style Interpretation,* (Appendix I).

Preparing a draft of an interpretation serves many purposes. In the process the counselor considers the data against his/her understanding of Adlerian theory and develops a basis for interpretative work with the client. Although the counselor

Reprinted by permission of the authors.

usually begins the subsequent session by asking the client what s/he considers particularly helpful or meaningful, the draft serves as a ready member of key concepts. Having studied the written interpretation should prepare the counselor sufficiently that s/he will be able to discuss rather than read the "report."

It is not unusual for counselors initially to experience difficulty committing interpretations to written form. Reluctant interpreters should note that drafts are not chiseled in granite and that even the most experienced of counselors can "guess in the wrong direction."

There is no recipe for selecting information from the draft to share with the subject. Presenting concerns, early recollections, metaphors, or other elements may be useful points of departure for interpretation. It is possible that the client may not remember some of the information gleaned in the first session or may recall additional information. Either actually may be an indication that the client is changing perceptions, but may be upsetting to the counselor who is preoccupied with procedure rather than dynamics.

As the process continues, the counselor uses the interpretation to seek a common understanding and confirm or not confirm the client's awareness of his/her own dynamics. In the process of interpreting, the counselor must keep in mind that building on the client's strengths and allowing him/her to gain insight are preferable to a direct interpretation. The counselor must use his/her best judgment in disclosing information that could be destructive to the client. If the counselor is in doubt about disclosure, s/he should confer with his/her supervisor.

As beginners in working with the life style, counselors are not expected to be skilled interpreters. It is not unusal to be clumsy at first. It is, however, necessary to be persistent and work through as many aspects of the interpretation as possible. Shortcuts are best used after the counselor has a more complete understanding of the process and has gained interpretive skills.

The subsequent or interpretive session serves still another purpose. It gives the client an opportunity to consider the information and to confer with the counselor. Since examining or changing perceptions sometimes is not easy, the counselor may be asked for clarification later in the term. The intention here is not to develop an ongoing counselor/client relationship, but for the counselor to clarify information already introduced. Counselors are reminded that it is generally not helpful to joke or hound a subject about his/her style of life. While it is easy to pass a person in the hall or within the company of others and comment on his/her life style, it may not be appropriate or helpful. At any time when interpretations are made the counselor should ask permission to disclose information to the client and be prepared to say nothing if the client states s/he doesn't want to know.

Staffing

The counselor uses the draft of the interpretation and video tapes of either the initial or subsequent session to prepare a presentation for staffing with other workshop members. The staffing is concerned with a selected issue arising out of the life style analysis session. The purpose of this assignment is to provide counselors with an opportunity to confer with the workshop members and instructor, and to provide a point of departure for group discussion. In addition, the counselor gains some practice in preparing information for staffing and discussion. The counselor might select for presentation a particular issue (e.g., "On what basis does the counselor decide to reveal life style information to a subject?"), a difficulty encountered (e.g., "How might a counselor use family constellation comparative ratings when the subject is an only child?"), or something done with skill (e.g., How did the counselor assist the subject in clarifying the presenting concern?"). Whatever the selection, the workshop discussion focuses on the skills of the counselor rather than the life style of the client.

When practicable, a four or five minute section of video tape might be included in the counselor's presentation. This gives the group some sense of the counselor's approach. It is important that the counselor preview the video tape and identify by tape number the part of the tape to be played. It is the counselor's responsibility to make sure the appropriate tape is brought to the workshop and returned immediately after the workshop session. The counselor's presentation and subsequent discussion usually are completed in a period of 30 to 40 minutes.

Final Copy of the *Life Style Interpretation*

In preparing the final copy of the interpretation, it is assumed that the counselor understands the difference between reporting data and writing an interpretation. Actual data is recorded on the *Interview Guide for Establishing the Life Style;* summary or general statements are included in the *Life Style*

Interpretation, with selected supporting data interwoven. An interpretation is not a transcript. Only statements supported by data from the life style interview should be included in the interpretation. The completed life style interpretation should approximate a clinical report and reflect thoughtful analysis and clarity of expression. Grammar, diction, coherence, and style are important. At the next workshop session following the counselor's presentation, s/he submits a final copy of his/her interpretation to the instructor for review.

Instrument for Assessing Competencies

Following the "total experience" of gathering, recording, and interpreting to the client the information pertinent to the life style, the counselor will prepare the *Instrument for Assessing Competencies in Establishing the Life Style*, (Appendix J). The instrument identifies characteristics or qualities considered essential to undertaking the life style analysis. Inasmuch as the process of developing the life style is but one aspect of Adlerian psychotherapy, the instrument is not to be used as an indicator of counselor competencies. A more inclusive instrument has been developed for that purpose and is utilized in the practicum, Adlerian Psychotherapy.

Observer

Initial Session

The observer completes the *Interview Guide for Establishing the Life Style* during the initial session. Whether the observer is in the same room with the counselor and client or behind a one-way mirror or views the session on closed circuit television, the observer is silent during the interview process. However, the observer actively hypothesizes about the client's life style and notes questions or observations about the counselor's approach and apparent understanding.

The observer, if appropriate, also reviews the video tape of the session with the counselor. In any event, they will confer about the session comparing information recorded on their respective interview guides. The observer then will draft an interpretation before the subsequent session.

Subsequent Session

During the subsequent session, the observer may participate in the interpretation process on a limited basis. The observer might play an important role in helping the counselor minimize the pitfalls of individual bias, generally contributing in any way that would help the counselor to provide more thorough information than otherwise might be the case. As is required of the counselor, the observer is expected to exercise professional judgement in disclosing information to the client. To assure him/herself of his/her appropriate role in this session, the observer should be well acquainted with the counselor's responsbilities during the session.

Staffing

Although the counselor is primarily responsible for selecting the topic, section of tape, and specifics for presentation, the observer may be a helpful resource in these matters. The observer also is expected to contribute to the staffing discussion. Here also, the observer may want to review the counselor's role in reading page 0.

Final Copy of the *Life Style Interpretation*

The observer meets the same requirements as the counselor for drafting, completing, and submitting the *Life Style Interpretation*.

Instrument for Assessing Competencies

The *Instrument for Assessing Competencies in Establishing the Life Style* is utilized by the observer as an aid to his/her learning. While it is not passed to the student counselor for his/her edification, it might well be used as a basis for discussion when the counselor and observer confer.

"Client"

Initial Session

Although a workshop "client" is not naive, s/he is asked to preserve whatever naivté exists by not rehearsing life style elements before the interview or being overly helpful to the counselor. It should be remembered that the client has not asked for professional assistance, but essentially provides a training function for the counselor.

Clients are reminded that they have the right not to answer any questions posed by the counselors and further, that their interpretations are just that—interpretations, not the final word on one's personality structure.

Subsequent Session

In the subsequent session the client is invited to explore the dynamics of his/her behavior and emotions. S/he may be asked to begin the session with his/her perceptions of what is stimulating, meaningful, useful, puzzling, and so on. During the session the client is asked to consider the counselor's interpretations and reflect upon them.

Staffing

The workshop staffing focuses on the skills of the counselor rather than the life style of the client. While the preparation and presentation of staffing information is primarily the responsibility of the counselor, the client may be asked to contribute to the staffing discussion.

Copies of Instruments Utilized by Counselor and Observer

The client is not required to prepare copies of the instruments required of the counselor or observer.

A Life Style
Thomas W. Allen

In the overview which serves as the introductory paper to this issue, the notion of life style is discussed. In the following article, Robin Gushurst, a clinical psychologist in private practice, articulates the interpretative procedures by which family constellation data and early recollections are processed to build an account of a person's basic orientation toward life, his "life style."

As a preface to Dr. Gushurst's discussion, it seems appropriate to present a "life style" in order to provide the reader with some concrete notion of where the interpretative stratagems described are leading him.

The life style summary is presented as a typical example, not as a virtuoso performance.

Family Constellation
Sibling Description

List all siblings in descending order including the patient in his position. Give patient's age and for each sibling the years of age difference with plus or minus sign. Include deceased siblings. Also include client's description of siblings.

Dan +10 *	Martha +7	Betty +3
Grown up Like an adult Out of my class Capable Sometimes crabby Sometimes nice Musically inclined	Called me a brat Made fun of me Thought I was a loudmouth Didn't like me at all Critical of the world Hateful at times	Serious She played nice She played fair Pigtails Funny teeth We had fun *During teen years* She was conscientious Worker at home; mom 　depended on her
Cathy 31	Andy −1½	Marion −3
Cute Chubby Happy Had fun	Devilish Cute Blonde	Quiet A rare gem Virginlike Fairy princess Untouchable Fragile She was there; but not there
Brenda −5½	**Debbie −9½**	
Chubby Cute Had a round face Long curls Sucked her fingers	The apple of my eye She was just "it" Sweet Gentle	*miscarriage

Thomas Allen, A Life Style, *The Counseling Psychologist*, 3(1), 1971, 25–29. Copyright © 1971 by *The Counseling Psychologist*. Used by permission.

Family Constellation

Ratings of Siblings

(A refers to Andy, B to Brenda, and C to Cathy)

Most to Least   **Most to Least**

Intelligence: B–C–Martha–Marion–Andy

Grades (Elem. Sch.): Same order as above

Industrious: B–Martha–C–A–Marion

Critical of others: Martha–Marion–B–C–A

Critical of self: B–Martha–C–A–Marion

Standards of accomplishment: B–Martha–C–A–Marion

Lived up to standards: Same as above

Helpful at home: B–Martha–C–A–Marion

Friends: Martha–C–B–A–Marion

Pleasing: B–Martha–C–Marion–A

Charm: Martha–C–A–Betty–Marion

Assertive: Martha–C–A–B–Marion

Bossy: Martha–C–A–B–Marion

Demanded way:.No one–It was useless

Got way: B–Marion–C–Martha–A

*Considerate: C–A–Martha–B–Marion

Selfish: Martha–B–Marion–A–C

Daring: A–Martha–C–B–Marion

Easy going: Marion–B–C–A–Martha

Sense of humor: C–A–Martha–B–Marion

Temper: No one as little kids; teen years: C–A–Martha–Marion–B

*Cathy didn't hurt others; was diplomatic and considered feelings of others.

Felt sorry for self: Betty–Martha (sometimes)–no one else

Athletic: We all enjoyed, no one outstanding, B–A–C–Martha–Marion

Looks: C–A–Marion–B–Martha

Feminine: All girls were, Martha–B–C–Marion (rating by age)

Masculine: Andy

Idealistic: B–C–Martha–A–Marion

Materialistic: Martha–B–C–A–Marion

Sensitive and easily hurt: B–Marion–Martha–C–A

Standards of right and wrong: B–A–Martha–C–Marion

Conforming: B–Marion–Martha–C–A

Made mischief: A–Martha–C–B–Marion

**Covertly rebellious: A–Martha–C–B–Marion

Complained at home: B–Martha–Marion–C–A

Punished: A–C–B–Marion

Spoiled: None

Over-protected: None

**Cathy would ask permission first; then if they said no and it was important enough she'd go ahead and do it anyway.

Family Constellation

Further Sibling Description

Sibling(s) most different from patient, and how?
  Betty and Marion. They were both quiet and less lively. Betty sometimes seemed unhappy.

Sibling most like patient, and how?
  Martha—we knew what we wanted; determined. Andy—we had fun, goofed around; stuck together in trouble and fun.

Which played together?
  Cathy and Betty; Cathy and Andy (he was the brains and I was the brawn); Marion and Andy.

Which fought and argued?
  Andy and Marion; Cathy and Martha.

Who took care of whom?
  Cathy of Andy; Martha of Marion.

Who had an unusual achievement? Talent?

Dan—trumpet; Martha—beautiful penmanship and wrote poetry; Cathy sang and acted in plays.

Who had a sickness (or surgery or accident)?
  Andy had pneumonia at 6 weeks. Almost died. Possibly dad gave him special exemption.

What was your role in the peer group?
  Flexible; never the leader but possibly "2nd in command."

What grade school subjects did you like best?
  Art and coloring.

What grade school subjects did you like least?
  Spelling.

Childhood fears?
  The dark.

Childhood ambitions?
    To get married and have kids.
What was your family's position in the community?

Middle-class.
What were the most important family values?
    Religion; be good (honest—don't cheat—play fair—don't hurt others); pay your own way, earn your keep, do your fair share.

For Female Patients

Age at menarche? **14.**
Was patient prepared for it, how? **Yes, by girl friends.**
Patient's feelings: Great, tickled, grown-up.
Menstrual difficulty? **No.**

Age at body development? **11–13.**
Patient's feelings? **Great.**
Were you a tomboy? **No.**
Did you ever want to be a boy? **No.**

Family Constellation

Parental Figures

Father	Current Age* 63 (+32) Occupation: Butcher	Favorite and Why? Cathy. He thought I was cute and sweet.

Cathy's view as a child:
Good-looking
Built nice
Radiates warmth
Million-dollar smile
Well-liked; fair
Intelligent
Desire for knowledge
Hard worker
Gentle
Understanding
		Ambitions for children?
		    Know how to behave; do what was expected of you; don't upset mom—be kind to her.
		
		Relationship to children?
		    Understanding, warm, friendly, dependable, comfortable. I loved to be around him and work with him.
		
		Sibling most like father, and in what ways?
		    Cathy. Warm, friendly, smiling, personable.

Mother	Current Age* 60 (+29)	Favorite and Why?
		    Dan, just because he was Dan.
		    Barb, (but she had to earn it).

Nice-looking
Well-kept (clean and neatly dressed)
Poised; stately
Emotionally strong
Loyal
 "Stick-to-it-ness"
Proud
Hard worker
Helped others (neighbors)
 	
*Place age in parenthesis if deceased.
		Ambitions for children?
		    Act like a lady; cleanliness; be dependable and reliable; do your fair share.
		
		Relationship to children?
		    Disciplinarian and dictator. We worked for her, not with her. She liked us a lot and was proud.
		
		Sibling most like mother, and in what ways?
		    Betty. Kept things inside; didn't show emotion; neat; good hard worker; clean; perfectionist.

Nature of Parents' Relationship

Very affectionate—cooperative and supportive. Mother's responsibility was the home and childrens' unbringing. Dad didn't interfere but would be disappointed* in us when we upset mom or made her unhappy.

*He wouldn't be upset—but just said he was disappointed.

Family Constellation

Additional Parental Figures

	Favorite? Ambitions for children? Relationship to children?	Why?
	Favorite? Ambitions for children? Relationship to children?	Why?
	Favorite? Ambitions for children? Relationship to children?	Why?
	Favorite? Ambitions for children? Relationship to children?	Why?

Early Recollections

1. Age: 5 or 6

Andy and I decided to get into some of Martha's keepsakes. He promised he wouldn't tell if I took one—so I did—and then he told mother what I'd done. I felt surprised and shocked that he told on me. He said he wouldn't tell but he did. I felt let down because now I was in trouble.

2. Age: 5

I ran away from home and hid behind a big bush at the neighbors for a long time. I decided I'd better go back home (I didn't know what else to do). As I was coming around the corner I looked up and Betty and Mom were looking out the window. They saw me coming. I knew I was in trouble and I was scared but I knew I had to go in.

3. Age: 5—

I was supposed to be watching Marion. She rolled down the basement steps in her stroller. I looked down the steps and the stroller was toppled over. I was stunned. I wondered how it happened . . . mother said I pushed her down and she sent me upstairs to wait for daddy. I remember sitting in a big green rocker waiting for him. I felt scared, but I knew I hadn't done it. I remember daddy talked to me and everything was OK.

4. Age: 5 1/2—

Andy, Marion and I were staying at grandmas. I was helping her set the table. She had a little blue and white cup that was different. She said we'd let Andy drink out of it and I said I'd like to have it. Grandma said OK. When I drank out of it, it didn't taste good. I thought I would like it but I didn't so I gave it to Andy.

5. Age: 5—

The first day of kindergarten. I had a new yellow tablet and pencil. I didn't know what to do. The teacher said we should do something so I drew some lines and was surprised and tickled when my picture turned out to be a pillow.

6. Age: 5—

I was getting ready to go to a birthday party and wore a new yellow dress with brown ribbon trim that mother made. I was all dressed up. Mother curled my hair with a hot curling iron and I had ribbons in my hair. I looked so pretty. I felt so happy and good.

7. Age: 5—

After the first day of kindergarten some of the men dad worked with gave me some gum (because it was my first day of school and I was like a big girl). Mom told me to say "thank-you." I felt uncomfortable. Then she said that if I didn't say "thank-you" she would take my new shoes back to the store. I waited a little while and then said "thank-you."

Life Style Summary

Summary of Family Constellation

She was the fourth in a family of 6 girls and 2 boys but psychologically she was the middle of 3 girls in a largely female populated and dominated household, a family in which domestic values and conformity to common cultural virtues were highly prized. The goodies in this family were to be had either by conformity to family standards or by cleverness. Assertion was a dead-end in this family. In this family the father decided the important things (like U.N. decisions) and mother decided the "small" home things. Since Betty had assumed the burden of living up to mother's expectations, Cathy was more free to follow her own desires. Betty was the windbreak, shielding Cathy from the full force of mother. Moreover, Cathy was more entitled to do as she pleased since Betty was more favored by the queen. She was pragmatic in regard to mother's dictums. Cathy cultivated her social skills (sense of humor, etc.) more than Betty who still hoped to find her fortune at home. Cathy followed father in this regard by generating warmth, by being gregarious, diplomatic and considerate but at the same time as a realist and a pragmatist she identified with mother, with her strength and her assertiveness.

Summary of Early Recollections

You can't fight city hall. My attempts to get my way by acting, by doing, by struggling against usually fell flat, leaving me worse off than I was before. When things do go well it's often just a matter of good luck, more luck than sense or because I'm attractive. In fact, happiness is being an attractive gal. Nonetheless, I deem it important not to acquiese to demands, even justified demands, which are put to me in what seems to me to be a high-handed manner. Outwardly passive but very determined resistance is my proper response to such insults.

I am a realist. I am practical and it is practical to be somewhat careful as to how much of yourself you share with others.

Life Style Summary

Mistaken and Self-Defeating Apperceptions

1. Cathy underestimates her strength to meet some problems of life head-on.

2. She may overrate the dangers or disadvantages of direct attempts to get what she wants.

3. She tends to discount her accomplishments, calling them happy accidents.

4. Cathy may overrate the importance of having her own way; of acting on her feelings. She sees demands placed on her, restrictions on doing as her feelings bid, as a sort of humiliation.

Assets

1. She is strictly a female female (she enjoys being a girl).

2. She is interested in other people and in having a good time.

3. She is down-to-earth (realist).

4. She has an artistic bent—a flare for color.

The Life Style and Career Counseling

William H. McKelvie
B. Udelle Friedland

Much of the vocational counseling done today is merely an extension of Parsons's (1909) turn of the century concept of matching client and job traits. While theories of vocational choice have been developed, techniques to explore the process by which individual's progress through the stages have been largely ignored. We believe that vocational counseling can go one step further and individualize the examination of exploratory choices an individual has made, his goals and strategies in doing so and his role in the process of his final career choice.

An individual's vocational goals and the behaviors leading toward those goals are an expression of the total person. A job is more than a collection of duties and responsibilities, it determines the kind of life led by the individual. His work satisfaction is in proportion to the degree it enables him to implement his self-concept and satisfy his salient needs (Super and Bachrach, 1957). Because occupations differ in their temperament requirements, career planning should take these differences into account. But, the goal of vocational counseling is to help the client solve not only immediate problems, it should help him become better able to deal with problems in the future as well. Thus, the vocational counselor should be sensitive to the individual's total development as it influences vocational choice and progress. He should help the client understand his capacities, interests and opportunities as well as the emotional attitudes which are interfering with rational choices or appropriate behavior.

The life style has as a basic premise the belief that all behavior is goal directed. The life style assessment is used to help label goals for clients and to help them explore the unique system which they have developed as a plan or strategy to move towards a self-determined goal. The individual may not be able to state this goal, but may merely feel the need for a sense of belonging, finding a place in a particular group or environment. How "finding a place" is defined differs with each individual and becomes his Life Goal. In order to facilitate utlization of the life style for career counseling, the counselor must delineate some of the "how to's" that the individual has been stumped by. We might rephrase the Life Goal as "I want to be _____ , but how the hell do I get there?"

If we assume that work is a means of achieving the Life Goal, a satisfying position, then fulfillment may come through a *Career Goal.*

Those variables which interfere with "getting there" are *Obstacles.* The client may build them to avoid attempting new things, he may over estimate them in order to deny they can be challenged, or he may have a realistic estimation of what is in his way.

He deals with Obstacles through *Strategies.* These may be effective or ineffective and the individual may or may not be aware of what they are. The counselor helps define them for the client before Obstacles can be dealt with.

The purpose of counseling is the *Evaluation* of both the reality of the Obstacles and the success of the current Strategies. The objective of this Evaluation is to generate more satisfactory *Outcomes* in terms of the individual's Life Goal.

Thus, the paradigm for counseling is:

LIFE GOAL

　　CAREER GOAL

　　　OBSTACLES ←→ STRATEGIES

　　　　EVALUATION ←→ OUTCOMES

The following case history is a synopsis of information obtained from a client who was concerned about career choice. The most significant information which the counselor used in making disclosures and evaluating her career problems has been retained. As we go through the description of utilizing the life style for career counseling, we will ex-

Reprinted by permission of authors.

trapolate from this information and relate it to the steps in the counseling paradigm.

Case Study — Hilda

Hilda is a married, 27 year-old mother of two sons. Her youngest child is now in kindergarten and she is interested in pursuing a career. Hilda dropped out of nursing school after completing her second year, in order to get married. She commented that she "should" probably go back into nursing, but felt it would place her in a subordinate position. She expressed confusion as to what field of work she should pursue.

A review of Hilda's early job choices included the following information:

Occupation	Age	Why Chosen
Forest Ranger	Elementary School	Provide freedom Allow me to be alone
Nurse	High School	Like to make people feel better

Her description of an ideal job listed these characteristics:

1. Respect—be accepted as a worthwhile person by people important to me
2. Usefulness—help others
3. Excitement and Freedom—variety, have a choice in what I do
4. Leadership—have an impact on others

Hilda felt she never quite lived up to her parent's expectations, she tried hard, but never impressed them while Jean didn't even have to try to get attention, especially from father. As a child Hilda spent a great deal of time in solitary activities, reading and working in arts and crafts. She fantasized about being the leader of a large group and getting her picture in the paper as a result of her accomplishments. Although she did become a leader in school, she still felt less sophisticated than the other kids.

Hilda went to parochial schools and was a good student who was interested in extra curricular activities. Her father did not pressure her about what course to take, but wanted her to go to college. Her mother felt strongly she should be a social worker or a secretary.

Her parents' relations with each other were "strained." Hilda felt her mother was concerned with status and never respected her father. The overriding family values were competence and independence.

After leaving school to get married, Hilda concentrated on being a wife and mother, utilizing her artistic ability in crafts projects. The pressures of raising two active boys, who were only 2 years apart, led her first to a parent study group and later to a women's consciousness raising group which she feels contributed to her personnel growth and has given her the courage to begin changing her life. Her husband is supportive of her career search, but she feels that his estimate of her ability is not high.

Hilda gave the following recollections:

1. I was 2 years old. Mother and I were walking. Mother was pushing a carriage with Jean in it. We came to a small hill and I asked if I could go

Family Constellation Diagram

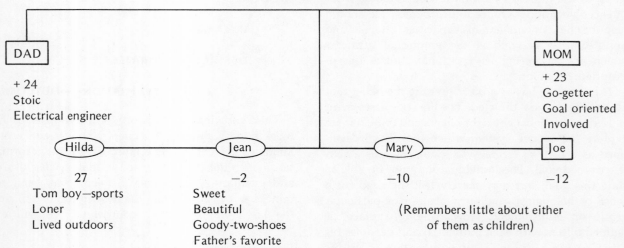

up and see what was on top. She said "Go up" and I crawled up and found a little fish pond. I decided to step on it, and fell in face first. The water covered my face, I started screaming and mother pulled me out. She took me home, put me in a hot bath and gave me hot milk.

> Focus—Looking up as mother pulled me out
> Feeling—Silly or foolish because the water was only 2 inches deep

> (She also remembered a second focus)

> Focus—At home sitting in hot bath, with hot milk
> Feeling—"Snuggly, good, floaty, cozy" because people were helping me

2. (This is not a recollection, but a recent incident Hilda related)

I brought home a dog from the pound. I had not told my husband I was going to, I knew he would be mad, but I decided that I was going to stand my ground. I got the dog for free, but had to give a donation. Also, we were going out of town for a couple days and would have to board the dog which would cost $50.00.

He blew up and I felt ridiculous and started to cry. He told me it was OK.

> Focus—Moment I started to cry
> Feeling—Angry with myself because I allowed him to make me feel like a half-ass.

The Life Goal

The underlying or ultimate goal of the individual, the feeling he has a place, is the focal point of all behavior. This is the *Life Goal.* It is reached through the day to day activities we pursue, or short range goals which we feel will lead to our ultimate objective. The paths by which the individual travels to his Life Goal can be considered *Intermediate* goals (Dreikurs). For example, the Life Goal of the individual may be to "be first" or "the best" in something. The Intermediate goals would include education, work experience, making the proper contacts, etc. These are more often the stated goals when the client comes for career counseling. *Immediate* or situational goals are the purpose behind the behavior we see at the moment; in a meeting, classroom, job situation or social setting. The individual is not aware that all behavior is directed toward his Life Goal, such clarification is part of the counseling process.

A goal is:

a. a subjectively set criterion of what makes individuals feel that they have a place, it gives a person a "plus" feeling,

b. always more visible to others than to the individual,

c. the why of behavior,

d. defined in terms of what a person does and can only be understood in a social context.

The Life Goal is the ideal state of "being." It cannot be used to predict specific behavior, but can predict the major themes or purposes of that behavior.

Let us look at Hilda's Life Goal(s) and how the counselor was able to determine what they were. Her ultimate goal was "to be special" which she felt she could reach by (a) being the center of attention, (b) doing something significant, and (c) making others happy.

Ideal Job Information Clues—She lists the need for respect for her accomplishments and usefulness to others, but also the desire to do as she wishes, not follow tight rules.

Family Constellation Clues—Hilda was never sure she was "good" enough and became special by being a loner. The loner in a group stands out and becomes special by being "different."

Although her description of herself belies it, Hilda is an attractive, warm individual who appeared to be enthusiastic about life. Her self depreciation may be used as a means to get "attention" by getting people involved with her.

Recollection Clues—Her fantasy as a child of having her "name in the paper" would cause people to recognize her specialness.

Her feelings of "snuggly, good, etc." occurred when her mother gave her the full attention she desired.

It is interesting to note that when the counselor disclosed the goal to Hilda her first response was a recognition reflex "Oh my God, that makes sense." Her next comment was "that's terrible." The counselor proceeded to explain that there are useful, productive ways to be "special" as well as useless ways and that an individual may choose how to go about working toward any goal. Being aware of a goal simply helps us to gain greater control over our lives.

Counselors should remember that it is important to get client acceptance of the correctness of the interpretation, but it is equally important that the client have a positive view of that interpretation. Regardless of how negative previous behavior has been, the client can be redirected toward effective strategies.

Obstacles

Obstacles can be defined as those things which currently stand in the way of a person working toward his goals. These may be subjective or objective in nature. Subjective obstacles are psychological absolutes—the "onlys," "musts," "shoulds" that lead to self defeating strategies. Properly verbalizing them for the client allows him to view the irrational aspect of expecting any human dimension to be an absolute.

Objective obstacles are situational variables such as training, talent, age, handicap, family responsibilities, job mobility, etc. The counselor initially deals with the subjective aspects in order to clarify them for the client. Then the focus shifts to the objective factors in order to assist the client to generate new alternatives.

One technique that the counselor may use in order to aid the client in developing skills to overcome obstacles is by invoking "magic." The counselor asks the client what would happen if the obstacles were magically removed? This allows both the counselor and the client the opportunity to see just how much of an impediment a stated obstacle really is.

Let's look at the obstacles which the counselor listed for Hilda.

1. Feeling that to be of worth she must measure up to her own standards and those of others.
2. Relying on others to judge when she is measuring up.
3. Feeling only masculine traits such as being independent, strong, etc. are of value and that feminine traits such as sweet, gentle, etc. are signs of weakness.

The counselor developed this list from the following clues in Hilda's life style responses.

The family value of achievement as a measure of self worth had served as a source of discouragement to Hilda.

Her comments throughout the interview about her husband not feeling she was smart, others being more sophisticated, etc. formed a pattern of her need to measure up and be evaluated by others.

In her recollections, she felt silly because she made a mistake when she tried to be independent, and angry that she allowed herself to be made to feel like a half-ass by crying.

The career of being a nurse (still usually associated with women) was seen as being a subordinate one.

Her mother wanted her to be a social worker or secretary (again female jobs).

Strategies

A *Strategy* is a behavior utilized by an individual to move toward a goal. In modern life we are bombarded with information and continually asked to make choices requiring it's use. Each of us develops strategies to help make these necessary choices, in accordance with our life goals and the obstacles we see standing in the way of reaching those goals. Sometimes, due to the complexity of the situation, we lose sight of the goals and focus on the strategies.

Strategies may be effective or ineffective. The individual may use as his strategy his "ability to solve problems." For him, each obstacle is seen as a barrier to be overcome. The individual has a positive view of himself and enjoys the challenge of "beating" external factors. Often ineffective strategies can be converted from an anti-social to a pro-social (Mozdzierz, Macchitelli, and Lisiecki, 1976) orientation. Then they become effective for the individual. For example, the client sees himself as "stubborn," the counselor reinterprets or rephrases this in a pro-social way as persistent. The purpose of disclosing strategies is to assist the person to see whether they serve as aids or deterrents in reaching goals.

Listed below are Hilda's strategies, with the positive and negative aspects of each. The counselor developed the original list of strategies from the life style clues which will be discussed later. The client was an *active* participant in listing the positive and negative aspects.

1. Be different

   Plus—am successful in being noticed, make original contributions, keep things exciting

   Minus—at times left out, at times it is hard work

2. Be helpless and emotional

   Plus—do get people involved, at times feel relieved after an outburst

   Minus—get angry with self because it shows weakness, causes others to underrate my abilities, lose respect of others, stay in same place

3. Be helpful

   Plus—I feel really good when I am

   Minus—at times over-commit myself

4. Be humorous

   Plus—I can laugh at myself, enjoy life

   Minus—none

5. Be persistent

   Plus—have faith that I can overcome, keep trying even when success is not sure

   Minus—may invest more than the goal is worth

6. Be confused

   Plus—appear to struggle, but take no risk

   Minus—get upset, stay in same place

Early in the interview the counselor noted Hilda's concern with her confusion as to what she should do, it was seen as a means to impress others with her struggle while she was provided with an excuse to do nothing. The initial period of the interview also clearly showed her concern with status—thus if she is confused and doesn't have to do anything she does not take the risk of not measuring up to her standard of status.

Her recollections show that when she appears helpless, a capable person steps in and by pampering makes her feel good again. Since her current attempts to impress people seem to fail, she feels better relying on helplessness.

The idea of being "different" came across in her wanting to be a forest ranger, 20 years ago girls did not do that, the "different" aspect of being a loner has already been discussed.

Helpful was shown in her desire to be a nurse, because that career helps others and gets a degree of respect for Hilda.

Her persistence and humor were strategies that came out in the general discussion with Hilda. Although she agreed with them being on the list, the pattern is not evident from the brief case study presented here.

Evaluation and Outcome

The *Evaluation* component of the paradigm is an examination of the pluses and minuses of the client's strategies to aid in movement toward the life goal. It is an integral aspect of the total counseling process, but it should be stressed that the counselor is evaluating the material about the client—*not* the client. Disclosures are statements about how a person operates, without a value judgment.

This integration between the client and the counselor is most difficult, if not impossible, to describe. There is no set format as the counselor responds to each client's unique needs. The counselor utilizes the information from the life style assessment in order to assist the client in evaluating current alternatives as he moves toward making a vocational decision. This is the ultimate objective of evaluation . . . it leads to the *Outcome* of counseling.

Let us return once again to Hilda and see what the outcome was. Hilda spoke to the counselor on three occasions and her final career decision was not made until after the second session. It is important for you to remember that if you do a good job in making guesses, the client needs some time to process this material before a definite decision is made. This was the case with Hilda. The information was gathered and disclosures were made during her first meeting with the counselor. The second session dealt with further relating this data to her career concerns and answering questions that had occurred to her. The final interview was a follow-up to discuss her vocational decision.

Here briefly are the major evaluation points and the outcomes of this case.

Hilda grew up in a situation where she felt it was impossible to live up to the expectations of her parents. She wanted to demonstrate that she was a special person by being competent. However, whatever she did was not enough to gain the degree of recognition that she desired. After the first session the counselor asked Hilda to make a list of 5 people she wanted most to please, placing them in rank order and including herself. Later they discussed the list and how Hilda could take some pressure off herself if these were the only people she was "always" concerned with pleasing.

As Hilda and the counselor discussed the obstacles she began to see they were largely her own creation. The realization that she had accepted the family value of measuring self worth through achievement helped her explain much of her discouragement. Additionally, she saw that her concern about what others thought had impeded her career decision because she wanted to select a career that would meet the standards of what she felt others would respect. Added to this were the cultural biases of "feminine" work being of less value. Thus, she was ruling out potentially satisfying careers.

Finally, Hilda concluded that whatever career she chose, those who really cared about her would still love and respect her. The session then concentrated on what factors were important to her in her career search. She said she wanted a profession where she could help others and that would allow her to enter the labor market in a reasonable length of time. The second session ended with her decision to check on local nursing programs to see how many of her college credits she could get transferred. About four months later the counselor contacted Hilda and was told she was in a nurses training program and truly enjoying the work.

Although the outcome of this particular case may have seemed apparent from the outset, Hilda did not feel that way. Her deep concern about her career choice was evident during the first session. If the counselor had merely recommended that she go into nursing because labor market trends projected there would be job opportunities, and she had the proper aptitudes, would she have been comfortable with the decision?

Let us quickly review the steps in using the life style for career counseling.

1. Assess Life Style—formulate goal statement "I want to _____ "
2. List Obstacles and Strategies
3. Develop Resource Bank for Client—list psychological assets and skills, this may include pro-social interpretation of previously negatively viewed attributes.
4. Action Planning—Re-assess ideal job, develop list of other jobs possible, use occupational in-

formation to further investigate jobs (the client is responsible for this)
5. Select Course of Action—set up specific actions and time limits
6. Evaluation and Follow-up—encourage client to check back and review his progress.

It is important that the client spend some time thinking over the life style information before making a career decision. The need to check back with the counselor should be emphasized to him. The total time for the process will vary, some clients will complete these steps in two or three interviews, others will need more. Remember that the time factor will be dictated by the client's feelings of readiness, you are not to do the investigating or deciding for him!

Bibliography

Dreikurs, Rudolph, "The Private Logic" mimeographed manuscript, no date.

Mozdzierz, Gerald J., Macchitelli, Frank J., and Lisiecki, Joseph "The Paradox in Psychotherapy: An Adlerian Perspective" *Journal of Individual Psychology* 52:2, 169–184.

Parsons, F. *Choosing a Vocation*, New York: Houghton Mifflin, 1909.

Super, D. E., and Bachrach, P., "Scientific Careers and Vocational Development Theory," New York: Bureau of Publications, Teachers College, Columbia University, 1957.

Life Style Concepts Applied to Correctional Counseling

Daniel G. Eckstein

Many counselors who work within correctional institutions, often become frustrated and discouraged when attempting to facilitate change within inmates or the system itself (i.e., *The Personnel and Guidance Journal*, 1974, pp. 128–168). Institutional and individual change is infrequent but, rather than become totally disenchanted with correctional institutions, it should be noted that growth *is* possible. The "dark ages of incarceration" *are* being dispelled slowly through innovative programs. Certainly much remains to be done, but needed changes *are* occurring within institutions as well as within the community.

In reflecting upon personal experiences in adult and juvenile correctional facilities, the author will discuss some general observations regarding correctional counseling. By utilizing insights from life style investigations, the article will conclude with a case history which will illustrate that personal change in both attitudes and behavior is possible within correctional institutions.

Needs

Maslow's (1954) hierarchy of needs provides important considerations for correctional counseling. He noted that there are basic needs which must be met before a person can consider other "higher" needs which he termed "metaneeds." For example, individuals starving from malnutrition probably will be focusing upon getting some food rather than dealing with such concerns as esteem, congruence, or genuineness. However, once such basic needs as food, shelter, and safety are met, then individuals may consider such "higher" needs as love, beauty, and ultimate self-actualization.

It is the author's contention that too often correctional counselors fail because the fundamental needs of inmates are never fulfilled. Basic nutritional needs are often neglected. For example, in many institutions supper is served at 4:30 p.m. and inmates are locked in buildings or individual cells with no additional food until 8:30 a.m. the next morning. Of course, correctional institutions have been notorious for poor health standards.

Providing that food services are at least minimally effective, inmates must then consider other needs which most people take for granted. Concerns for safety, clean sheets and towels, and even soap and toothpaste generally precede questions regarding honesty or truth. In fact, for many inmates, life becomes a constant obsessional struggle to meet such basic needs.

A constant concern for most inmates relates to personal safety. Counseling a timid male after being sexually assaulted by other inmates is a grim ordeal, but too often such activities occur frequently within correctional facilities. Counselors trained in traditional "one-to-one client-seeking-help-with-a problem" must realize it is often a different world inside the prison walls. Fear, discouragement, mistrust, and misinformation are typical feelings for incarcerated inmates.

Counselors who are not willing to facilitate fulfillment of such basic food, shelter, and safety needs will probably experience difficulties in correctional institutions. Brodsky (1974) describes the attempts of two beginning counselors at making their roles more meaningful: "Rather than spending their time counseling or addressing the system, they spent their first two weeks in the institution setting rat traps. They caught most of the rats that had been running around the living quarters for years. This brought them a better relationship with the inmates and made the institution a much more human place" (p. 164).

General William Booth, founder of the Salvation Army, coined the slogan: "soup, soap, and salvation" to describe his work with down-trodden individuals. Counselors who are not willing to become involved with "soup and soap" concerns may never have an opportunity to facilitate an inmate's personal "salvation."

Quest for Meaning

Lest the author be mistakenly perceived as advising beginning counselors merely to set mice traps and provide adequate food and clothing, it should be noted that crucial metaphysical questions relating to purpose and meaning in life can aid an inmate in transcending the bitter reality of incarceration. Such an existential dilemma is vividly described by Viktor Frankl in *Man's Search For Meaning* (1963). During three harrowing years of confinement in a Nazi prison camp, Frankl found that some prisoners lost all hope, literally lying down and dying. Other prisoners were able to endure the most hellish times because of deep personal commitments. For Frankl, the love of his family and the desire to complete a manuscript provided the meaning necessary to endure the agonizing prison camp experiences. In a diary reflecting upon his confinement, Frankl writes: "A man who becomes conscious of the responsibility he bears toward a human being who affectionately waits for him or to an unfinished work, will never be able to throw away his life. He knows the 'why' for his existence, and will be able to bear almost any 'how' " (p. 127).

Thus, while working within the institution to improve living conditions, counselors may also facilitate a transcendence of the most depressing situations by helping inmates find ultimate purpose and meaning in their lives. Values clarification and self-exploration should aid in establishing needed personal identity and commitment.

Adlerian Contributions

Alfred Adler has made important contributions to the helping professions by focusing on the necessity of social interest, the goal directed or purposeful nature of behavior, plus the unified "holistic" striving of all individuals. It is interesting to note that he described inmates as having "pampered life styles." Adler (in Ansbacher & Ansbacher, 1970) notes that:

"In criminals we invariably find evidence of the pampered life style. Delinquents who have committed one or more crimes picture the world as a place where everyone else exists for their exploitation, where they have the right forcibly to take possession of the goods, health, or life of others and to set their own interest above the interest of others. In such cases we can always find a certain attitude which can be traced through the life history of the delinquent back to childhood. Delinquents are always individuals whose social interest suffered shipwreck in childhood, whose social interest did not attain full maturity. They begin very early to take forcibly anything which seems to them to belong to them" (p. 257).

Incarcerated inmates often feel unfairly treated by society. A frequent notion held by such individuals is that they can break societies rules, but not have to suffer the "logical consequences" of such inappropriate behavior. They generally have failed to gain attention in socially accepted way, thus resorting to socially unacceptable but personally enhancing delinquent behavior.

Two specific Adlerian techniques found to be useful included what Nikelly (1972) described as "stroke-and-spit" tactics. "Stroking means that the therapist gives of his time and effort to help the client listen to himself and to cultivate an active, social interest. In spitting, the therapist discloses the skillful maneuvers of the client, who may be seeking to avoid intimacy or who is directly hostile to others, and thereby exposes his ineffective ways of behaving (i.e., 'Look what you are actually doing"). Spitting implies that the disclosure is unpleasant enough so that the client no longer desires to continue this behavior." (p. 88).

Through encouragement, a trusting relationship between the counselor and inmate becomes more possible. A psychological investigation follows, including a life style and other relevant psychometric information. The crucial interpretation of the life style plus re-orientation phases involve sharing possible mistaken goals (i.e., undue attention, power, revenge, inadequacy), while encouraging the use of more socially appropriate ways of fulfilling the unique life style.

Inmates often resent "society-oriented" counselors "unfairly" trying to change their lives; yet, they are often encouraged upon gaining insights as to possible reasons for engaging in delinquent activities. Discussing more socially appropriate ways of fulfilling the same needs is similarly encouraging.

Adler's personal illustration concerning the useful and useless nature of life styles has been appreciated by many inmates. As a child, Adler had an intense fear of death, resolving to overcome it by becoming a physician. However, another man with a similar fear of death became a grave digger, burying others and not being buried himself. Just as inmates can realize the useful-useless side of the same need, so they often decide to utilize more socially appropriate means of attaining their goals. It seems futile for counselors to argue that an individual's incarceration is fair; rather, encouragement in fulfilling their goals through more useful ways has appeared to be more effective.

Life Styles

Through the use of a life style investigation the following important family atmosphere characteristics are analyzed: birth order, interpersonal relationships between members of the family, the siblings main competitor, and unstructured early recollections from childhood experiences which are in harmony with an individual's present outlook on life. Dreikurs (1953) followed Adler's "holistic" notion by writing that "the life style is comparable to a characteristic theme in a piece of music. It brings the rhythm of recurrence into our lives" (p. 44).

Although each individual's own style is unique, Harold Mosak, (in Nikelly, 1972) has identified fourteen different commonly observed life styles. Particularly relevent to the following case history is Mosak's (1959) description of the getter: "The 'getter' exploits and manipulates life and others by actively or passively putting others into his service. He tends to view life as unfair for denying him that to which he feels entitled. He may employ charm, shyness, temper, or intimidation as methods of operation. He is insatiable in his getting" (p. 194).

Additional information concerning the use of life styles may be found in *The Counseling Psychologist* (1971, 3, 2–72) or in a programmed workbook, *Life Style: What It Is and How to Do It.*

Representative Case History

A. Family Atmosphere

John is an eighteen year-old Negro male, having three older brothers, one older sister and two younger sisters. His brother, David, is six years older than he, while Webster and Andrew are four and two years older respectively. Compared to the females, John is two years younger than Juanita, while one and two years older than Teresa and Denise. Thus, he is the fourth brother and fifth of seven children in the family.

In sibling interrelationships, John feels that Webster was most *different* describing him as a "good boy," having more friends, liking school, not cursing, but drinking more than John. Conversely, John states he was most *like* Andrew, describing him as a "trouble maker" who would "jump on people if he had to." John also says that Andrew did not get along well with his friends, didn't like school, and that, although he doesn't drink, he smokes. All of these characteristics were shared by both Andrew and John. John describes Webster as being "prejudiced" regarding interracial relationships.

As a child, John describes *himself* as playing and fighting a lot, pulling jokes on people he did not like,

attending school when he felt like it, and, when in school, having constant conflicts with his teachers. It also appears that John was encouraged by his three older brothers to fight other students.

John seems to have had the closest relationship with his older sister, Juanita, specifically stating that "she gave me confidence." Conversely, he and his younger sister, Teresa, were constantly at odds with one another. John specifically resented her achievement in school, the fact that she was "bossy," and that she criticized him when he was wrong. Thus, Teresa served as the main competitor for him.

Compared with the other siblings, John found his place by being a hard worker, rebellious, considerate, wanting his own way, feelings easily hurt, very quick temper, few friends, and very spoiled. He also saw himself as having the least intelligence, making the poorest grades, doing the least amount of work around the house, the least selfish, the lowest achiever, and the shortest.

None of the siblings appear to have been responsible for the others. John and Andrew played together, as did Juanita and Teresa. John states that Webster was his father's favorite, believing himself to be his mother's favorite.

John describes his father as being "mean, with a quick temper." Conversely, he views his mother as "nice" noting that "she wouldn't let my father beat me." Thus, it appears that his parents often disagreed concerning methods of discipline for John. During such disagreements, the mother seemed the most dominant, preventing her husband from disciplining the children, prompting John to boast "I've never been whipped in my life."

The quarreling between his mother and father reached a zenith when John was six years old. His parents were upstairs arguing, John being the only other person in the home. Suddenly, he heard a gun shot, upon which he ran upstairs. Opening the door to his parent's bedroom, he saw his mother lying on the floor dead. His father made a motion towards him, whereupon John ran. He then heard another shot, returning to find his father dead also.

After the death of his mother and father, the family remained together for two years. Then the oldest brothers went to live with other relatives, while Juanita went to Baltimore. John, Teresa, and Denise went to live with his grandmother, currently his legal guardian.

B. Early Recollections

1. Age 5: John, Andrew, and Webster "picked on" a midget; called him "midget, shorty." He got mad, I laughed. He called us bad names, then we

ran him down the street. He tried to get the police on us, but we hid. Felt: thought it was fun.

2. Age 5: Ran down alley throwing down trash cans, making noise. Someone called police. They snuck up on Andrew, Webster, John. Took us to station. Wouldn't talk. Warned if caught again would lock up. When got home, Dad wanted to whip us, but Mom wouldn't let him. Felt: when throwing cans felt happy and fun-liked playing; when caught, still happy, didn't know what was happening, when home still laughing—just followed gang.

3. Age 5: Andrew and me playing in house—he hit me—I become cross-eyed, people made fun of me—I didn't understand how I got cross-eyed. Felt: didn't like it—wasn't laughing when I came up.

4. Age 6: Fought with anyone—for example, me and white boy got in fight. He passed me and said something—called me "nigger," my brothers told me to beat him up, and I beat him up with a stick. He went home crying—I went home laughing; his mother came over to my mother—she took up for me. My brothers came to the rescue also. His mother went home saying she would call the police. He was 8, I was only 6. Everything brothers told me to do or say, I did. Felt: when it happened I was mad; I felt like killing him; got carried away. Next day wanted to get him again. A few days later, Juanita got on me for following older brother's advice. Felt bad after that.

5. Mother and Father's death—Age 6; I was downstairs—I heard a gun go off—went upstairs—saw mother on floor—father looked at me—I ran—then heard another shot—went back up again. He was on floor—went downstairs—didn't know what to do—few minutes later, went to get uncle. Felt: confused, didn't know what happened. (didn't realize death until 10)

C. Possible Interpretations based on Early Recollections.

1. It is satisfying to get the best of other people, especially those whom I consider inferior.

2. I can do as I please, and don't have to worry about the threats of others, nor do I have to abide by "the rules of the game;" I enjoy having fun at the expense of others.

3. People generally don't care about me, and I am especially upset by criticism, because this causes me to lose peer approval.

4. It is important to gain recognition, and essential not to let others put me down, thus causing me to "lose face" in the eyes of others; I often follow the advice of others, but do not want to disappoint people whom I love.

D. Life Style Summary

John seems to be an individual for whom a stressful situation consists of losing face in the eyes of others. It appears that John is sensitive to criticism, seeking the approval of other peers. As the youngest male in the family, he describes himself as the mother's favorite and admits to being spoiled and having had his own way. When frustrated, he then uses his temper and rebellion to have things go his own way. It also appears that John rates himself low on attributes of productivity. However, one exception which should be used as a source of encouragement is his ability to work hard at a task.

From his early recollections, John seems to feel that people are critical and out to "put me down." When this happens, he says it is "important for me to get back, or not to stand for it." It also appears that John needs the approval of others. His general mistaken notions of life seem to include the ideas that he can do as he pleases, disregarding society's rules, not having to worry about the consequences of his actions.

Assets for John include his concern for others and his willingness to work hard. He appears to be very concerned about the opinion of others, finding it upsetting to lose face in the eyes of others.

Future goals of counseling include helping John gain peer approval in productive ways. One possible way is through his leadership in a dormitory singing group. It will also be pointed out to John that there are many other ways to gain proper approval, but that in the past, he has chosen undesirable activities such as picking on midgets and knocking over trash cans to gain such recognition. The disadvantages to such actions are that they lead to being incarcerated in a correctional institution.

Another counseling goal will be to enhance John's own self feelings in minimizing the need of antisocial peer approval. Instead of reacting with anger when he feels put down, hopefully John can come to realize that he doesn't need to enhance himself at the expense of others.

E. The Turning Point

Three weeks after sharing the life style summary with John, including encouraging him to become aware of situations where he felt "put down" and suggesting some alternative behaviors, a major incident indicated that change is possible. John was arguing violently with a correctional guard, insisting he had not been involved in stealing food from the kitchen. As the dispute grew more heated, the guard seized John. Breaking free, John grabbed an empty soft drink can, splitting it into two sharp jagged pieces.

Suddenly fifty other inmates surrounded John and the guard in their game of "confrontation," shouting encouragement to John and obscenities at the guard. It was obvious that John faced critical choices; putting down the now deadly "weapons" involved losing face with his peers, being placed in maximum security, and probably not being paroled for another thirty days. The other alternative involved two split aluminum fragments and an unarmed but angry guard similarly unwilling to be "put down." At age 18 the stakes were deadly for John.

In the midst of the struggle, John stopped; and a crucial decision was made; moments later the "weapons" lay harmlessly on the ground. He was smiling broadly realizing that a major victory had been won. A few weeks later, John returned home a free man.

Bibliography

Adler, A. *Superiority and Social Interest*. Edited by H. L. & R. R. Ansbacher, Evanston, IL: Northwestern University Press, 1970.

Brodsky, Stanley. "Personal Commitment: Challenge for Change," *The Personnel and Guidance Journal*, 1974, 53, 164.

"Counselors in Corrections," *The Personnel and Guidance Journal*, 1974, 53, 128–168.

Dreikurs, Rudolf. *Fundamentalf of Adlerian Psychology*. Chicago: Alfred Adler Institute, 1953.

Eckstein, Daniel; Baruth, Leroy; Mahrer, Dave. *Life Style: What It Is and How To Do It*. Dubuque, IA.: Kendall/Hunt Publishing Company, 1978.

Frankl, Viktor. *Man's Search For Meaning*. New York: Washington Square Press, Inc., 1963.

Maslow, Abraham, *Motivation and Personality*. New York: Harper & Row, 1954.

Mosak, Harold, "The 'Getting' Type: A parsimonious social interpretation of the oral character," *Journal of Individual Psychology*, 1959, 15, 193–196.

Nikelly, Arthur. *Techniques For Behavior Change*. Springfield, IL: Charles C. Thomas, 1972.

Concise Counseling Assessment: The Children's Life-Style Guide

Don Dinkmeyer, Jr.
Don Dinkmeyer, Sr.

If school counselors are to effectively influence children's attitudes and behavior, they need to understand the perceptions of those children. In order to understand these perceptions school counselors must utilize all available sources of information. This includes the data in the children's cumulative school folders. When counselors have massive work loads, they often reach first for this data because it is easily obtainable. The materials contained in such folders provide substantial information, but unfortunately reveal very little about children's views of the world. Perhaps the only truly legitimate way to know a child's perception is to ask the child directly. The Children's Life-Style Guide (CLG) is a technique to help counselors with this process.

CLG standardizes the counselor-child discussion and focuses on an investigation of the child's perception of his or her world. It is essentially a questionnaire that serves as the basis for a structured interview with a child. Subjectivity is the key to the CLG, since it is intended to provide unique information about each child. Normative information is pertinent only to the extent that some children may hold similar life perceptions. The CLG is particularly useful for elementary school counseling because children are free to respond in their own language. Thus the CLG allows both the counselor and the child to become highly involved in the assessment process.

The CLG presented here was developed from the work of Dreikurs (1967) and subsequent adaptations by Mosak (1973). This CLG has eight major sections, six of which are completed with information from the child while two are summaries by the counselor. The following case study illustrates a counselors' use of the CLG with a child named Lisa and presents typical data and counselor summaries.

Children's Life-Style Guide

I. Family Constellation

Mr. W.	44 years old
Mrs. W.	42 years old
Lisa (F)	12 years old
Harry (M)	8 years old

Who is most different from you? How? Harry—everyone gives in to him; he's the favorite of Mom and Dad.

Who is most like you? How? Harry—he tries to make people laugh, likes to tell stories like I do.

What was life like before you went to school? I was the only one and life was beautiful. I always got my way and people spent a lot of time with me.

II. Functioning at Life Tasks

Socially: How do you get along with adults? children? With teachers, O.K., but you can't trust them. They expect you to cooperate all the time. I have a few friends, but I'm not popular.

Work: How do things go for you in school? I have some trouble; teachers think I'm not doing what I should.

What subject do you like best? Like least? Why? I like social studies, because we get to read. I don't like arithmetic or spelling, because they are too much work.

Don Dinkmeyer, Jr. and Don Dinkmeyer, Sr., Concise Counseling Assessment: The Children's Life Style Guide, *Elementary School Guidance and Counseling*, 12(2), 1977, 117–124. Copyright 1977 American Personnel and Guidance Association. Reprinted with permission.

What would you like to be when you grow up? Why? I would like to own a business and make a lot of money.

What do you fear the most? Nothing in particular.

III. Family Atmosphere

What kind of a person is your father? He is friendly but not consistent. Sometimes he tries to hassle me.

What kind of a person is your mother? She's moody, crabby, and demanding; a lot of the time I don't know what to expect.

Which of the children is most like your father? In what ways? Harry—because they share some of the same hobbies.

Which of the children is most like your mother? In what ways? I am, because we both like to talk.

IV. Sibling Characteristics

A series of questions (such as "who is the most intelligent?") are asked until the child makes a response to each item.

a. Intelligent—Lisa
b. Hardest worker—Harry
c. Best grades in school—Harry
d. Conforming—Lisa
e. Rebellious—Harry
f. Helps around the house—nobody
g. Critical—Harry
h. Considerate—nobody
i. Selfish—Harry
j. Tries to please—Both, but Harry usually wins
k. Sensitive, feelings easily hurt—Lisa
l. Temper—Lisa
m. Materialistic, likes to get things—Lisa
n. Most friends—Harry
o. Most spoiled—Harry
p. High standards of achievement—Lisa
q. Athletic—Lisa
r. Strongest—Harry
s. Attractive—Lisa
t. Most punished—Harry

V. Early Recollections

"What can you remember that is a specific event—like a picture of one certain time—from when you were younger? What were you feeling at the time?"

1. Making a house from building blocks, after it was finished another girl came and smashed it. I felt very angry.

2. In kindergarten one day they told me that I could play with the toys. When I started to make something the teacher took them away from me. I felt cheated.

3. Mom brought home a clarinet for me. I tried to blow in it, but nothing happened. I was embarrassed.

VI. Three Wishes and Fantasy Animal

If you could have three wishes, what would they be:

1. That I didn't get picked on in school
2. That my teachers wouldn't make me do so much math
3. That I could stay home and read

If you were going to pretend to be an animal, which would you choose? Why? I would like to be an alligator. I could bite people and make them afraid of me.

VII. and VIII. Summary and Assets

Lisa is the older of two children. She has been referred to the counselor by her homeroom teacher for failing to get along with her classmates and having power struggles with the teacher.

Lisa sees herself as intelligent, easily hurt by criticism, and the victim of demanding teachers and inconsistent parents. She feels it is unfair that special privileges are granted to her younger brother. Lisa is deeply discouraged about her inability to get along with peers and also is aware of her conflicts with teachers.

She is confused about her position in life. Despite great skill in reading, teachers demand that she concentrate on her weaker areas, math and spelling, and deny her the pleasurable subjects. Her early recollections about life suggest that Lisa believes life is unfair, confusing, and demanding.

Her faulty assumptions are that: (a) Life is unfair and unpredictable. (b) I cannot count on people to do as they should. And (c) I am not as capable as I should be.

Lisa's assets are her high intelligence, interest in certain school areas such as reading, and her sensitivity to her own feelings.

Interpretations

In section I, Family Constellation, children are asked to reveal how they see themselves by sharing the ways in which they are similar or different as siblings. Thus, "My brother is more talkative" is also saying "I am more reserved."

It should be emphasized that all individuals make their own decisions as to how they will find a place (or psychological position) in their family. These general characterizations are not firm stereotypes nor hard and fast rules. Such a claim would deny the unique creativity to choose that each individual brings to the world.

The second section focuses on functioning at life tasks. Dreikurs (1950) and Adler (1969) identified certain tasks of life that people are faced with as they grow. How individuals choose to deal with each of these tasks is indicative of their psychological movement, goals, and purposes.

The first question in this section investigates the social tasks of life. Lisa recognizes her troubles with peers and describes a lack of trust with her teachers.

Question two is useful in assessing the child's approach to schoolwork. It also provides insight into the child's personality. Dreikurs (1971) indicated that children who have difficulty with spelling indicate a disregard for order, while problems with arithmetic point toward poor problem-solving skills in all tasks of life. Our example, Lisa, dislikes both of these subjects, indicating a possible lack of skills with others and herself.

Questions three and four give indications of the amount of realism in a child's goals and concerns. It also provides insight into the child's self-ideal. It is essential that the counselor determine the reasons a child chooses a certain type of work. For example, some may choose to be airplane pilots because it is exciting, others because of the anticipated free time. The child's perception of a certain type of work is obtained so that counselors are not biased by their own ideas about the values of various jobs.

The third section, Family Atmosphere, allows the children to share their subjective impressions of family members. Questions three and four are followed by the specific "In what way?" The answer to these questions tells about the children even if they are not the one most like father or mother. For example, if children see a brother as being like father because they all like people, the children also are saying that they are more reserved towards others.

The fourth section, Sibling Characteristics, allows children to indicate which of their siblings they see as possessing the most or least of a list of characteristics. This section also allows children to share themselves in personality areas since their descriptions are useful in compiling their assets and liabilities.

The Early Recollection section (V) is subjective interpretations of children's ideas about life (Kopp and Dinkmeyer 1975). Early recollections are an economical technique for gaining insight into children's goals, attitudes, and beliefs. An early recollection is a specific event the child can "almost see." It is a singular, captured rememberance that the child chooses to remember.

Early recollections tend not to be unusual events, but instead reveal a pattern of attitudes that are consistent with broad based beliefs about life. Lisa, for example, chose to remember incidents in which life was unfair, where life was demanding and confusing. It is important that the counselor get a specific feeling the child was experiencing at the time of the event. This feeling often reveals the child's attitude about life. Accordingly, counselors should ask for enough recollections (usually three to six) until the child reveals a pattern of attitudes towards events. In some cases prompting may be necessary to give the child an idea of the type of desired responses but care should be taken not to bias the child's responses in any particular direction. One might ask for recollections about school, or interactions with siblings, or friends, or parents, but only after presenting the request in an open-ended manner.

The sixth section, Three Wishes and Animal Question, allows the children to express traits they value. In order to obtain accurate information, it is essential that the counselor ask children why they would like to be certain animals. For example, Lisa chose to be an alligator so she could be ferocious and dangerous; not to be able to sit in the sun all day.

The last two sections, Summary and Assets, capsulize the information gathered from the child. The summary section enables the counselor to gain an overview of the situation. The assets section is useful in formulating consulting strategies for interactions with parents and teachers. Together they help the counselor formulate the most effective counseling strategies. If the CLG is used correctly, their strategies will be highly personalized.

Conclusion

The Children's Life-Style Guide provides structured examinations of childrens' movements in life; the way they see themselves, and their ideas about getting along with peers and adults. This diagnostic tool creates a basis for understanding children's perceptions about life that counselors can build on in future interventions. The CLG helps counselors see the world through the eyes of children and that should make their jobs more meaningful.

References

Adler, A. *The science of living.* (H. L. Anshbacher, Ed.). Garden City, New York: Doubleday, 1969.

Dreikurs, R. *Fundamental of Adlerian psychology.* Chicago: Alfred Adler Institute, 1950.

Dreikurs, R. *Psychodynamics, psychotherapy, and counseling.* Chicago: Alfred Adler Institute, 1967.

Dreikurs, R., Grunwald, B; & Pepper, F. *Maintaining sanity in the classroom.* New York: Harper & Row, 1971.

Eckstein, D., et al. *Life-style: What it is and how to do it.* Chicago: Alfred Adler Institute, 1975.

Kopp, R. R., & Dinkmeyer, D. Early recollection in life-style assessment and counseling. *School Counselor,* 1975, *23,* 22–27.

Mosak, Harold. Life-style. In A. Nikelly (Ed.), *Techniques for behavior change.* Springfield, Ill.: Charles C. Thomas, 1971.

Shulman, B. *Contributions to individual psychology.* Chicago: Alfred Adler Institute. 1973.

The Moral Dimensions of Life Style

L. Shannon Jung and Patricia B. Jung

Morality is often associated with momentous decisions: the responsibility of extramarital sex; problems of scarce medical, nutritional, or energy resources; or a church's response to social injustice. Surely these questions throw moral issues into vivid relief. However, even when the crisis situation evokes a self-conscious decision, that decision results not so much from a disembodied rational calculation as it does from the way in which a person's everyday decisions have already been made. Clearly the psychological self one has become penetrates even the rational decision-making process. Morality has more to do with one's everyday style than is generally thought.[1]

A popular area of social scientific investigation—that of life style analysis—has an affinity with this emphasis on the morality of everyday life. This is particularly the case when it is understood that one's life style is not simply a matter of insignificant preferences—snow skiing over water skiing, for example. In contrast, one's life style overarches most of the decisions a person makes; it is a mode of moving through the world, of relating to others, and of identifying one's own commitments. Hence, it necessarily entails moral dimensions.

In this essay, therefore, our focus will be on the morality of life style. Rather than examining the morality of extramarital sex, we look at one sexual context, the life style of shyness; rather than dealing with the criteria for determining how scarce medical resources should be distributed, we look at the life style of careerism; rather than taking up the relationship between the church and social action, we look at the life style of Unification Church membership. Each of those three decisions would be worked out in a matrix where the decision-maker's life style would be an important feature.

Shyness, careerism, and Unification Church membership represent three life style choices. Beyond being merely whimsical preferences or partial commitments, they embody a holistic gestalt—the lens through which people view the world and themselves. Our contention is that they also represent moral choices; and, in fact, embody styles of morali-

ty. Indeed, the purpose of this essay is to suggest that life style analysis is an approach to personal and group morality which offers the psychologist, the sociologist, and the ethicist unique advantages.

The essay begins by comparing the psychological stance towards "life style" with that of a prominent Christian ethicist. It moves then to an analysis of three contemporary life-styles: those characterized by shyness, careerism, and membership in the Unification Church of Reverend Moon. In conclusion, it will document the advantages offered by life style analysis, and suggest directions for further study and correlation.

Alfred Adler (1929) in psychology, and Max Weber (1946) in sociology, can both be credited as progenitors of the notion of "life style." Because Weber's work centered on cultural style and this article will focus on personal and psychological style, attention will be directed towards Adler's work. Adler (1929, p. 98) asserted that a feeling or complex of inferiority drove people to movement and action, and ultimately to a goal. He originally called this consistent movement towards a goal "a plan of life," but modified that term to "style of life." Ansbacher and Ansbacher (1967) understand Adler as later equating this "style of life" with the self, one's own personality, the method of facing problems, and the person's whole attitude towards life. Clearly Adler's notion was that life style is the holistic way in which the individual relates to himself, to others, and to the world. As he (in Ansbacher and Ansbacher, 1956, p. 172) writes, "The style of life is the more general concept comprising, in addition to the goal, the individual's opinion of himself and the world and his unique way of striving for the goal in his particular situation." Gushurst (1971, p. 30) summarizes this concept as "the total system which accounts for the

Reprinted by permission of the authors.

1. This emphasis on everyday style is one that is shared by life style analysts and ethicists who focus on moral character, "being good" rather than "doing good," and the virtues. Currently there is a revival of interest in the ethics of character (Gustafson, 1975; Hauerwas, 1974) within the discipline of ethics.

consistency and directionality of an individual's life movement."[2]

Some Adlerians use a tripartite technique for analyzing life style. (See the use of this tool suggested by Eckstein, Baruth, and Mahrer, 1978.) They suggest that responding to the three statements "Life is . . . Others are . . . I am . . ." will enable a person to categorize his or her life themes. This interpretative device corresponds to Adler's own conception of the relational nature of the self, which is perhaps most evident in his work *The Science of Living* (1929).

The relational base which is prominent in Adler's psychology also undergirds the work of a significant Christian theological ethicist, H. Richard Niebuhr. It is not all surprising, therefore, that Niebuhr was interested in the concept of "life style" (1963, pp. 149–151). Though he used the concept explicitly only late in life, Niebuhr's system of thought and methodological approach make manifest the fact that his interest in life style was a logical extension of his thought rather than merely an accidental figure of speech.

Niebuhr (1963, p. 45) writes that, "The object of the inquiry is not, as in the case of Christian ethics, simply the Christian life but rather human moral life in general." He understands the Christian style of life as "continuous with other modes of human existence" (p. 45); this is reflected in the phenomenological—rather than theological—base which he uses to analyze moral responsibility. Only in later chapters do his religious commitments enter into the substance of his work. For this reason, Niebuhr's relfections on moral life style seem to be methodologically compatible with the psychologist Adler who similarly employed a method based on phenomenal observation.

Niebuhr draws on social psychology, particularly that of G. H. Mead, to make the case that human life can most accurately be described as life-in-response. He suggests that the image of "man-the-answerer, man engaged in dialogue, man acting in response to action upon him" (p. 56) is implicit in the idea of moral responsibility. This should not be taken to mean that the self is only responsive, as opposed to being also initiating and creative. Niebhur builds this image on a relational base, as did Adler.

In his Earl Lectures, Niebuhr attempted to interpret the style of the Christian life with the aid of the symbol of responsibility. He is interested in the form and character of that life style, and also in how it differs from other life styles. As he inquires (1963, p. 149), "How does the general Christian character and form manifest itself in specific activities such as those in

which Christians, like all other people, engage when they marry and raise children, eat and drink, obey civil laws and help enact them . . . when they make all the countless daily evaluations, decisions, and choices that human beings must undertake in their inescapable freedom?" Thus he wants to describe the style, form, or gestalt which grounds the manifold activities of Christian believers.

His concern with the category "life style" reflects a conviction that an individual's identity is a matter of what he or she believes, is, and does. He affirms that being and doing arise inseparable from the same core; they are reciprocal processes (1963, p. 150). Thus, Niebuhr differs from those philosophical ethicists who identify one's morality as synonymous with what one thinks to be moral. He focuses instead on the psychological and sociological dynamics which figure in the process of decision-making. Two directions of movement are emphasized: creative reflection on what one ought to do, and the conditionedness of morality by what one has already done and become. Morality is a result both of one's social and psychological rootage in a situation and also of "what one is as a result of the values and beliefs which one self-consciously holds" (Miller, 1976, p. 77). The affinities with those psychologists and sociologists who employ the category "life style" are obvious.

The thought of Niebuhr and Adler converge at very crucial points. Both men based their interpretations on the recognition that human life is lived in relationship—to self, to others, and to life-in-general, or nature. The similarities—and one significant difference—can be illustrated graphically:

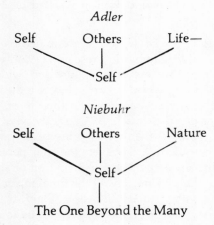

The One Beyond the Many

2. One difficulty with the concept of life style is that the term refers to such a broad canopy that it may not be too helpful in describing behavior. Another difficulty is that human behavior may not be so consistent or unambiguous as the category life style seems to suggest.

Both thinkers realized the important role that self-identity and self-concept plays in a person's life. Both recognized the influence of others in shaping one's own identity and behavior; particularly noted are the relationships which form and inform our life styles. The categories "life" and "nature" are more similar than they initially appear. Both men are suggesting that our lives have to do with our relation to broader entities than ourselves or others.

Up to this point, both men have described human existence in essentially the same way. Niebuhr clearly goes beyond Adler in saying that the Christian understanding of God, "the One beyond the many," (1970, pp. 110–113) qualifies and informs all aspects of Christians' life styles. He does not think, however, that this ultimate commitment somehow makes the Christian's human existence discontinuous with that of other people; he stresses the continuity of Christian and general human experience. As he wrote (1963, p. 150), "Christianity represents a qualification of human practical existence, or at least of Western moral life, rather than a new and wholly different way of living; it may represent a species rather than a genus of human moral existence."

Following Niebuhr's lead, we will look at the morality manifested in three life styles, first from the viewpoint of general humanitarianism, and then from a religious and Christian perspective.

The Life Style of Shyness

"I am lonely beyond belief. I live in complete solitude without a friend in the world, neither male nor female. I have been betrayed many times over and my experiences in life have left me very unhappy and bitter. I spend the holidays in complete solitude."
—A 50-year-old businesswoman (Quoted in Zimbardo, 1977, p. 19)

The first life style to be examined is that of shyness. Philip Zimbardo's research (1977, p. 13) indicates that shyness is common and widespread; more than 80 percent of his subjects indicated that they were "shy at some point in their lives," 40 percent considered themselves "presently shy," and 25 percent reported themselves "chronically shy." We will be considering, however, the four percent—the "true-blue shys"—whose self-definition of shyness is based on their feeling shy *all* the time, in *every* situation, and with virtually *all* people. Only such a comprehensive frame of reference enables us to consider shyness a life style.

Because shyness generally appears to be a very personalistic trait, it is appropriate to mention that our cultural matrix also feeds into its development. Certain kinds of American social and cultural values—the norms that overemphasize competition, individual success, and personal responsibility for failure—"lead people to imprison themselves within the egocentric predicament of shyness, and to torture themselves with that culturally determined sensitivity" (Zimbardo, Pilkonis, and Norwood, 1975, p. 72). Parents and teachers often help to transmit this social disease, apparently with greater frequency to the first-born. (See the discussion of ordinal position in Forer, 1976; Miller and Maruyama, 1976; and Zimbardo, 1977, pp. 60–62.)

In describing the life style of shyness, one characteristic stands out as fundamental: an excessive preoccupation with the self, an over-concern with being negatively evaluated. This extreme self-consciousness leads the chronically shy to build a world of protective isolation from others. From the outside, the shy person appears silent, passive, and noncommunicative. Inside, the shy person is obsessed with avoiding evaluative situations, concerned about what others think, and feels overwhelming anxiety when asked to do anything in front of others. This style corresponds most nearly to the one which Mosak (1971) labels the "inadequate."

Experiencing both loneliness and extreme dread of people, the shy isolate themselves from the warmth of human contact and thereby condemn themselves to remain strangers within their narrow prison of self. They choose the security of isolation over the risk of rejection. By controlling situations tightly, they eliminate possibilities for intimacy. This results in the shy person's having few outlets for the expression of his or her feelings. Often the shy person loses his individuality in the presence of authorities; he feels no alternative but to obey them. Zimbardo (1977, p. 114) says that it has become clear to him that "shy men and women have abdicated responsibility for taking the risk of freedom, for keeping the life force flowing." Thus, shyness is an extreme example of what James Gustafson (1968, p. 254) calls "excessive scrupulosity." The life style of shyness may become, at its worst, a severe form of neurosis that results in depression and may even influence a person towards suicide.

Having described briefly the life style of shyness we undertake an analysis of the form of morality that is embodied in it from a general humanitarian viewpoint. Most striking is the fact that the world of the shy is morally constricted. Both descriptively and normatively the relational range of the self is reduced to include only the self. Because the self's relations to others are seen as threatening, the shy person would find it difficult to adopt morally responsible ways of interacting with them. Hence even basic moral obligations, much less morally "heroic" actions, are neglected because they might involve consequences that are perceived as too personally revealing.

The shy person also neglects his or her responsibility to himself. Tragically the shy person lacks the basic self-esteem and confidence to treat him or herself as a worthwhile object of care. The life style of shyness prohibits the person from enjoying many growth experiences and from realizing his potential abilities. For example, true sexual intimacy is almost out of the question for the totally shy.

It may be, ironically, that the shy person can relate to broader community issues and take up his communal responsibility, so long as that does not require intimate face-to-face relationships or social performance. Obviously these qualifications restrict the range of community activities that could be undertaken.

We have in this instance a case where the life style itself has precluded many "normally" requisite actions. Consequently, those narrow experiential parameters make the fulfillment of many moral responsibilities virtually impossible. The shy person need not continue to choose that life style, however; individuals do have the freedom and the means[3] to break out of their social conditionedness.

From the specific viewpoint of Christian ethics, the life style has to be seen as unfortunately egocentric. Though shyness may appear to exhibit characteristics similar to humility and meekness, that is only the coincidental result of an underlying fearfulness. In terms of consequences, shyness may permit a miscarriage of justice, and fail to exhibit love assertively. Even though the sources of that neglect are far removed from the egocentricity of rapacious self-interest, it is hard to imagine the shy person actively seeking the good. The sin entailed by this life style is that of omission rather than commission; shyness rests on an underestimation of the self and a lack of trust in the goodness of God and the created order.[4]

The Life Style of Careerism

"He's a doctor, you know. When he finally does get home at night, all he wants to do is stretch out. How can the kids and I compete with the noble duties and responsibilities of his career?"
　　　—a 35-year-old wife and mother (Personal interview)

A second life style choice is characterized by an emphasis on upward vertical mobility in one's career. We shall call this pattern "careerism." Its external traits include the spending of time, money, and energy on one's career. "Such an emphasis is often accompanied by actual movement into social positions of greater prestige, property, and power, but the important criterion, from the perspective . . . of style of life involved, is that a person engages in career-relevant activitiss to the partial exclusion of alternative activites" (Bell, 1968, p. 147). Those alternatives mentioned by Bell include familism and consumership.

As in the case of shyness, the life style of careerism involves the pouring of one's energies into one container, to the virtual exclusion of other alternatives. Men have adopted this life style far more than women;[5] therefore, we will focus on male careerism. Particularly in their twenties and thirties are men oriented to achievement; the life style of careerism represents an extreme case of a cultural norm. As Sheehy writes (1976, p. 127), "If he burns with the desire to gain recognition as well [as earn the credentials that will win him societal approval], a man must be faithful and attentive to his real loved one: the career. All our traditions and institutions help to pave the way by recommending, applauding, and giving full permission to men who pursue such a course." In terms of the commonly observed life style themes which Mosak (1971) has identified, the pattern of careerism corresponds to that of the "driver." Ambitious and goal-oriented, the careerist comes to identify himself with his career; alternative courses of action are measured in terms of their promotion of the career.

Often accompanying this life style is the professionalization of the person. Concerned as he is to "make it," the careerist pays inordinate attention to the standards, procedures, and methodology of the profession. The activities of ordinary life become absorbed in the career drive; awareness of one's family and even of one's own needs and feelings may be lost in fulfilling vocational responsibilities. As Whitehead (1925, pp. 196–197) suggested, "The remainder of life is treated superficially, with the imperfect categories of thought derived from one profession." Furthermore, many careerists have adopted professions that provide genuine public service; this contributes a noble rationalization for their total absorption. After all, if a husband or father comes in at 10:30 p.m. from a medical emergency or some crisis counseling, what wife or child could impugn the validity of saving a life or helping to avert trauma?

3. The second half of Zimbardo's *Shyness* (1977, pp. 118–222) is entitled "What To Do About It" and consists of exercises and activities designed to enable a shy person to break out of that life style.
4. Clearly this analysis makes the assumption that a shy person can change his or her life style.
5. For an experiential understanding of the social and personal reasons why women have not, see Sheehy, 1976, pp. 82–85, 91, 126–129, and 136–137. But see pp. 262–276 for examples of women who do adopt a careerism pattern.

From a general humanitarian perspective, the morality of this life style must be judged ambiguously. Devotion to public service and relieving suffering or anguish are certainly positive attributes of the careerism style. Indeed, as a whole, the professions—be they medical, legal, ministerial, business, or educational—are highly regarded in our society and not without cause. The whole struggle for social advancement and dedication to common good are morally good, occasionally even noble.

However, careerism can also produce a monstrous drive for personal career advancement, insensitive to the cost of such achievement for society—for example, the "Robber Barons" of the nineteenth century. Furthermore, professional progress "for the sake of progress" can and has already produced many social problems—e.g., irreparable damage to the natural environment, a lowering of the quality of production, and the development of "life-saving" medical technology which only prolongs the dying process. Careerism untempered by a general concern for the common good and individual happiness is a leviathan.

In regard to one's responsibility to self, careerists certainly do not exhibit the key deficiency of shyness: underestimation and failure to respect oneself. Like shyness, however, the wholeness of the self is reduced to one dimension by careerism: in this case, that of external advancement and service. One's responsibility to growth in interpersonal sensitivity and awareness of one's own feelings (particularly the not-wholly-pure motivations and drives which compel the careerist onward) is stunted by this life style.

In the sphere of relationships with others, the careerist is usually benevolent to those who are his patients, clients, parishioners, customers, and students. These relationships are integrated into the careerist's role, however; seldom are the personal lives of those who are seen or dealt with professionally taken into account. This may be due to the fact that the careerist seldom takes his own personal life into account. The family relationships of careerists are slighted; familial responsibilities are often displaced.

Professional interaction often involves both professional etiquette and a nonprofessional human encounter grounded in reciprocity and trust. It is Larry Churchill's contention (1977, p. 49) that "interpersonal and social dimensions of professional actions can become habitually secondary, even tertiary." For example, medical techniques may become more important than the patient's anxieties and fears. Preoccupation with correct procedure often constitutes a "blind spot" which narrows the range of ethical con-

siderations to those that are professional. Reciprocity and trust are overriden.

It is in relation to the community that the careerist appears morally most luminous. Justifiably commended for his public ministrations, the careerist may nevertheless restrict his own standards of accountability to members of his or her own profession (Churchill, 1977). He may be insulated from any community needs that are not strictly pertinent professionally. This may in some cases be the result of a happy coincidence of self-interest and community public service needs.

From the perspective of Christian ethics, this life style can be judged as morally absolutist. Rather than opposing "objective relativism," Christian morality may "require it in view of its fundamental dogma that none is absolute save God and that the absolutizing of anything finite is ruinous to the finite itself." (Niebuhr, 1970, pp. 112–113) Careerism, thus, involves the immorality of idolatry; it skews the moral life in its compulsive worship of career and personal advancement. While appearing to be morally upright, and justifiably so in one area, it neglects several other aspects of the moral life. Careerism, however unintentionally, can lead to moral surds. Finally, careerism plays several moral chords so intensely that the melody of the careerist's life is dissonant.

The Life Style of Unification Church Membership

"I've been looking for something like this for years. It answers all the questions I was asking."
—A Unification Church member
(Quoted in Rice, 1976, p. 40)

The third life style to be examined is that adopted by the members of the Unification Church of Reverend Moon. The ascetic nature of the life style manifested by converts to that cult is its most evident characteristic, in correlation with the totalistic demands of membership. The life style theme which Mosak (1971) calls the "need to be good" comes closest to describing this style.

Best classified sociologically as a youth sect (Yinger, 1963, pp. 23–24), the Unification Church has established rigid standards for admission to membership. The first prerequisite is willingness to abide by the teachings and living patterns specified by Reverend Moon. Extensive and rigorous training, and adherence to a stringent moral code follow. Disciples are expected to exhibit unswerving loyalty to Moon.

Like most sects, the Unification Church began in response to a social problem, or in this case, a plethora of social problems including crime, alcoholism, divorce, suicide, drug abuse, and communism. Its twin goals are to solve these problems, and to "mobilize an ideological army of young people . . . to unite the world in a new age of faith" (President Niel Salonen, as quoted in Rice, 1976, p. 40). New converts give their possessions to the Church; the Church in turn takes care of their daily needs. The life style of adherents is strictly specified: no drugs, no alcohol, no sex, no money, no problems, no choices, and no decisions. Tasks are assigned to each person; these usually involve recruitment, fund raising, or working in one of the movement's businesses.

Despite their spartan existence, adherents demonstrate an evangelical zeal. Group prayer, interaction, and worship services fill believers' leisure time. Very noticeable is the segregation of members by sex and also their indoctrination in the dangers of communism. Though membership is freely chosen, the life style of the initiates does not include the making of decisions; one's decisions are made by group leaders and church officials.

Two perspectives are helpful in understanding this phenomenon. William James's description of the nature of religious conversion fits the procedures employed by the Church. According to James conversion occurs most often to those beset by a "sense of incompleteness and imperfection," often during a "state of temporary exhaustion." It brings a new sense of "spiritual vitality," new energies, and a sense of peace and harmony (James, 1941, pp. 217–258). Robert Lifton's thesis on "Protean man" (Lifton, 1969, pp. 37–63) suggests that youth today long to attach themselves to a movement that will provide answers to the complexity of life questions. Often that conversion is intense but short-lived; one possible explanation is that such conversion is affiliative, more motivated by a desire for social intimacy or belonging rather than by ideological commitment. Apparent attractions of the life style include feelings of fellowship, freedom from problems, and relief from the pressures of a confusing and bewildering world.

Looking at the morality of this life style from a humanitarian perspective, we can affirm the loyalty and industry of its adherents. Clearly this style is not materialistically self-seeking.

In terms of one's responsibility to self, however, this life style smacks of escapism and intellectual dishonesty. One of the attractions of the style is its provision of answers to the perplexities of everyday living. The adherent is provided with a life program incorporating everything from basic physical needs to spiritual beliefs. Converts buy the whole ideology

or none at all. Individuality is suppressed; deviating in attitude or idea is forbidden. For young people seeking self-identity, the Unification Church offers instant community and a comprehensive handbook of answers. The complexity of the questions which are so facilely answered by this movement requires that the convert be intellectually dishonest. The pain of the search is dissolved by accepting the received dogma, no questions asked. The isolation of the member from mental inquiry and from many normal everyday processes restricts the growth of the self; furthermore, it borders on moral cowardice in confronting life questions.

In relation to others, the believer's life style is also constricted. One's moral responsibility to others becomes reduced to encounters with fellow believers; warmth and intimacy are shared with like-minded believers. Responsibility to nonbelievers, parents included, almost disappears in this life style. The zeal with which believers attempt to recruit and convert others could possibly be construed as an exception to that statement.

Despite its professed purpose, the Unification Church expends little effort toward producing social change or the alleviation of social problems. In fact the movement relates to the greater community primarily as objects for conversion. "Most of its resources are directed inward, producing more money and more recruits, who in turn will recruit more members and raise more money" (Rice, 1976, p. 45). We cannot judge the Church's effort towards meeting communal responsibilities very charitably.

From the standpoint of Christian ethics, the life style of Church members involves compliance in heresy. Moon can be viewed as a modern anti-Christ, for he promotes the implication that he is the Messiah. Even more importantly, the life style of believers undercuts human freedom and substitutes for it heteronomous adherence to a programmed script. The activities of the Unification Church members are geared solely towards personal ends and the enhancing of the Church. Others are treated warmly either because they are fellow members or because they are potential recruits or customers; there appears to be no drive to love one's neighbors simply for their intrinsic worth as fellow beings. Certainly there is no institutionalized thrust towards a corporate and social ministry. This life style is characterized by a retreat from intellectual struggle with the complexity of modern life—a struggle undertaken with intellectual honesty in the ideal Christian life style.

Benefits of Analyzing the Morality of Life Style

The psychologist or sociologist can realize significant benefits from including the moral dimension in his or her analysis of life styles.

One important benefit to be gained is simply a more comprehensive description of human experience, a primary goal of the social sciences. The moral dimension is present in virtually all of human behavior, whether or not it is recognized. Therefore, the life style analyst who includes an explicit discussion of that dimension can hope to be both more comprehensive and more illuminative in his or her treatment of attitudes and experience. There have been advances in this area beyond Freud by Erikson, Piaget, and Kohlberg, of course. It seems, however, that such discussions of moral development are left largely segregated from other aspects of human life, e.g., personality, attitude change, altruistic behavior, conformity, social change, and urbanization. An analysis of the moral dimensions of life style could integrate these aspects of the self.

A second benefit accrues from the first. The life style analyst has a perspective which is especially able to integrate the moral dimension. He or she focuses on the personal style which is a product of both psychological and sociocultural dynamics; at the same time, he or she emphasizes the intentional and purposeful thrust in human behavior. Like H. Richard Niebuhr, the life style analyst recognizes that our lives are both conditioned and also intentional. The interrelation of these two forces becomes particularly conspicuous when conditioned messages come into conflict with intentional goals. That tension usually involves a moral question; the interplay between the ideal and actual self has a moral dimension. The analyst of life style is aware of the balance between these two elements—conditionedness and freedom—in such a way that he or she can integrate them.

The analyst also recognizes the way in which decisions flow out of a person's daily or habituated style in conjunction with conscious decision-making. Thus the life style approach could also investigate actual and ideal *moralities*. Consonance between a person's actual and ideal morality may be a sign of mental health; extreme dissonance between actual and ideal morality may be a sign of mental illness. We suspect that employing such a perspective could be of real help in a therapeutic setting.

Incidentally, the formulation of a distinction between *actual life style* and *ideal life style*, and the exploration of that distinction, is an area which may prove fruitful to those in counseling or other helping professions.

A third benefit to be gained from analyzing the morality of life styles comes from recognizing morality as part of one's self-concept. Adler's recognition of the importance of one's attitude to oneself, which usually contains an element of moral evaluation (Wrightsman, 1972, p. 258), has been collaborated by the extensive use being made of the notion of self-concept. The consideration of individuals' moral identity in examining life styles would illumine areas which may have seemed impervious to measurement or comprehension. Since the moral element in one's self-concept has been largely overlooked, behavior that seemed inconsistent before may be explained through a sensitivity to that feature of one's self-concept. The helpful work of Leon Festinger (1957) on "cognitive dissonance" comes to mind as a theory which might be expanded and refined to include this moral dimension.

One drawback of this approach is that the moral elements in one's self-concept will be difficult to measure. This drawback should not deter the social scientist from recognizing a human dynamic which we all know to be operative. Indeed, if quantifiability is a prerequisite for social scientific consideration, many important aspects of human experience will go unrecognized.

Benefits of Life Style Analysis as an Approach to Morality

There are several advantages of using the category "life style" for other groups—philosophers, ethicists, cultural analysts, and religious professionals.

One cultural force presently influencing the work of ethicists is social and personal tolerance. While that force is generally to be applauded, ethicists have been so concerned to avoid even the semblance of prescribing for others that relatively little attention is being focused on personal morality. Social analysis and theoretical work abound. An advantage of the use of life style as an approach to morality is that life style pertains to personal morality, but in a way that need not be *heavily* prescriptive and that also avoids an extreme personalism.

The category life style points to the influence of both psychological development and social forces; as such, it connects personal and social morality. All moral issues have life style implications or can best be understood as facets of a particular way of life or mentality (Miller, 1976, p. 76). No matter how broad the issue—war, racism, sexiam—it has its context within the life style of individuals or communities. It is in relation to the whole social context that one's personal life style becomes comprehensible to the outside observer. Because life style focuses on both the personal and social levels, it enables the ethicist to deal with personal morality without ignoring the person's social context or social morality.

A second benefit to the ethicist results from the concrete and practical locus of life style analysis. We can readily identify and understand life style because we all live out a particular life style. For the ethicist this focus on the concrete shifts the emphasis from monumental crisis decisions to include the everyday style out of which we live. It enables him or her to gain distance from occasional crisis decisions to understand the continuous interplay between a person's life style and the decision-making process. It is more helpful to understand the whole as a process rather than to analyze the elements of the moral life separately. Therefore, an astute analysis of life style enables the ethicist to illumine the integrated nature of the moral life. Furthermore, it can promote clarification of the unintentional as well as the intentional commitments reflected in a life style. A person's moral quandries may stem from not being able to discern what is going on more often than they do from not knowing right from wrong. For that reason, the illumination offered by life style analysis can be of practical moral importance to any conscientitious person. It can also reveal areas where change is needed.

A third benefit emerges from the emphasis on character, disposition, and the virtues which life style analysis promotes. With this analysis certain features of the moral life, which tend to be obscured by the decisional model, can be uncovered. The agent's moral identity is brought into the foreground. The agent is revealed to have a unique scheme of values, an effective deportment, and a web of loyalties. His or her orientation towards life and vision of the good is that of the participant, an important perspective that is neglected if the analyst is only taking the spectator's point of view. Often philosophers and ethicists have operated from the spectator position, emphasizing logical rules or reasoning and the particularities of the specific situation. Left obscured has been the way the participating agent acts out of his or her own character, in accord with his or her own life style. Life style analysis offers a corrective emphasis; it highlights the prescriptive and orienting functions of the moral agent's own character.

For the Christian ethicist, life style analysis is one way that he or she can make sense out of the claim that Christian commitments do have everyday consequences for the way a person lives. It enables him to explore the specificity of the Christian's moral life, both descriptively and normatively (See Hauerwas, 1974).

Finally, however, the most important benefits of incorporating an analysis of morality in the consideration of life style are practical and of benefit to anyone. Such an analysis can offer anyone another way of understanding him or herself. It can assist us in understanding why we feel guilty, or upstanding; inadequate, or competent; negatively, or positively about ourselves.

It can also reveal those elements in our actual life styles which are destructive and which we want to change. Thus, it can assist all of us in the pilgrimage towards moral growth and humane benevolence, and can help those interested in developing a Christian life style.

References

Adler, Alfred. *The science of living.* New York: Greenberg Publishers, Inc., 1929.

Ansbacher, H. L., and Ansbacher, R. R., editors. *The individual psychology of Alfred Adler.* New York: Basic Books, 1956.

———. *The individual psychology of Alfred Adler.* New York: Harper & Row, 1967.

Bell, Wendell. "The city, the suburb and a theory of social choice." *The new urbanization.* Edited by Scott Greer. New York: St. Martin's Press, 1968, 132–168.

Churchill, Larry R. "The professionalization of ethics: some implications for accountability." *Soundings,* 60/1 (Spring 1977), 40–53.

Eckstein, Daniel, Leroy Baruth, and David Mahrer. *Life style: What it is and how to do it.* Dubuque, Ia.: Kendall/Hunt Publishing Company, 1978.

Festinger, Leon. *A theory of cognitive dissonance.* Stanford: Stanford University Press, 1957.

Forer, L. *The birth order factor.* New York: McKay Publishing Company, 1976.

Gushurst, R. S. "The technique, utility, and validity of life style analysis." *The Counseling Psychologist,* 3/1 (1971), 30–39.

Gustafson, James M. *Christ and the moral life.* New York: Harper & Row, 1968.

———. *Can ethics be Christian?* Chicago: University of Chicago Press, 1975.

Hauerwas, Stanley. *Vision and Virtue.* Notre Dame: Fides Publishers, Inc., 1974.

James, William. *The varieties of religious experience.* London: Longmans, Green, and Company, 1941.

Lifton, Robert Jay. *Boundaries: psychological man in revolution.* New York: Random House, 1969.

Miller, Donald E. "Life style: A category for the analysis of moral identity." *American Society of Christian Ethics: Selected Papers 1976.* Edited by Max Stackhouse. Missoula, Montana: University of Montana Press, 1976, 75–88.

Miller, N. and G. Maruyama. "Ordinal position and peer popularity." *Journal of Personality and Social Psychology,* 33 (1976), 123–131.

Mosak, Harold H. "Lifestyle." *Techniques for behavior change.* Edited by Arthur G. Nikelly. Springfield, Ill.: Charles C. Thomas, 1971, 77–81.

———. *On purpose.* Chicago: Alfred Adler Institute, 1977.

Niebuhr, H. Richard. *The responsible self.* New York: Harper & Row, 1963.

———. "The center of value." *Radical monotheism and western culture.* New York: Harper & Row, 1970, 100–113. First appeared in *Moral principles of action.* Edited by Ruth Nanda Anshen. New York: Harper & Brothers, 1954.

Rice, Berkeley. "Honor thy father Moon." *Psychology Today,* 9/8 (January 1976), 36–47.

Sheehy, Gail. *Passages: Predictable crises of adult life.* New York: E. P. Dutton & Company, Inc., 1976.

Weber, Max. *Essays in sociology.* Translated and edited by H. H. Gerth and C. W. Mills. New York: Oxford University Press, 1946.

Whitehead, Alfred North. *Science and the modern world.* New York: Macmillan Company, 1925.

Wrightsman, Lawrence S. *Social psychology in the seventies.* Monterey, California: Broks/Cole Publishing Company, 1972.

Yinger, J. Milton. *Sociology looks at religion.* New York: The Macmillan Company, 1963.

Zimbardo, Philip G. *Shyness: What it is: What to do about it.* Reading, Massachusetts: Addison-Wesley Publishing Company, 1977.

Zimbardo, P. G., Paul A. Pilkonis, and Robert M. Norwood. "The social disease called shyness." *Psychology Today,* 8/12 (May 1975), 69–72.

Pictorial Mini Life Style: A Method for Democratic Group Psychotherapy

Bill and Kathy Kvols-Riedler

Martha Asks for It!

It was session #1 of our 8 week mini life style group. Martha was the second individual to volunteer. When we asked what we should put in the "situation to be improved" square, she broke out in tears and proceded to tell us this story. "My husband beats me about once a week. I want to leave him but I'm afraid that if I tried he might really hurt me." We asked Martha if she was willing to let the group help to find what she could do, or stop doing to improve the situation. She agreed. By asking Martha questions about her family constellation and early recollections, we led the group discussion. As a result of that discussion, we drew the following mini pictorial life style for Martha (see illustration). In the process of drawing the sketches and answering the "I am" series of questions, the group helped Martha recognize how she allowed her husband to impose on her to gain the payoff of moral superiority. This was the same goal which was vividly pictured as the method used in her childhood to defeat her brother and domineering father. This also won the admiration of her younger sister.

The group then listed Martha's assets. One of which was "I'll bet you're not afraid of saying whatever you want to anybody you want." That comment led us into our next step, recommending alternative responses.

We asked Martha if she could tell when she was going to get beat up. "Oh, yes!" she grinned. "He always gets this certain gleam in his eye."

We suggested that when she saw that certain gleam in his eye, that she be kind and firm at the same time. We also asked if she could withdraw from the power struggle. Martha said she could. The group suggested that she should role play how she would tell her husband what she was going to do. She picked a member of the group to play his part. This is what she said to him: "Tony, the next time you hit me I'm leaving!" Everyone, including Martha laughed as she recognized how she was "asking for it" again.

The group encouraged Martha on her effective eye contact when she was talking to "Tony." Then we asked the group how they thought Tony would feel about Martha's tone of voice. They said that they would feel threatened. We suggested an alternative statement. After several practice runs, Martha said, "Tony, sometimes when we argue I notice I get upset and say some things which make you angry. I don't want to do that anymore. So from now on, when I catch myself doing that I'm going to take a walk to cool off. Please don't think that I'm leaving you. I'll be back. I just don't want to say things to hurt you." The group commented on how effective it was when she reached out and touched his knee. We told Martha to try it this week at a time when Tony and her were NOT fighting and let us know next week what happened.

Before we tell you what happened to Martha, we would like to explain why we choose to use pictorial mini life styles and describe the process we used with Martha and the group.

Why Mini Life Styles?

Just as traditional parenting methods, in order to be effective, are being revised to coincide with today's evolution toward democracy, we also see a trend toward devising new methods of psychotherapy which are not based in discouragement and intimidation. We have developed the pictorial mini life styles to contribute toward democratic group therapy.

The mini life style, in a short period of time, gives each member of the group an accurate understanding of the life styles of the other group members. This insight gives them the tools to operate with the therapists in the tasks of helping each individual recognize how his current behavior relates to patterns which no longer result in positive payoff.

Reprinted by permission of the authors.

Life Is: Exciting when I'm hurt by others.
I Am: So good. —hurt a lot
Men Are: Mean
Women Are: They always have to do it all!
So Therefore: I can be special by doing more than my share and showing how the others mistreat me—then I look "better."

Situation to Be Improved

Tony Beats Me Up!

Assets

Responsible
Hard Worker
Dependable
Very Helpful
Good Sense of Humor
Not Afraid to Say What She Wants

Each group member can then function as a skilled contributer, avoiding the traditional "patient-therapist" relationship which hinders the democratic process.

The mini life style enables the group to visualize the life style. As the group proceeds from week to week, it acts as an instant reference. It also creates a humorous atmosphere our human imperfections aren't taken so seriously.

The Process

We use 6 steps in the mini life style process. All of these steps are done with the assistance and participation of the group. They are:

1. Determine the "situation to be improved."
2. Draw mini life style.
3. Answer the following questions.
     I am _____.
     Men are _____.
     Women are _____.
     Life is _____.
     So therefore _____.
4. List assets.
5. Recommend alternative behavior.
6. Have the individual practice alternative behavior in the group.

All confrontations must be put in a way that does not discourage the individual or the group. If discouragement becomes apparent, it is the groups responsibility to improve on the situation. This may need to be modeled and guided by the leaders at first. However, the leaders should arrange to step out of this responsibility so the group can gain the satisfaction of maintaining a positive atmosphere.

Suggestion

Look back and see if you can pin point each of the six steps in the "Martha Asks For It" Example.

What Happened to Martha?

Martha reported the first week that she had told her husband what she was going to do and they hadn't even quarrelled! However, three weeks later she got her first chance to use her new skill. She told the group that that weekend they were going to have company and both Martha and Tony were feeling tested. They were concerned about whether or not their hospitality was going to be "good enough" and were both sensitive to each other's imperfections. They started to argue. Martha, at first added fuel to the fire of their argument and then remembered her new alternative. She got up, walked calmly out the door, and took a walk around the block. She came back finding the situation to flare up shortly after her return. This time she took a longer walk. She came home and returned to her project. About a half an hour elapsed before round three began! This time she took a load of laundry to the laundromat! Martha again returned home to temporary peace and quiet but, it appeared that her husband was pretty determined to enter the battle ground again. This time Martha started to get up from her chair to leave again when her husband said, "Oh, never mind, I'll go this time." She said, "Would you? I was getting awfully tired." At which point they both started to laugh. Needless to say, neither of them left the house! About a year later we gave Martha a call to see how things were going. She said she had left the house a few times during arguments with her husband but has never gotten hit since she began using her new alternative. She said, "Sometimes I take out my mini life style sketch to remind me . . . and I laugh!"

"The Willhite":
A Creative Extension
of the Early Recollection
Process

Robert G. Willhite

Fantasy is but another creative faculty of the soul . . . Just as the projection of certain memories into the sharp focus of consciousness, or the erection of the bizarre super-structures of the imagination, fantasy and day-dreaming are to be considered part of the creative activity of the soul. (Adler, 1927, p. 57)

Each of us has no doubt had occasion when the interpretation of an Early Recollection did not flow smoothly, or despite best efforts, the client could not (or would not) comprehend the interpretation. I found myself facing such a situation in 1975 while working with an anxious, self-doubting client, Gil. He had not given me a well-defined overall feeling for the Early Recollection, and I was stuck; I couldn't get him to accept my explanation. In an attempt to clarify the meaning for him, I went to the board and wrote out the recollection verbatim and broke it into logical segments, thus:

1. I am playing catch with my father on the front lawn.

2. It's a very soft ball— a big padded ball.

3. We are throwing it back and forth.

4. I realize he's not having fun.

5. He's teaching me. He's looking down on me. That's the reason he's doing this.

6. It's his responsibility to make me better.

7. I don't know how to be better.
   [Overall feeling:]

8. I'll never be able to do it well enough.

To my chagrin, he still did not grasp my explanation. Since he was elaborating about how life is for him, it occurred to me to ask him how he wished life would be, and I wrote these statements in a second vertical column, opposite to those of the original recollection. Because I knew the way situations worked out for him were consistent with the original recollection—not the revised story in the second column—I assumed that the revised recollection represented his self ideal, while the original memory was consistent with his self-concept. What I now had on the board was:

Self-Concept	*Self-Ideal*
1. I am playing catch with my father on the front lawn.	I am playing catch with my father on the front lawn.
2. It's a very soft ball—a big padded ball.	We're throwing the ball back and forth.
3. We are throwing it back and forth.	He throws the ball to me and I fumble it.
4. I realize he's not having fun.	I run after it, pick it up and throw it back to him.
5. He's teaching me. He's looking down on me. That's the reason he's doing this.	We're laughing and having a good time.
6. It's his responsibility to make me better.	We start talking about things.
7. I don't know how to be better.	He's listening to me.
[Overall feeling:]	[Overall feeling:]
8. I'll never be able to do it well enough.	Loved

Reprinted by permission of the author.

Returning to the original Early Recollection (the *Self-Concept*), I had Gil tell me the emotions appropriate to each of the frames. Then I had him imagine what emotions would be involved in the idealized story in the second column (the *Self-Ideal*). By this means I was able to tune into what feelings and emotions he would use in the *Self-Ideal* to effect change. Recall that the original memory and the *Self-Ideal* were written opposite one another; therefore it was quickly evident at what point he would have to create different emotions in order to avoid the pattern shown in the Early Recollection.

Self-Concept	*Self-Ideal*
1. I am playing catch with my father on the front lawn. (*apprehensive, nervous*)	I am playing catch with my father on the front lawn. (*joyful, warm*)
2. It's a very soft ball—a big padded ball. (*"a fact"*)	We're throwing the ball ball back and forth. (*caring, closeness, warmth, trust*)
3. We are throwing it back and forth. (*fear, anticipation of what is going to happen next*)	He throws the ball to me and I fumble it. (*disappointed, frustrated, impatient*)
4. I realize he's not having fun. (*fear, confusion, concerned*)	I run after it, pick it up and throw it back to him. (*confident, proud, energized*)
5. He's teaching me. He's looking down on me. That's the reason he's doing this. (*inferior, small, tight*)	We're laughing and having a good time. (*accepted, elated, energized*)
6. It's his responsibility to make me better. (*"a fact"*)	We start talking about things. (*warm, worthy, trust*)
7. I don't know how to be better. (*helpless, abandoned, lonely, inadequate*)	He's listening to me. (*understood, content*)
[Overall feeling:]	[Overall feeling:]
8. (*I'll never be able to do it well enough.*)	(*loved*)

Since that day two years ago I have used this same basic technique—which has come to be known as "The Willhite"—with hundreds of clients. Out of this experience I have developed some refinements which help the client to quickly grasp the hidden logic and his/her unique psychological modus operandi.

I always have the client dictate the *Self-Ideal* frame by frame (comparing it to the *Self-Concept* while doing so) so that each column has the same number of action-emotion components. This format prevents the client from skipping over those portions which are indicative of anxiety and/or denial. At the conclusion of the Early Recollection the client gives me a word or phrase which is descriptive of the overall feeling of the memory. I also get an overall feeling to write in as the last frame of the *Self-Ideal*, so that the two are graphically analogous. I number the frames for convenience.

Although the original Early Recollection (the *Self-Concept*) is not to be changed in any way, I instruct the client that (s)he is free to add or delete emotions as I am writing it on the blackboard. The *Self-Ideal* (revised Early Recollection) can also be re-worked. It is often a bit of a struggle for the client to develop the *Self-Ideal* fantasy and it is necessary to encourage him/her to be innovative and flexible.

One simple and useful therapeutic tool is my "Feelings List." This is a piece of paper on which I have listed about 150 emotions, plus a section briefly describing commonly used defenses. A person who is highly defensive, or comes from a family which had a "no-talk rule," or who is experienced in behavior-oriented therapy may sincerely not know how to identify specific feelings or emotions. I have the list available for the client to refer to during our sessions. The person who is searching for a descriptive word for a feeling will skim the list and will consider only those words which are consistent and appropriate; words that are irrelevant will be disregarded.

Before the emotional component is added to the Early Recollection I instruct the client that if one of the thought-units does not elicit any emotion whatever it will be called "a fact." Other words may be used by the client which are essentially equivalent to no recalled emotion—such as "confused," "blah," or "bored."

When the client uses "a fact" or an equivalent term in place of an emotion, it is a tip-off that this is precisely the point at which (s)he is blocking. At that moment in the past the person probably could not identify what the feelings were. His/her subsequent behavior was a cover-up act, making it impossible for others to know what the feelings really were. The client deceives himself/herself and others at the same time, which feeds into and amplifies the self-delusion.

When working with "The Willhite" it is important for the therapist to record everything the client says from the beginning of the recollection to the end. The inclusion of supposedly objective explanations, parenthetical information, distracting phrases, etc., is crucial to a correct and poignant analysis. It is precisely this apparently inconsequential data which often reveals where the client is repressing, blocking or resisting getting in touch with his/her feelings. In so many instances these nervous or distracting comments directly precede a painful part of the memory—softening its impact and easing the pain. This may also mark the point at which the person unconsciously decided to skew the interactional process by using his/her emotions as a manipulative tool. When reviewing the emotional sequence with the client, I spend some time trying to get him/her in touch with what the feeling really was at that point.

I explain to the client that where "a fact" or other non-emotion word is inserted in place of an actual emotion that at that moment in the episode (s)he was probably behaving in such a way that (s)he could not identify what the feelings were. The conscious picks up that as no feeling; therefore, the frame gets labeled "a fact" or some such innocuous term. Now I help the client search more deeply for a believable feeling and reconstruct the episode. (S)he is then able to realize that this part of the memory had been purposively discounted or repressed.

The next step of "The Willhite" is to list just the emotional sequence on the blackboard. This graphically illustrates in a terse and easily comprehensible form his/her personal interactional style and perception of life. I explain to the client that this is an emotional set-up which (s)he has created—leading to a self-fulfilling prophecy that invariably confirms one's expectations about life. A quick reading of the sequence of emotions reveals the psychodynamics which the client typically employs toward the outcome of relationships, and I can pinpoint where the negative or pathological attitude and accompanying behavior is first manifested. (This is invariably near the beginning of the Early Recollection of a troubled person.) I explain that this emotional set-up—and the progression of events which ensues—is designed to confirm one's expectations about life. The client nearly always responds to this with quick recognition—that "Aha!" response which is a prelude to opening up to insight and change.

Returning to Gil's case, the emotional sequence for the *Self-Concept* reads:

1. Apprehensive, nervous
2. "A fact"
3. Fear, anticipation of what is going to happen next
4. Fear, confusion, concerned
5. Inferior, small, tight
6. "A fact"
7. Helpless, abandoned, lonely, inadequate
   [Overall feeling:]
8. I'll never be able to do it well enough.

The emotional sequence is typical for Gil; this theme—and variations on it—appears repeatedly in his life. Without being cognizant of it he sets himself up for the same denouncement in a variety of guises—"I'll never be able to do it well enough."

I teach clients that emotions are not random physical events nor merely responses to environmental stimuli, but rather that they are a vital force which can be harnessed and used to enhance relationships and realize positive personal goals. A clear understanding of emotions is a prerequisite to putting new feelings onto behavior patterns. By discovering and affirming various emotions people can become responsible for controlling their behavior.

At this point it is very helpful to have the client describe a current interactional problem with which (s)he is having difficulty. Going beyond the statement of the problem, the client also describes how (s)he imagines the episode will unfold and what the conclusion will be. As with the *Self-Concept* (the original Early Recollection) and the *Self-Ideal* (the revised Early Recollection), I write the client's description out word for word (on paper), separating it into thought-units, and add the emotions appropriate to each unit. Now the client has revealed in detail how his/her private logic is going to be put to work to reach a negative or unhealthy outcome. I then transfer the current problem to the blackboard. I do not, however, write it out literally as I did for the *Self-Concept* and the *Self-Ideal*. In order to expose the underlying pattern I fit the episode into a format involving the same number of frames as the *Self-Concept* and the *Self-Ideal*. This usually involves compressing the data. Occasionally there is an apparent gap in the sequence; I simply ask the client to fill it in for me. This rather arbitrary reconstruction of the current example (which I call the *Private-Logic-at-Work*) is necessary; most clients are more verbal about current events (*Private-Logic-at-Work*) than about memories (*Self-Concept*) or possible alternatives (*Self-Ideal*).

When we compare the *Private-Logic-at-Work* sequence to the *Self-Concept* it is usually remarkably analogous. Because the *Self-Concept* is a prototype for the private logic, the dysfunctional pattern persists. The client is again drawn down into the familiar transaction and unhappy conclusion. (S)he sincerely believes in the inevitability of the outcome which speciously "proves" that the private logic is unalterable.

Let's take a look at Gil's *Private-Logic-at-Work* (which was adjusted somewhat to make it fit the pre-existing eight-frame format):

	Self-Concept	Private-Logic-at-Work	Self-Ideal
1.	I am playing catch with my father on the front lawn.	I try to keep a dialogue going with my wife when I really don't want to.	I am playing catch with my father on the front lawn.
	(apprehensive, nervous)	(worthwhile; putting myself forward)*	(joyful, warm)
2.	It's a very soft ball—a big padded ball.	I try to be correct—to say something correct so she can't argue with me.	We're throwing the ball back and forth.
	("a fact")	(anticipating trouble)	(caring, closeness, warmth, trust)
3.	We are throwing it back and forth.	She wins by changing the issue.	He throws the ball to me and I fumble it.
	(fear, anticipation of what is going to happen next)	(anger, frustration, betrayed, vulnerable)	(disappointed, frustrated, impatient)
4.	I realize he's not having fun.	I realize I am going to lose.	I run after it, pick it up, and throw it back to him.
	(fear, confusion, concerned)	(apprehension, fear, confused)	(confident, proud, energized)
5.	He's teaching me. He's looking down on me. That's the reason he's doing this.	I sense the futility of the discussion.	We're laughing and having a good time.
	(inferior, small, tight)	(despair, inadequate)	(accepted, elated, energized)
6.	It's his responsibility to make me better.	She seems to have a corner on irrefutable truth.	We start talking about things.
	("a fact")	(frustrated, angry)	(warm, worthy, trust)
7.	I don't know how to be better.	I want to leave.	He's listening to me.
	(helpless, abandoned, lonely, inadequate)	(useless, inadequate)	(understood, content)
8.	[Overall feeling:]	[Overall feeling:]	[Overall feeling:]
	(I'll never be able to do it well enough.)	(She always wins—abandoned, lonely)	(loved)

*The apparently inconsistent feeling in this frame is explained in the following interpretation.

Interpretation of "The Willhite"

Self-Concept:

The *Self-Concept*—Gil's original Early Recollection—shows that he has strong feelings of inadequacy but does not know how he sets himself up to carry off the pattern. The Early Recollection, with the feelings inserted, is a revelation of how the process is set up.

The first step in the analysis is to look at the end—because the last frame or two will state, usually quite literally, the person's goal in life and his/her basic perception of what life is like. Knowing this makes it easier to comprehend the private logic which is employed to attain this goal while subtly disguising the mechanics involved. The Early Recollection gives us a candid glimpse of the person's personality with the underpinnings laid bare. Remember that behavior has two purposes: (1) to achieve the goal per se; and (2) to hide the interactional mechanics sufficiently so that the person's private logic—erroneous as it may be—is left intact. Gil's intended goal is to avoid taking responsibility and to justify that avoidance. This goal is obvious from the feelings in Frame 7—"helpless, abandoned, lonely, inadequate," and from the succinctly stated conclusion in Frame 8—"I'll never be able to do it well enough." Since these are Gil's own words he is not in a position to deny their validity as part of his behavior pattern. Notice that the last two frames of the *Private-Logic-at-Work* (center column), which is a description of a current relationship, highlights the same conclusion. Gil's private logic—seemingly so fragile—is iron-clad; this design is the "scarlet thread" which keeps appearing in his life. Other memories and current relationships will also unwittingly fall into this same pattern unchallenged, since Gil unconsciously engineers the outcome. Compare this with the outcome Gil fantasizes in Frames 7 and 8 of the *Self-Ideal* (third column)—to be content, understood and loved.

Returning to the *Self-Concept*, we see that he enters the interaction with an apprehensive and nervous feeling (Frame 1), probably because he sees the other person (his father in this case) as awesome and overwhelming. We know that he does not deal with the feeling because he inserts the mundane sentence, "It's a very soft ball." When I asked him to identify a feeling or emotion for this sentence he could not; to him it was merely "a fact." I have found that whenever "a fact" appears in the emotional sequence it shows precisely where the person is not in touch with his/her feelings; it can also be an indication of which specific feelings the person is afraid to express. In this case, the position of the "fact" tells me that Gil does

not deal with his apprehension and fear of not being able to measure up—products of his low self-esteem. This was the hunch I played, and he confirmed it with a recognition response. I can now show Gil how—by not dealing with his fear—he is setting himself up to fail.

Frame 3 of the *Self-Concept* shows what happens even when the other person cooperates; Gil still shows apprehension and fear about what is going to happen next. Gil's attitude, "I'll never be able to do it well enough," supports the low self-esteem. Gil is putting himself down by elevating his father; father is elevated by Gil's rationalization in Frame 4 that father is not having fun. This further supports his feelings of inadequacy. The first four frames show how Gil has carefully set up this process—filtering the action through his predetermined perceptions about life—so that it appears to be someone else's fault (father's) that he feels inadequate.

Frame 5 reinforces his low self-worth with the statement, "He's teaching me. He's looking down on me." The feelings associated with this frame—inferior and small—clearly feed into the intended goal. Since this is now an absolute for Gil he carries his self-deception one step further by making the whole thing father's responsibility (Frame 6). Since the feeling of inadequacy is so strong Gil won't take responsibility for it himself; rather he assigns the responsibility to his father. This frame was labeled "a fact"; Gil had no awareness of an accompanying emotion. We can conjecture that he doesn't dare confront the person he is so dependent on, probably because of fear of losing the relationship. The "fact" no doubt also covers his anger which he must desperately conceal and deny.

Frames 7 and 8 show the total emotional bankruptcy with the declaration, "I don't know how to be better." The feelings of helplessness, loneliness, inadequacy and abandonment now potentiate the low self-esteem, and also reinforce the fear that if he asserts himself he will be rejected or abandoned. "I'll never be able to do it well enough" (Frame 8) is his erroneous conviction about life.

The *Self-Concept* as a whole reveals the self-fulfilling behavior pattern in detail; Gil has an opportunity to learn by examining the step-by-step process.

Private-Logic-at-Work:

In the *Private-Logic-at-Work* sequence (center column) we analyze a specific on-going situation with which the client is having difficulty. In Gil's case we see how his persistent low self-concept colors his relationship with his wife. Gil—not his wife—

initiates the attitudes and concommitant behaviors which will once again confirm his belief about life: he doesn't measure up, but it's someone else's fault.

In Frame 1 he takes the lead in the interaction—''I try to keep a dialogue going with my wife when I really don't want to. He has now shown us how he controls the opening gambit with his negative attitude; the self-fulfilling prophecy is already set in motion. The feelings he states for this frame, ''worthwhile; putting myself forward,'' indicate he is not consciously aware of the apprehension and nervousness indicated in the recollection; he is denying these very discomforting stirrings by using the defense of false feeling of worthness. He carries this self-delusion into Frame 2 and sets himself up by ''trying to be correct'' so she can't argue with him. This defensiveness is an effort to protect himself from the feelings of inadequacy which are threatening to surface. The emotion he states is ''anticipating trouble.'' One can guess at this point that he will emerge from this encounter in a one-down position. He does not deny his feelings quite as vigorously in this instance as he did in Frame 2 of the *Self-Concept*, which was ''a fact.'' This observation can be used to help Gil gain insight into how he sets himself up for another failure.

Next (Frame 3), ''She wins by changing the issue.'' This is the ploy by which he deceives himself into believing that his wife is responsible for the impending interactional disaster. How artfully this fits into Gil's goal in life—avoidance of responsibility and justification for that avoidance. His feelings here of anger, frustration, betrayal and vulnerability combine to set the stage for Frame 4: the apprehension and fear of realizing that he is going to lose. His confusion is a device to smoke-screen his emotional bankruptcy. In Frame 5 he ''senses the futility'' (with supporting feelings of despair and inadequacy) and gives up any power he might have had when he says, ''She seems to have a corner on irrefutable truth.'' His frustration and anger are more out front here than in the *Self-Concept* where this frame was labeled ''a fact.'' Nonetheless, at this point he is self-victimized and can do very little about it. His only recourse (as he perceives the situation) is to leave, which he expresses a desire to do in Frame 7. This is the feeling of uselessness and inadequacy that Gil promotes leading to a ''such is life'' conclusion of: ''Others always win, and I am abandoned and left to feel lonely.'' This is consistent with Frame 8 of the *Self-Concept*—''I'll never be able to do it well enough.'' Many times a client is not consciously aware of this progression, but with this method he/she becomes aware of the subtle ways in which the progression is predetermined by the fictive goal. The *Self-Concept* revealed

by the Early Recollection and the life story revealed by the private logic are analogous because they are based on the biased perceptions the person has learned and nurtured.

Self-Ideal

The feelings of the *Self-Ideal* form a different pattern than those of the *Self-Concept* and *Private-Logic-at-Work*, yet they are still within the framework of the person's potential for interacting. This set-up has also been created by the client and is available to get him out of the self-fulfilling emotional bind. Gil's *Self-Ideal* shows—via his fantasy about how he would like life to be—how he would be willing to consider modifying his behavior to reach a better conclusion.

Sometimes people have the perception that in order for life to be different for them, others have to change. This is particularly true of the person who has chosen the victim role; he feels that no matter what he does ''they'' will keep him from succeeding. In Gil's case he is still willing to risk playing catch with his father (Frame 1), indicating he is willing to try to do something different with the relationship. The significant difference is that Gil has chosen a joyful, warm feeling to replace the feelings of nervousness and apprehension of the *Self-Concept*. This in itself initiates a shift in the pattern of behavior, setting him up for what he wishes for—caring, closeness, warmth, and trust (Frame 2). This attitude is an appropriate one and can lead to his fantasized goal—to be loved (Frame 8).

The key to the behavior change is the identification of the emotions or feelings involved; when Gil gets in touch with these he can volitionally alter his behavior pattern. It is this identification of feelings permitting the shift to new behaviors which is the strength of the Willhite method. I have found that people don't change until they are given alternatives backed up by feelings that are consistent with their private logic.

Frame 3 of the *Self-Ideal* shows Gil still flirting with failure, but just having been fortified with caring, closeness, warmth, and trust (Frame 2) he can now respond to fumbling the ball appropriately with disappointment, impatience, and frustration. This is quite different from the corresponding feelings in Frame 3 of the *Self-Concept*—fear, anticipation of what is going to happen next. The disappointment of fumbling the ball, however, opens up the opportunity for him to run after it and throw it back to his father (Frame 4). Here Gil assumes the courage to take a risk. With the feelings of confidence, pride and being energized, he has now set into motion the new pattern of behavior which facilitates change.

Now he is faced with considering a new conclusion as a result of his efforts. Many times a client wishes to stop in the construction of his/her story at this point, but to allow him/her to do so would overlook handling the feelings and emotions in the remaining frames; in both the *Self-concept* and the *Private-Logic-at-Work* these are devastating. By being forced to fill in all the open frames Gil has to create a new ending for the story—and so he continues. In Frame 5 both he and his father are laughing and having a good time; this reinforces feeling accepted, elated, and energized. Frame 6 shows Gil sharing equally again—"We start talking about things." The feelings of warm, worthy, and trust fortify this behavior and allow him to progress to Frame 7 to entertain the notion that someone would want to listen to him. And this leads to feelings of being understood and contentment.

The overall feeling of the *Self-Ideal* is that of being loved. The way Gil got there was by counting himself as an equal and being able to risk trusting and being close (Frame 2). The task of therapy now becomes an effort to encourage Gil to factualize the fantasy of the *Self-Ideal* by deliberately creating the emotions that were identified.

As a therapist my goal is, of course, to disrupt that sequence which leads to dysfunctional behavior by changing the conclusion about life. By using the information the client has provided for the *Self-Ideal* it is clear just how (and how much) the client is willing to change. And it is clear how the pattern of emotions must be altered in order to effect a new and more desirable outcome.

The Early Recollection, in addition to being a diagnostic aid for the therapist, contains within itself the seeds of a dynamic phenomenological process, therapeutic in and of itself, and made possible by the creative use of fantasy on the part of the client.

I have found this method to be an excellent tool for uncovering psychological mechanisms as well as an opportunity to become closely involved with the client in a situation where (s)he is comfortable, interested, and relatively non-defensive. A meaningful therapist-client interaction is the most effective way of building trust and effecting change.

Inherent in this process is a belief in the creative potential of human beings, with the opportunity for expressing that creativity given the client through the fantasy of the *Self-Ideal*. Related to this is implied faith in the ability of the client to change, to take charge of and be responsible for his/her own life, with the therapist providing encouragement. "The Willhite" is an exercise in change, an experiential introduction to the therapeutic mode.

As an Adlerian psychotherapist I subscribe, of course, to an ideographic philosophy based on the following axioms:

1. All behavior is purposive and goal-oriented.
2. We use emotions and specific emotional sequences creatively to facilitate reaching personal goals.
3. Motivations may be on an unconscious level and may effectively hide the person's goals from consciousness.
4. Behavior and life style are determined by and consistent with each person's unique system of private logic.
5. Differential behaviors comprise and reinforce the life style, and the life style in turn ostensibly substantiates one's private logic.
6. Behaviors, life style and private logic—in concert as they must by definition be—can occlude a person's awareness of alternative possibilities.
7. This lack of awareness confirms the private logic and leads to delusions and self-fulfilling prophecies.

In order for the client to change, (s)he must acknowledge the dysfunctional behavior which prior to the Early Recollection demonstration may not have been available to him/her consciously—thus protecting the hidden private logic mechanisms. The first step of the therapeutic change process is an experiential awareness of behavior patterns.

Since the possibilities for change have been stated by the client—not just arbitrarily imposed by the therapist—(s)he is more readily willing to accept the responsibility for trying out the new behaviors and to work on developing appropriate emotional response patterns. (S)he has provided every word on which the interpretation is based; therefore (s)he must accept that the sequence is accurate and take responsibility for it. Even in the revised Recollection—the *Self-Ideal*—I explain that (s)he could not possibly have given me data which was beyond the scope of the private logic.

In the following example, given to me by a passive and responsibility-dodging woman, Alice, notice the consistency between the *Self-Concept* and the *Private-Logic-at-Work* when she portrayed her unsatisfactory sexual relationship. By using the data drawn from the *Self-Ideal* I was able to help her develop appropriate alternative attitudes and behaviors which resulted in a more positive and fulfilling outcome.

Self-Concept	Private-Logic-at-Work	Self-Ideal
1. My brother was sick.	My husband and I have a sex problem.	My brother is well.
(lonely, scared)	(cheated, lonely)	(content, relaxed)
2. He had spinal meningitis.	He doesn't initiate any action, and I figure, "To hell with you, buddy, I don't need it either."	He is outside playing.
(scared, trapped, overwhelmed)	(rejecting, defiant, irritated, proud)	(relief—he's not bothering me)
3. They came with an ambulance and took him away.	I don't give any ground; he doesn't give any ground. A stand-off.	His friends come over to play with him.
(It doesn't bother me.)	(It doesn't bother me.)	(pleased, happy)
4. Mother was in the bedroom sitting in a chair.	I can get all the attention I need from work.	Mother is cooking dinner.
(sad, sorrowful)	(sad, sorrowful)	(satisfied, warm)
5. She was crying. I didn't want to see her cry.	I won't show him I'm hurt, by damn!	She is laughing and talking; I am laughing and talking with her.
(Hurt, but I don't want anyone to know)	(Mad, angry, hurt)	(Joy, fulfilled)
6. Overall feeling: I can't do anything to change the situation.	Overall feeling: I can't do anything about it.	Overall feeling: I am involved.
(Helpless)	(Helpless)	(Warm, close)

Interpretation of "The Willhite"

Self-Concept

The Self-Concept column shows how Alice gets herself into the helpless position (Frame 6) which is her interactional goal. In Frame 1, her brother is sick. From the onset she is an observer of the action; distance is set up. She reacts to the situation by feeling lonely and scared. The function of describing the illness—spinal meningitis—in Frame 2 is to repeat the emotion of scared and add the feelings of trapped and overwhelmed. It is interesting what she does with these feelings in Frame 3. The denial and covering up of her feelings is obvious; she takes the feelings of loneliness, fear, trapped, and being overwhelmed and then boldly states, "It doesn't bother me."

After experiencing her brother's movement away from her, she looks for support and closeness from her mother. Again she finds no solace because mother is in the bedroom crying (Frames 4 and 5) and

Alice is again left alone emotionally. She is sad, sorrowful and hurt, but again this is denied: ". . . but I don't want anyone to know." As long as Alice skillfully denies her feelings—as she does in Frames 3 and 5—she can logically conclude, "I can't do anything to change the situation." The resulting feeling is one of helplessness—but remember she has gone through a cleverly designed five-step process to get there.

Private-Logic-at-Work

The private logic story parallels the *Self-Concept*; there is the same step-by-step progression toward Alice's preconceived conclusion of "such is life." She starts out in Frame 1 stating that she and her husband have a sex problem. The emotional response—cheated, lonely—is a dead giveaway to how she will conclude her story. Whenever she gets this feeling with someone she finds a way to withdraw and emotionally isolate herself. She does this in Frame 2 by blaming him for not initiating any action; she says,

"To hell with you, buddy. I don't need it either." This is her way of building her road to helplessness because of the accompanying feelings of rejection, defiance, irritation and pride. Pride is probably the emotion she uses to justify the others, and it also allows her to drive these painful feelings underground. Note in Frame 3 she follows on course by saying, "It doesn't bother me," in response to the phrase, "I don't give any ground; he doesn't give any ground—a standoff."

Again, according to the plan of the *Self-Concept*, Alice turns her attentions elsewhere to find solace (Frame 4). She says, "I can get all the attention I want from work." The feelings, however, sadness and sorrow, belie this statement. She must now deal with these feelings—and again she follows here preordained path by covering them over: "I won't show him I'm hurt, by damn!" This is the denial of the mad, angry, hurt feelings and leads her to her personal conviction of, "I can't do anything about it." The resultant emotion is, once again, helplessness.

Self-Ideal:

The *Self-Ideal* reveals to what extent Alice is willing to consider changing her style of life. It also helps her identify what feelings and emotions she will need to make the new behavior believable. In the *Self-Ideal* Alice reveals that even in fantasy she chooses to promote her distance from others. In the first frame we see that brother is well, and she feels content and relaxed. The therapist could well speculate that she will construct the fantasy so he will pay attention to her—but, as we see in Frame 2, this is not the case. Alice places him outside playing and expresses relief that he is not bothering her. This shows her inability or unwillingness to get close. It could mean that she sees males as too threatening to get close to; she may have a need to maneuver them out of the picture because the thought of a close relationship is too threatening. This is a good exanple showing why the therapist—no matter what his/her guess might be—should not interfere with the client in constructing his/her own logical fantasy process.

The distancing is even more clearly revealed in Frame 3 where she has her brother's friends come over to play with him so she gets off the hook from having to be too close and still does not have to take the blame or responsibility for it. In this case she feels pleased and happy. The story follows her pattern—for at the end of Frame 3 she has completed one relationship transaction and immediately turns to another to find satisfaction. She is perfectly free to continue the single relationship with her brother, yet she chose to switch the focus to mother. Alice still maintains her lack of intimacy by having mother cooking dinner; she feels satisfied and warm (Frame 4). Frame 5 finds mother laughing and talking, and Alice is laughing and talking with her—yet one still gets the impression of distance, even though the emotional component reads, "joy, fulfilled." In Frame 6 Alice sees herself as involved and feels warm and close—but she has accomplished this with minimal or no risk to herself. This method of analysis gives the therapist this expanded data to work with—and is also a warning that Alice is not willing to take risks in intimacy, while at the same time she will complain long and loud that the significant others are not intimate with her.

The therapeutic intervention in this case can well be made by contrasting Frame 2 of the *Private-Logic-at-Work* with Frame 2 of the *Self-Ideal*. The former reads, "He doesn't initiate any (sexual) action," and the feeling is "rejection"—the latter reads, "Relief—he's not bothering me." She needs to be faced with this discrepancy and to realize that her alternatives are to either risk getting close to a male to find pleasure and happiness, or to decide it is too risky and then she will intentionally promote distance in the relationship. When she does this she must realize her own responsibility for the decision and accept that she still can be OK. Maybe then she can stop blaming others, thus feeling rejected and irritated, and stop the denial—"It doesn't bother me."

It is helpful when analyzing an Early Recollection (or any column of "The Willhite") to gain a better perspective on the clients private logic by being aware of the overall pattern of the event. Each memory contains the following data:

1. The setting;
2. The person's place/position in the setting. (e.g., involved, a spectator, on the fringe of the action, etc.);
3. The person's perception of what is happening;
4. The sequence of events;
5. The person's private predetermined (often unconscious) goal;
6. The overall feeling or conclusion—one's personal view of the world—"such is life."

In Alice's Early Recollection these six factors are:

1. *The Setting*—"My brother was sick." Here we see Alice setting up illness as a distance-producing device and the accompanying feelings confirm it—lonely and scared.
2. *Place/Position*—Here Alice is very much a spectator all the way. Everything is observed

and there is absolutely no interaction and no direct involvement on her part. This is another way she has of promoting her helplessness.

3. *Person's Perception of What is Happening*—Alice sees all of the things happening to her brother, but also becomes acutely aware of her mother's reaction and is aware of the fact that she cannot do anything about her mother's crying.

4. *Sequence of Events*—Alice is immobilized and helpless to change the outcome. *He* has spinal meningitis; *they* come with the ambulance; *she* was crying. There was nothing poor Alice could do (so she thought) to change the course of fate.

5. *Person's Private Goal*—In Alice's case this is to avoid risk-taking; she accomplishes this goal by believing she is helpless and by creating interpersonal distance.

6. *Conclusion*—"I can't do anything to change the situation."

The *Self-Concept* represents the past, and the *Self-Ideal* speaks to the future; nonetheless, we must focus on the present pain, problems, hopes, fears, motivations, strengths and weaknesses. Using this process—"The Willhite"—the client is able to existentially experience the possibilities of change. Notice that specific emotions and feelings are identified which, when embodied in new believable behavior patterns, can reveal to the client a new perspective on how life can be. This is the encouragement factor that is so essential in the growth process. This extended Early Recollection technique helps to clearly pinpoint and identify erroneous attitudes so that the client is consciously aware of the new growth direction.

Since trying out new responses and behaviors in real-life situations does not always lead to the predicted and hoped-for conclusion, I encourage the client with the advice that (s)he is responsible only for making the effort—not for the outcome.

Another way I encourage the client is by helping him/her risk developing a fantasy for the *Self-Ideal*—a risk which challenges the old dysfunctional behavior. As the client becomes excited about the prospect of defying his/her own mistaken opinion of life, (s)he takes on the responsibility of making the new behavior functional and believable. The therapist and client work closely in this process, promoting trust, cooperation and respect. The client can readily see that it is through his/her own creative powers that new behavior evolves. (S)he can take charge of his/her life; one's past experiences need not prophesy doom but rather challenge one's ingenuity and imagination. At this point the client recognizes that there are alternatives—choices—and with

choices comes the freedom to choose. "The past is dead, he is free to be happy and to give pleasure to others," a quotation I find very meaningful and which I believe is in the spirit of Adler, but for which I cannot find the source.

Summary

"The Willhite" process is holistic because its individual parts—the *Self-Concept*, the current *Private-Logic-at-Work*, and the *Self-Ideal*—contribute to a whole which is dynamic, flexible, and synergistic. The chronological realities of past, present, and future merge into a viable, mutable experience which denies none of these realities but is more than all of them.

The process is compatible with the tradition of brief psychotherapy, which quickly get to the heart of the matter, presenting the client with a recognizable picture of his/her behavior and a blueprint for change which (s)he has designed.

In order for the client to change, (s)he must acknowledge the dysfunctional behavior which prior to the Early Recollection demonstration may not have been available to him/her consciously—thus protecting the hidden private logic mechanisms. The first step of the therapeutic change process is an experiential awareness of behavior patterns.

Emotions are created—on an unconscious level—which are consistent with the private logic and which serve to reinforce it. The early memories which a person retains are retained precisely because they serve as a statement of one's private logic and goals. It is my belief, however, that the Early Recollection reveals not only the private logic and goals but also the *emotions* a person uses to give impetus to the logical sequence leading to the preordained conclusion.

"The Willhite" adds a new dimension to therapy by allowing for much more involvement on the part of the client. It establishes a much clearer and better defined contract between the client and the therapist.

There are several unique features of "The Willhite" which extend and enhance the usefulness of the Early Recollection process:

First, by having the client specify which emotion(s) are appropriate to each segment of the recollection it is revealed what sequence of emotions (s)he employs to confirm the private logic—that sense of "such is life." The person whose behavior is dysfunctional tends to utilize the same general pattern over and over again in problem solving.

Second, in addition to the original recollection I have the client reconstruct the episode the way (s)he would like to have had it happen; this is called the *self-Ideal*.

Third, by developing the *Private-Logic-at-Work* section the client has an opportunity to discover the bottleneck of his/her psyche and can consider the alternatives suggested in the *Self-Ideal*—since this is consistent with the person's system of private logic.

And, finally, "The Willhite" creatively uses fantasy as a vehicle for making the transition from diagnosis to treatment. Indeed, it serves as the catalyst for a process which, I believe, exemplifies Ansbacher's statement: "There is in Adlerian therapy no sharp distinction between diagnosis and treatment." (Ansbacher, 1972, p. 141)

References

Adler, A. *Understanding Human Nature.* New York: Greenberg: Publisher, 1927.

Ansbacher, H. L. Adlerian Psychology: The Tradition of Brief Psychotherapy. *Journal of Individual Psychology,* 1972, *28* (2), 137–151.

Psychodrama and "The Willhite"

Jay Colker and Elaine Funk

In the previous chapter, Robert G. Willhite presents his approach to early recollection interpretation in which he lists the client's sequence of emotions as the client relates them. Willhite maintains that the emotional sequence, which is unique to each individual, is employed in problem solving and may lead to dysfunctional behavior. "By having the client specify which emotion(s) are appropriate to each segment of the recollection, it is revealed what sequence of emotions (s)he employs to confirm the private logic—that sense of 'such is life.' The person whose behavior is dysfunctional tends to utilize the same general pattern over and over again in problem solving." (Willhite, 1978, p. 81) The emotions are used by the client to initiate behavior that confirms the client's convictions (values). "We now see why we need emotions. They provide the fuel, the steam, so to speak, for our actions, the driving force without which we would be impotent. They make it possible for us to carry out our decisions. They permit us to take a stand, to develop definite attitudes, to form convictions: (Dreikurs, 1967, p. 207)."

In "The Willhite" problem—solving stage, the recollection is recreated with the same structure but with an ideal setting, ideal actions, and new related emotions. This revision creates a new set of expectations for the client and disrupts the old pattern seen both in the early recollection ("self-concept") and in the "private logic at work" (presenting problem). This new set of expectations gives the client alternatives to his present dysfunctional system. "Since the possibilities for change have been stated by the client—not just arbitrarily imposed by the therapist—(s)he is more readily willing to accept the responsibility for trying out the new behaviors, and to work on developing emotional response patterns [to implement them]. (Willhite, 1978, p. 78)." Finally, the therapist can evaluate the usefulness of the ideal ER by seeing the movement toward social interest. When one feels that he belongs as he is, then he acts on the basis of social interest without the need for personal superiority.

Psychodrama puts the recollection in action and enables the client to relive the experience and the related emotions vividly. The recollection then becomes experiential rather than only an intellectual rememberance. If we assume that emotions have the purpose of moving the person through an established sequential pattern of behavior, then psychodrama can help to focus more quickly on that recurrent pattern. Because actions speak louder than words, having the client relive the recollection can help to magnify and to highlight his recognition of his private logic and mistaken goals. This can speed the diagnostic and therapeutic processes and enable both the counselor and the client to reach the problem-solving stage more quickly.

Combining psychodrama and "The Willhite" enhances the client's ability to adapt to new alternatives by enabling him to see and experience alternative behaviors. Psychodrama helps the client to experience those alternatives so that he can actualize those most comfortable to him. In having found viable alternatives, he feels encouraged because he has a sense of direction and goal attainment.

Format

The idea for combining "The Willhite" and psychodrama came to Jay Colker after watching Gloria Lane, an Adlerian counselor from Wilmington, Delaware, demonstrate the technique and after having worked with Elaine Funk, a Certified Director of Psychodrama and Psychotherapy from the Moreno Institute and a faculty member at Bowie State College. Funk had been working with Colker, utilizing psychodrama with mental patients. The format for the workshop was developed by Lane, Funk, and Colker, with the latter acting as facilitator. Although the following incident is true, the names of the clients have been fictionalized.

Reprinted by permission of the authors.

Diane, the primary client, was thirty seven years old, married to Bob for seventeen years, and had two children, ages ten and seven.

I. *Interview with the client*—conducted by Gloria Lane, the counselor
   A. *Format*
      1. First the presenting problem was discussed and the client was asked why she felt that it was a problem.
      2. Once she had indicated a specific example of her problem, it was discussed.
      3. The client was then asked to think of a similar episode from high school, then from grade school, and finally she was asked for an early recollection (ER). The purpose of moving the client back in stages through the years was to get an early memory based on the problem. (If the client had had trouble thinking of similar examples in high school or grade school, she would simply have been asked for any ER.)
   B. *Workshop Presentation*
      1. Diane recounted, "My main concern is that I more often than not react and interact from a defense stance, a stance aimed at protecting myself from attack, ridicule, showing them how foolish and stupid I am, from being hurt as well as hurting others. The defensiveness? I don't let people get close to me. I'm very quiet, and if someone does approach me, I keep it at a surface level. I don't really let them know me. I've only let my sister and my husband know me. I consider myself shy. I don't have very many friends. I don't get into a discussion very much with people. The reason why I'm here today is that I want to change. I've joined a women's group and have just tried to get out around people more."
      Specific example—"My husband and I come home from a movie. I have expressed an opinion about one of the characters. I may catch an expression from him, a quizzical look—that's enough to set me off. He's wondering what I'm talking about. I immediately question why is he looking at me like that? Is what

I said that stupid? Or if he doesn't understand what I am trying to express, I get highly excited. What's the matter? I immediately launch into a defense. I'll repeat it, elaborate on it, go on and on and on. I catch myself five minutes later in an agitated monologue and Bob hasn't said anything. "Couldn't you see it? I saw it." Sometimes Bob will give up or he may tell me why he is right. I immediately tell him why he is wrong. It ends in one of three ways. He will drop it. Or he may continue to hold to his opinion and I redouble my defense. Or Bob decides to leave and I will follow him. Then it ends in a big fight. I'll keep defending my position until he says maybe I'm right. He will walk away and I feel discounted."

      3. *Similar situation in past*—Diane could not come up with a specific example from the past. She seemed very self-protective and defensive. Therefore the counselor just asked for any ER. Diane then recounted,

      "I was about five. All of us kids and my mother and the whole neighborhood were raking leaves. My mother was tired. It was evening, suppertime. I went into the kitchen to take a cookie, and she came in and told me I couldn't do that because it was suppertime. I said, 'You're mean. I hate you.' She sent me upstairs to my room and said, 'Wait for your father.' He came home and he came upstairs and started beating me like he usually did. He was really excited and went into the bedroom and came out with a black suitcase and told me he was going to send me away from the family because the family didn't want me anymore. I thought I was going to prison or somewhere that they send bad people that nobody wanted. I panicked and snuck downstairs and begged her not to send me. He took the suitcase back but decided that my sisters didn't want to share the room. He put a mat on the hallway floor and that is where it ended. My older sister snuck out and told me that she didn't want me out of the bedroom."

II. *Presenting problem in action*—directed by Elaine Funk, the psychodramatist

  A. *Format*

   1. The psychodrama was based on the client's perception of the presenting problem. The psychodramatist kept the client in role reversal as much as possible, because this important tool helps the client to get a better and different perspective of herself and intimate others.

   2. When the action from the presenting problem had run its course, the psychodramatist stopped the enactment. The counselor then asked an ER. The ER triggered by the psychodrama was earlier, more concise, and clearer than the one originally reported.

  B. *Workshop Presentation*

   1. The psychodramatist started by focusing on Diane's mouth, because of her tight-lipped delivery. When questioned about it, Diane recognized tension in her lip, jaw, and cheek muscles, but stated that she had never noticed it before because it had been habitual. The psychodramatist pointed out that tension in these areas acts as a muzzle and prevents people from talking freely.

The stage was then set for the presenting problem. The first scene was with Diane and Bob at the movies. Questions focused on Diane's perception of herself and Bob. (It is important to note that Bob was in the audience. However, Diane said that she would feel more comfortable if he did not participate in the psychodrama.) Diane verbalized her thoughts on the characters while watching the movie' "I really feel sorry for her. She's really in a state right now. He's not hearing what she is saying. He's coming on the opposite of what she needs. She's counting on him understanding and he isn't. She's desperately trying to explain how she feels."

The psychodramatist then checked with Diane on her body tensions, and she expressed feelings of tension in her mouth, fluttery legs and stomach. The psychodramatist then put her in role reversal and Diane verbalized her feelings as "Bob." "These characters are irritating me. They are acting crazy. That women is distraught." The psychodramatist noted that "Bob's" foot was jerking. On checking "his" body movements, "Bob" said, "I have a feeling of tension in my legs. I want to smash my impatience with these people, the way they are acting crazy. Pounding my foot will break this connection between their craziness and me." The movie ended and "Bob" said, "That movie gave me a headache. I really feel agitated all over."

The scene was then switched to the car while driving home. Diane role reversed between herself and Bob. The psychodramatist reminded "both" of them of their feelings of tension and had "them" reenact them. Diane's extreme agitation in the role of herself was noted and she was asked to verbalize her feelings toward Bob. She said that she was not sure if she wanted to say these things to Bob because it might "really start something."

To facilitate the action and to help Diane to overcome her resistance, the psychodramatist had her pick a double from the audience to verbalize her inner thoughts and feelings. The double talked directly to Bob, saying, "I really want you to talk about this. I feel worthless when you don't respond. I feel you are discounting me." Diane nodded her head in agreement, and stated that the double was expressing her thoughts and feelings accurately.

The scene was switched to the home where Diane and "Bob" (Diane still in role reversal as Bob) discuss the movie (characters).

Diane: Why do you think she is crazy?

"Bob": They are both crazy. He's crazy too.

Diane: How?

"Bob": I don't know. He's always ranting and raving at her. It's like old home week again.

They argued back and forth, until "Bob" cut off the argument by saying that he was going to sleep. Diane "gave" permission by saying, "It's alright! I'll be alright! Go ahead and leave!" The psychodramatist then had Diane state her real feelings in a soliloquy. "Damned bastard! Leaving me here to stew, and he just wants to drop it. How will we ever get this solved if he is going to go to sleep on it. But I guess it's for the better because the only thing that would happen is it would end up in a big fight. I'll stay here until I cool off and then I'll go to sleep."

At this point, Diane's body muscles were extremely tense and she seemed to be shrinking down into herself. The psychodramatist then had Diane maximize her body feelings and go all the way with them. Diane went halfway to the floor. The psychodramatist then put her hands over Diane's eyes and said, "How old are you?" Diane immediately responded, "Three!"

2. Diane said, "I am three. I am with my sister. We came home from Sunday school. Father was at the top of the stairs and asked, 'What did you do at Sunday school?' I answered, 'Oh we sang songs and colored in coloring books.' He said, 'What song did you sing?' 'I don't remember the name of it,' I answered. He said, 'Sing it for me.' I didn't want to sing it. He came flying downstairs angry because I wouldn't sing and he smacked me. He hit my face as he always does. It got to the point where I couldn't breathe. I was gasping for air and then he quit and I went my own way."

III. *"The Willhite"* with Diane's recollection—conducted by the counselor

A. *Format*

1. The ER was then interpreted with "The Willhite" (see Table I). Because of the brevity of the workshop, the original recollection was not dramatized.) (The emotion elicited by the psychodramatic presentation made them more easily recognized for use in "The Willhite." This quicker recognition of the emotions further justifies use of the two techniques conjointly.)

2. The client was then asked to recreate the recollection with an ideal setting, ideal actions, and new related emotions. (see Table I)

B. *Workshop Presentation*

1. Table I shows how the recollection was set up for interpretation using "The Willhite." For each thought phrase in the recollection, Diane was asked to associate a feeling. From the feeling content expressed by Diane, the counselor pointed out the sequence of emotions causing the presenting problem and hypothesized how this pattern recurred in other similar situations. (Diane exhibited recognition reflexes to these hypotheses.)

Diane generally feels fine, comfortable, and content until she sees someone else as superior (Father at the top of the stairs) and herself as inferior. Then she feels uncomfortable, on edge, and angry. She begins to feel fear and fury at being "put on the spot." Her feelings exacerbate to defiance, noncooperation, and inflexibility. When these feelings explode into rage, she accepts her punishment (the payoff) and then is relieved that "it is over for this time." But she anticipates that it will happen again. Thus, as Willhite says, the pattern becomes a self-fulfilling prophecy.

2. The counselor then led Diane through the recollection and had her change it to her ideal situation. (see Table I) In comparing the ideal ER with the original, it is noted that

TABLE I

"The Willhite" Interpretation of Diane's Recollection

	Self-Concept	Emotions and Feelings of Self-Concept	Self-Ideal
1.	I was with my sister.	felt fine, contentment, comfortable	I was with my sister.
2.	We came home from Sunday school.	comfortable, contentment	We came home from Sunday school.
3.	Father was at the top of the stairs.	Why was he there? Uncomfortable, on edge, What does he want?	Father is in the bathroom shaving and mother is getting out an early lunch.
4.	Father asked, "What did you do at Sunday school?"	Will we be drilled? scared, angry, If I don't cooperate, I'll be in trouble. uneasy	Father comes downstairs and asks, "How did things go at Sunday school?"
5.	"Oh, we sang songs and colored in coloring books."	Now I can go off and play. That's what he wants. Relief	Sister answers, "Fine."
6.	"What song did you sing?"	Oh, oh, here we go again. I wish I could remember. apprehension, feel like I'm on the spot. Trapped by bully. Fear, Rage.	Mother says food is ready.
7.	"I don't remember the name of it."	Really scared, defiant	"I'm really hungry," I say.
8.	"Sing it for me."	I wasn't going to do it. On the spot. Don't have way out. Defiant, angry	Everyone starts eating.
9.	I didn't want to sing it.	Won't let him bully me. Uncomfortable, trapped, angry	
10.	He came flying down the stairs angry because I wouldn't sing and smacked me. He hit my face as he always does.	Scared, anticipating, I won't cooperate. outnumbered, helpless only defense is to be defiant	
11.	I couldn't breathe. I was gasping for air.	hurt, rage, fury, I won't be forced.	
12.	He quit and I went my own way.	He is satisfied for today. Relief, That is it for this time. Isolated and extremely alone. He and I and then the rest of the family. Now I can go off but I'll go off by self. Feel defiant but anticipate future.	

when Diane feels inferior, her discomfort will trigger her movement through her dysfunctional sequential pattern.*

Thus, when Bob says, "Crazy people," she perceives that he is including her with those "crazy people." She sees him as judging her and acting superior. Diane then suckers Bob in, using her old system. "I can bring him down. He can victimize me but he can't make me change my mind."

It is interesting to note that Diane changes the recollection so that she would have people equal to her. Only when she perceives that people are being superior will she lash out. If she could see it differently, then she might not feel threatened.

IV. *Psychodramatically Acting Out the Self-Ideal of the ER*—directed by the psychodramatist
   A. *Format*
      1. The "ideal" ER was reenacted psychodramatically so that the client would recognize and experience the alternatives.
      2. The psychodramatist had Diane set up the scene of the ER, incorporating the changes for the ideal situation.**
   B. *Workshop Presentation*
      1. Diane chose people from the audience to play the roles of her sister, father, and mother who participated in the following:
      2. "Father is in the bathroom shaving and mother is getting out an early lunch. We come in the front door. Mother greets us. Father comes downstairs and asks, 'How did things go at Sunday school?' Sister answers, 'Fine.' Mother says that food is ready. 'I'm really hungry,' I say, and everyone starts eating."

The psychodramatist noted the relaxation in Diane's face and body and asked how she was feeling. Diane said, "I feel comfortable. He accepts what we said about Sunday School and he doesn't need to dig any further."

V. *Examining the Alternatives in the Here and Now*—directed by the psychodramatist

A. *Format*
   1. The scene was then changed to the movie and Diane was asked if she now felt comfortable enough to bring the real Bob in for the scene. With her agreement, Bob left the audience and joined the psychodrama.
   2. The psychodrama continued, relating the changed ER to the presenting problem. Alternatives generated from the discussion of the self-ideal were role trained.
B. *Workshop Presentation*
   1. Diane acted out the movie situation with Bob, but with the focus on the new alternatives and on feeling relaxed and equal. Diane had a hard time deciding what she could do to feel comfortable when she perceived Bob being upset (foot tapping). She couldn't find a way to feel comfortable!
   2. The psychodramatist then changed the scene to the car. Diane was told that as soon as she felt uncomfortable, she was to stop herself and to find a way to feel comfortable. She said that when she knows that Bob is agitated, she can't feel comfortable.

She was therefore unable to find her own alternatives and the audience was asked for suggestions. Diane could then draw on these alternatives as a recourse to succumbing to her old established pattern of reaction.

VI. *Encouragement and Closure*—conducted by Jay Colker as facilitator, and by the counselor and psychodramatist
   A. *Format*
      1. Because of the group's identification with Diane's problem, their aid was enlisted in suggesting alternatives. Each person who volunteered a sug-

*We used "The Willhite" at an early stage in the development of the technique. We did not elicit emotions for the self-ideal nor did we follow through with the appropriate number of frames to keep it consistent with the self-concept (see "The Willhite," p.73). We were still able to use the material to constructively work with the client. We examined patterns of emotions in the self-concept and were able to point out similarities in her presentive problem.

**It is important to watch the movement in the self-ideal. It is important to see an increase in social interest, otherwise the ideal could be equally dysfunctional.

gestion was asked to enter the psychodrama and role play the alternative. The psychodramatist checked with Diane for the acceptability of each alternative.

2. Closure was completed by asking the audience to list the resources that Diane and Bob could draw upon to successfully overcome their problem.

B. *Workshop Presentation*

1. The following are some of Diane's alternatives which were role-played: "I could take responsibility for myself and not worry about Bob's being upset;" "I could think to myself, 'You're a male, but that doesn't make you a son of a bitch;' " "I feel way down sometimes, but if I can look at you as not so perfect, then I think I could probably enjoy the movies with you."; "I don't have to view this as winning or losing. It's alright for Bob to see it differently."; "I could recognize when I begin to feel uncomfortable, wait a minute, and then say what I am feeling."; "All I can say is what I would like. I can state my feelings in terms of I messages, such as 'When you turn off and don't talk, I feel like you are wiping me out. I feel awful bad about that.'; "I can respect Bob's choice NOT to talk. I can accept the fact that he doesn't like to be pressured. I should not use authoritarian words because that closes Bob up."

2. Diane's resources included courage, tenaciousness, willingness to try something new, creativity, good observational abilities, humor, and a willingness to change.

   Bob's resources included courage, a sense of humor, warmth and care for others.

VII. *Followup*—conducted by the facilitator

A followup session with both Diane and Bob took place five days after the workshop to get their comments about the day and about the combination of the techniques. The following are exerpts of the session;

Diane: I was concerned that I had stretched out the workshop without being able to come up with what they were asking me to do. I worked the counselor and the psychodramatist very hard. I would have liked to clear up where exactly I start the process going, where I turn the whole thing the way I want it to go. I want to see more clearly so I know how to change the old; "I may get smacked but at least he hasn't beat me down morally." I realize that one strategy I use is to go to battle verbally. When I perceive that he's not enjoying the movie, or he's upset about it and I picked the movie, and he's making less of me because I picked it—the maneuver I pull to show him that I'm not as low as I assume he's assuming is to confront him and do battle on it. I try to convince him that I'm not what he's thinking. That is one strategy I use.

Facilitator: What did you learn from the day?

Diane: I saw very clearly how we get what we ask for. We arrange our lives so we get what we know how to cope with. At the start of the psychodrama, I was very nervous about being in front of all those people. I was concerned with letting people see what kind of fool I am. As things progressed, it was difficult for me to role-play and remember what I was doing. What was most comfortable was when the doubles spoke for me, when they verbalized what I was feeling or thinking. It really was helpful to hear myself and be objective. I have to be aware of what I'm feeling. I don't connect what I'm feeling with what I am saying. If I let someone know what I'm feeling, it is like handing them something that they can use against me. So I am extremely cautious of that. I have to trust people more.

After the workshop, I didn't dwell on it too much. Something came to me the other day and it was a complete surprise and I thought, "Oh no! It has opened up a whole Pandora's Box for me." I was fixing dinner and I was muttering "damned bastard" to myself without any connection to anyone. Then it connected with my mother. I would say "damned bastard" while I was cooking the spaghetti sauce, and my mother was attached to it. I thought, "What is happening here?" and I began to realize that during the workshop all the discussion was me and my father, and once in a while my sister would come into it. But all the time, my mother was always there and I left her out completely and I always have because she was so passive. I always thought that her passive part meant that she wasn't in it. I realize that she was very active in a very unhelpful way to me. These things were going on right under her nose, and she let them go on for years and years and she never stepped in. By the time I got dinner on the table, I wanted to run to my mother and shake her and say, "God damn it. Where were you? What was the matter with you? Couldn't you see?" This was a total surprise to me.

I realize that I cause the difficulty and I want to pursue this further. Before the day (of the workshop), I thought this idea was a credible one, but I hadn't realized the extent to which I am involved.

Facilitator: What about the combination of techniques?

Diane: I was in doubt how much I influenced the situation. But seeing my recollection on the board and then putting it into action, I realized that I had major input into it. The program helped me to see it.

Facilitator: What about your perceptions of Bob?

Diane: I was amazed that he participated as much as he did. I chose not to use him at the beginning because I thought that he would be uncomfortable.

Facilitator: Bob, do you have anything to add?

Bob: I tried to keep an open mind. I'm surprised that I was able to stick to it without being pinpointed. I guess it will take a matter of time to sort these things out. I don't like being pinned down. That's a characteristic of mine unless I know what I'm being pinned down for. I was surprised that I went through with it.

Willhite's comments on Diane's recollection

Using "The Willhite" it is relatively easy to pinpoint Diane's emotional sequence. First she feels comfortable and contentment and continues the feeling of comfort to try and reinforce it. Immediately there is a feeling of discomfort—"on edge." She feels scared, angry and uneasy until she finds a way to get out of the situation—relief. This does not work for her for she immediately goes into fear and rage and is "really scared—defiant." She carries this defiance and anger into the next frame. From this she feels uncomfortable, trapped and angry. This seems to get her to her prophecy of a feeling of helplessness with the only defense of being defiant. She justifies this defiance by thinking she "won't be forced." We can see, however, that her private view of the world is that she is isolated and extremely alone . . . I'm in this alone. She never deals with her defiance (anger) because of her aloneness and isolation. She sets herself up not to deal with life thru self-assertion for fear she will be rejected. The irony is she sets up the rejection herself thru isolating.

The self-ideal column gives us a clue as to how Diane will deal with her dilemma. She maintains the feelings of contentment and comfort in the first two frames by not changing the story. The third frame reveals the first change in behavior—that of changing father's behavior, not hers. She learned a lot by being able to see her behavior unfold as she dealt with it in the self-image and the feelings and emotions. Now I would like to have her put feelings and emotions to the self-ideal story. She then would have specific feelings to tune into when she wanted to consciously change her behavior. When he (father) finished shaving she could have felt pleased, rather than the counter part of feeling on edge and when he asked, "Did you have a good time at Sunday School?" she could have felt encouraged or hopeful. These are specific feelings she will have to focus on to break from the "such is life" conviction of loneliness and isolation.

It is also important to have Diane finish the story in the self-ideal column because by not doing so in this particular sequence she avoids dealing with the trapped, angry, outnumbered, helpless feelings she has and she also does not have to deal with her rage. The self-ideal fantasy is a comfortable way of looking for avenues of expressions to deal with painful feelings such as trapped, helplessness, etc.

Colker and Funk have put "The Willhite" to an interesting test and found it helpful in enabling the client to relive the experience—especially as the recollection reveals the feelings and emotions the client uses. I am extremely pleased to have been able to make a contribution to this process. Colker and Funk have made a useful adaptation of "The Willhite" to a particular therapeutic modality. It is gratifying to watch the process unfold as they implement it.

Robert G. Willhite

Summary

"The Willhite" assumes that emotions move the person through an established sequencial pattern of behavior which ultimately confirms the life style. "The Willhite" examines the emotions in an early recollection to establish the sequence of behavior. "The Willhite" then helps the client to develop an ideal ER which creates a new set of expectations and disrupts the old pattern.

Psychodrama puts the recollection in action and can help to magnify and to highlight the client's recognition of his private logic and mistaken goals. This can speed up the diagnostic and therapeutic processes and enable the counselor and the client to reach the problem solving stage more quickly.

Combining psychodrama and "The Willhite" enables the client to see and experience alternative behaviors and to actualize those most comfortable to him.

We have given a step by step process of how we combined psychodrama and "The Willhite." We recognize that this is preliminary conjecture and that there is no empirical basis to assess the combination.

References

Dreikurs, R., "The Function of Emotions" in *Psychodynamics, Psychotherapy, and Counseling,* Chicago: Alfred Adler Institute, 1967.

Willhite, R. " 'The Willhite': A Creative Extension of the Early Recollection Process." *Life Style: Theory, Practice, and Research* by Leroy Baruth and Daniel Eckstein. Dubuque, Ia.: Kendall/Hunt Publishing Company, 1978, 72–82.

Early Recollections in Life-Style Assessment and Counseling

Richard Royal Kopp
Don Dinkmeyer

The idiographic approach to assessment presented in this article is based on the Adlerian approach to life-style assessment (Ansbacher 1967; Ansbacher & Ansbacher 1964; Dreikurs 1967; Mosak 1958, 1971; Shulman 1973). The idiographic method focuses on the individual case or person, whereas the nomothetic method is designed to discover general laws which are true for groups of individuals. Life style is defined as the characteristic patterns of an individual's responses. Thus, the idiographic approach identifies the uniqueness of the child.

As Adler (in Ansbacher & Ansbacher 1964) states, "The goal . . . with each individual is personal and unique. It depends upon the meaning he gives to life" (p. 181). Too much of the data available to the school counselor is nomothetic; that is, it is related to norms and averages and thus does not help the counselor understand the individual student.

Relevance of Life-Style Assessment to the School Counselor

Life-style assessment not only enables both the student and teacher to become aware of the student's goals, but it also points to specific changes. For example, if the student is especially motivated by the desire for attention, the teacher may be helped to find active and constructive ways in which the student can obtain attention by contributing to the group. With the student who seeks power and control, it may be possible to give that student leadership responsibilities in the school setting.

This approach to assessment is of particular value insofar as it reveals the pattern of the individual. Instead of dealing with unrelated test scores and observations, the idiographic approach presents a holistic picture of the basic beliefs and motives of the student. As we become aware of these beliefs and motives, the individual's behavior makes sense and is also more readily modified.

Assessment Using Early Recollections

The rationale for using early recollections as an assessment tool is based on the idea that people remember only those events from early childhood that are consistent with their present view of themselves and the world (Adler 1958; Kelly 1963; Mayman 1968; Mosak 1958). In remembering and telling a specific incident, the person reconstructs in the present an experience he or she once had.

The person selects only certain events from the countless number of experiences that occurred during early life and enphasizes certain aspects of each memory while diminishing or omitting other details. Because it is a product of these selective and evaluative processes, the memory can thus be used as projective data from which we can infer the basic elements of the current life style (i.e., beliefs and motives) that influenced and shaped the recollection as it is told to the interviewer.

Collecting Early Recollections

Mosak (1958) suggests guidelines that are useful for defining an early recollection. These include: (a) the use of only those memories that can be visualized (or vividly recalled) and that are described as single events; (b) omitting incidents (termed "reports") that happened many times and/or that are vague with respect to details of action, feeling, or the setting in which the memory takes place; and (c) using only those memories of experiences that occurred before the individual was eight years old.

Our experience indicates that an individual eight years of age and older can usually produce early recollections which are of value. Because the pro-

Richard Kopp and Don Dinkmeyer, Sr., Early Recollections in Life Style Assessment and Counseling, *The School Counselor*, 23(1), 1975, 22–27. Copyright 1975 American Personnel and Guidance Association. Reprinted with permission.

cedure is not common to the student's experience, it is essential to follow the guidelines for collecting recollections precisely.

Kopp (1972) developed a procedure for collecting early recollections in writing, thus enabling memories to be collected in groups. This procedure is standardized and can thus be used for research purposes. The format presented below, which is a verbal procedure, is derived from this wtten procedure and can be used by the counselor when collecting recollections in a personal interview.

Think back as far as you can to the first thing you can remember . . . something that happened when you were very young (it should be before you were seven or eight years old). It can be anything at all—good or bad, important or unimportant—but it should be something you can describe as a one-time incident (something that happened only once), and it should be something you can remember very clearly or picture in your mind, like a scene.

Now tell me about an incident or something that happened to you. Make sure that it is something you can picture, something specific, and something where you can remember a single time it happened.

As the student begins to tell the memory, listen for the visual and specific part of the memory. Some background details may be appropriate. Do not, however, spend too much time setting the stage with facts leading up to or surrounding the incident itself. Instead, concentrate on what actually happened.

Phrases such as "We were always . . .," "would always . . .," "used to . . .," or "would happen" suggest incidents that occurred repeatedly. Ask the student to choose one specific time which stands out more clearly than the others and tell what happened that one time. If one particular incident does not stand out over others, eliminate this event and choose a different early memory which can be described as a single incident.

Before moving on to the next memory, ask the following questions and write down the student's response:

Do you remember how you felt at the time or what reaction you had to what was going on? (If so) please describe it. Why did you feel that way (or have that reaction)?

Which part of the memory stands out most clearly from the rest—like if you had a snapshot of the memory, it would be the very instant that is most vivid and clear in your mind? How did you feel (what was your reaction) at that instant?

Our experience indicates that although we can begin to see a student's basic beliefs and motivations in the first memory, the accuracy of these interpretations increases when they are based on additional memories. The counselor's assessment thus should be based on at least three memories. Typically, from three to six memories are collected.

Using Early Recollections in Counseling: An Example

Ernie, a second grader, was referred to the counselor because he drew nude pictures of women and showed them to his teacher. The teacher asked the counselor what to do.

In order to be able to help the teacher and Ernie, we must first understand the meaning of Ernie's behavior. Let's see how the following early recollections can help.

Recollection A: Age one year. "Once my dad came in from work and I just bit him on the knee. That was telling him 'hello.' He giggled when I did it. He picked me up and sat down beside me and my leg was under him—he did it on purpose. I told him to get off—I was mad at him. Biting him stands out most—I wanted to say 'hello' and I didn't know how to say anything then."

Interpretation. The counselor must first focus on the action sequence described in the memory. In this memory, the initial action sequence is: Dad comes in; Ernie bites dad on the knee; Dad giggles. Having identified the sequence, we next focus on the messages and metaphors that the action expresses.

We are struck by the inappropriate and even contradictory method of communication expressed in the action, and we can infer that (a) Ernie believes that he must do the unexpected in order to communicate with others and get their attention, (b) he wants to make an impression. Since we are regarding the memory as a metaphor that is indicative of a general pattern, "saying 'hello' " suggests a specific instance of a communication style between people. Similarly, this pattern probably applies to most of Ernie's relationships with others, although it may be especially characteristic of the way he relates to males.

An action sequence can also reveal the child's self-image, image of others, motivation, and typical behaviors. For example, the second action sequence—Dad picks up Ernie; Dad sits on Ernie's leg (on purpose); Ernie tells him to get off—suggests that (a) Ernie sees himself as small (needing to be picked up); (b) Ernie perceives others (perhaps men especially) as pinning him down; and (c) when he is (or feels) pinned down, Ernie gets angry and will protest overtly, in effect telling others to get off his back (or his leg in this case!).

"Biting him" stands out most for Ernie, indicating the main motivational theme of this memory: He wants to make contact with and impress others. It also suggests that Ernie chooses inappropriate and aggressive methods for doing this, methods which will impress others. (The act of biting literally makes an impression!) Further, the memory suggests that Ernie chooses this method because he feels that he doesn't know how to get others to notice him through appropriate methods.

Having formulated these initial impressions from the first memory, we turn to the second recollection.

Recollection B: Age one year. "James [Ernie's brother] climbed up in the barbecue. I saw him get in and I got in and took a bath in it. James got the ashes in his hands and rubbed it all over my face and hair. As soon as my mom and dad came out to see what we were doing, I just took a bunch and threw it at my brother and he threw it at my mom and dad. They spanked him and sent him to bed. I thought it was funny because he got in trouble."

Interpretation. Early recollections can suggest the social role frequently played by a child. The initial action sequence in this memory is: James climbs in the barbecue; Ernie watches; Ernie also gets in; Ernie "takes a bath" in the barbecue ashes; James rubs Ernie with ashes. Ernie's role here is as an observer and willing follower when seeking mischievous fun. Note, however, that this memory suggests that Ernie has the ability to cooperate and join with others (peers) in an activity (albeit a mischievous one).

The remaining action sequence is: Mom and Dad come out; Ernie immediately throws ashes at his brother; his brother throws ashes at Mom and Dad; Mom and Dad spank James and put him to bed. The main significance of this sequence is that James gets punished while Ernie does not. Ernie emphasizes this part of the memory as the part that is most vivid for him. This emphasis suggests the following about Ernie's life style: (a) He wants to have fun (motivational goal), but does so in mischievous ways (method of reaching the goal); and (b) Ernie prefers that others get into trouble while he escapes the consequences of his behavior (this doubles his pleasure and doubles his fun!). As with the first memory, this recollection suggests that Ernie sees communication between people in basically nonverbal and aggressive terms.

Note that the question of whether or not these events actually happened in the way Ernie remembers them is unimportant for our purposes. Since he selects these events and details from the uncountable number of experiences he had as a small child, what Ernie does tell us reflects the present way he sees himself in relation to the world and others and the current things that are important to him. This is the rationale which allows us to interpret the memories as we have.

Life-Style summary. An important final step in the life-style assessment process as described by Adler (1935), Ansbacher (1967), Ansbacher and Ansbacher (1964), Dreikurs (1953), Shulman (1965, 1973), Mosak (1954), and Allen (1971) is formulating a summary that includes the basic elements of the life style. The life style consists of (a) beliefs about self, the world (life), and others; (b) motivation (goals, purposes, and intentions); and (c) the choice of behaviors designed to reach life goals. Also included in the summary is an assessment of strengths and weaknesses (i.e., beliefs, goals, or methods which facilitate or interfere with successful functioning and development).

We can summarize Ernie's life style as follows:

Self-concept: I am small and sneaky.
World image: The world is a place to have fun and make mischief.
Image of others: Others (adults) are strong and powerful; they can overpower and punish me.
Motivational goals: I want to impress others, to make mischief without having to pay the consequences, to defend myself when I feel pinned down.
Behavior for achieving the goals: I will do the unexpected, be sneaky and clever, protest when I'm overpowered.
Strengths: Ernie is bright and assertive; he is capable of enjoying life, wants the recognition of others, is able to cooperate, has a good sense of humor, and knows how to get a response from others.
Weaknesses: He overemphasizes mischief and surprise tactics as a method for getting others to notice him and probably doesn't believe he can impress others in more constructive ways; he overestimates the power of others and their intent to use that power against him; and he expects inconsistent and even contradictory messages from adults.

Drawing nude pictures is but one method of impressing others by being mischievous and doing the unexpected. We are likely to find additional instances of behaviors that fit this life style pattern. The counselor can suggest to the teacher that the pictures be ignored (thus eliminating the desired payoff) and that attention be given to constructive behaviors. Ernie's strengths also suggest that he is capable of being a leader and thus should be given an opportunity to direct the class in some activity. By sharing the life-style summary with Ernie, the counselor is able to (a) formulate counseling objectives; (b) quickly develop rapport with Ernie by demonstrating that the counselor understands how Ernie sees himself, life, and others; and (c) focus immediately on the probable reasons for Ernie's present behavior.

References

Adler, A. The fundamental views of I.P. *International Journal of Individual Psychology, 1935, 1*(1), 5–8.

Adler, A. *What life should mean to you.* New York: Capricorn Books, 1958. (Originally published 1931.)

Allen, T. (Ed.) *The Counseling Psychologist: Individual psychology, 1971, 3*(1). (monograph)

Ansbacher, H. The life style: A historical and systematic review. *Journal of Individual Psychology, 1967, 23,* 191–212.

Ansbacher, H., & Ansbacher, R. (Eds.) *The individual psychology of Alfred Adler.* New York: Harper Torchbooks, 1964.

Dreikurs, R. *Fundamentals of Adlerian psychology.* Chicago: Alfred Adler Institute, 1953.

Dreikurs, R. *Psychodynamics, psychotherapy, and counseling.* Chicago: Alfred Adler Institute, 1967.

Kelly, G. *A theory of personality: The psychology of personal constructs.* New York: W. W. Norton, 1963.

Kopp, R. R. The subjective frame of reference and selective memory. Unpublished doctoral dissertation, University of Chicago, 1972.

Mayman, M. Early memories and character structure. *Journal of Projective Technique and Personality Assessment, 1968, 32*(4), 303–316.

Mosak, H. H. The psychological attitude in rehabilitation. *American Archives of Rehabilitation Therapy, 1954, 2*(1), 9–10.

Mosak, H. H. Early recollections as a projective technique, *Journal of Projective Techniques, 1958, 22,* 302–311.

Mosak, H. H. Lifestyle. In A. G. Nikelly (Ed.), *Techniques for behavior change: Applications of Adlerian theory.* Springfield, Ill.: Charles C. Thomas, 1971. Pp. 77–81.

Shulman, B. H. A comparison of Allport's and the Adlerian concepts of life style. *Individual Psychologist, 1965, 3*(1), 14–21.

Shulman, B. H. *Contributions to individual psychology: Selected papers.* Chicago: Alfred Adler Institute, 1973.

Family Constellation and Lifestyle: Educational Applications

Terrance D. Olson

This article illustrates the use of the assumptions of Individual Psychology for therapeutic purposes in educational settings. Ideally, an atmosphere of mutual respect and concern can be generated in any classroom, regardless of the subject matter. This article, however, specifically focuses on using Adlerian concepts, i.e., family constellation and lifestyle, in teaching courses that deal with human relationships, marital interaction, and personal development.

In these educational contexts, the primary goal is not particularly to diagnose an individual lifestyle, but to present the principles of Adlerian psychology in ways that illustrate how they apply to a person's current patterns of behavior and interpersonal interaction. For example, in examining family-Oconstellation factors related to "personality," the fundamental idea presented is that the family is the laboratory where a person conducts his or her first experiments in living; that is, the family origin serves as an internship for future relationships. The goal in the human relationships classroom is not so much to teach *why* as it is to teach *how* a person can use insights gained from an understanding of family constellation to modify current patterns of thinking and behaving.

In many instances, accomplishing these goals should not be limited to class lecture or discussion. Often, the concepts can be illustrated by the behavior or atmosphere present in the classroom, by structured exercises, or by outside-of-class experiences. In any case, the classroom is considered a proper place for pursuing therapeutic goals.

Hopefully, using specific theory and general teaching strategies will achieve therapeutic goals—such as helping students understand their own lifestyles, thus opening the possibilities of choosing choosing healthier behaviors (Papenek, 1972)—and, concomitantly, achieving two classic goals of Adlerian therapy: increasing both courage and social interest (Ansbacher & Ansbacher, 1967).

Both Adler and Dreikurs illustrated the use of clinical practice for benefiting great numbers of people, inasmuch as both clinicians worked "in public," hoping that the example of one person or family learning to cooperatively solve problems and strengthen relationships might be useful to observers. Conversely, educational settings should also be therapeutic, especially since, in this paper, the goals of both the educational and clinical settings are assumed to be identical.

Family Constellation

College courses designed for marital preparation or strengthening provide examples of how to generate insight into one's lifestyle. Although numerous concepts related to family constellation and lifestyle can be reviewed, the purpose of the following examples is to demonstrate what can be presented and how classroom interaction can be used to generate insight, action, courage, and social interest.

The concept of family constellation may be introduced in a variety of ways. A typical class experience is grouping students by birth-order categories, requesting that each group develop a "composite personality" that describes every member of the group. Youngest children, for example, are grouped together to share their observations of what youngest children are like. Only those tendencies and qualities on which everyone in the group agrees should be included as components of that specific lifestyle.

In the reporting phase of this exercise, students generally become willing not only to report on their conclusions about their own group, but also to offer opinions about other sibling categories. Typical directions of discussion can be identified.

Terrance D. Olson, "Family Constellation and Lifestyle: Educational Applications," *The Individual Psychologist*, June 1978, pp. 5–10. Reprinted by permission of the publisher.

1. There are comments that support family-con-stellation theory: oldests feel "only" and mid-dles feel "average" or just "middle."
2. In a group of second-born individuals, consid-erable trait oppositeness is acknowledged with respect to themselves and their older siblings, regardless of the sex of the siblings.
3. During the process of asking each group to report its conclusions, there is often behavior that humorously illustrates, in vivo, the im-pact of family constellation on current behav-ior. For example, when a youngest group is asked to report, choosing a spokesperson is tossed like a hot potato from one group mem-ber to another; or, in a heated exchange be-tween oldest and youngest groups, the middles complain about being "left out." Often, these here-and-now illustrations of pat-terned behavior become the springboard for discussion. Once, a very meaningful exchange occurred when the "only" child in the class raised her hand to share how she felt about being "only." The exchange she had observed in the groups sensitized her anew to her goals of belonging.

An extension of this exercise in a marriage-prep-aration class is to ask for predicted strengths and weaknesses in marriage relationships composed of people from various family constellations. Even more directly, class members who are going steady, are engaged, or are married may be requested to identify a current behavior pattern in their love relationship that is related to their family of origin and to discuss these insights with their companion.

An additional outside-of-class activity involves class members to identify a component of their lifestyles (defined simply as a patterned way of behaving) that they can link to their own family constellation and then share their insights with a family member (if geographically available) or with a close friend. This kind of assignment helps link real-world relationships and experiences with class study and discussion.

Inferiority Feelings

The concept of inferiority feelings generates in-terest and has wide applicability. Two goals of dealing with inferiority feelings in the classroom are to teach that such feelings are universal and that they can be beneficial. As an initial step, class

members may be asked to identify one way in which they feel inferior to others. Interestingly, when the responses to such a question are com-piled, answers are predictable by sex. Females identify some physical quality as inferior (legs, nose, face, body—with *overweight* being the most common response), while males identify some-thing that involves interpersonal competence ("I'm not confident," "I don't talk enough," or "I have few friends"). With this kind of data in hand, the idea that everyone feels inferior in some way becomes a reality for the class, and the discussion can then proceed to a general level (what we have in common in our feelings of inferiority suggests something about our cultures, our families, and ourselves) or can be applied more specifically to current relationships. Students may be asked, "What are the benefit and the liability of your in-feriority feeling to you?" The ensuing discussion helps illustrate the purposes of people's attitudes, as well as offer insights into current patterns of behavior. Even more directly, class members may be assigned some outside-of-class "lab" exercises, such as: (a) sharing an inferiority feeling with someone to whom they feel superior, (b) for 3 days acting as if they were competent in that quality they assume to be one of personal inferiority, and (c) answering the question "What would be the consequence of my giving up this feeling of in-feriority?" and then sharing the insight with some-one they trust.

Social Interest

Social interest is a cornerstone of personal de-velopment. A fundamental concern for others is a prerequisite to establishing fulfilling marital rela-tionships; and, in a marriage-preparation class, de-veloping social interest is of prime concern. One class exercise illustrates a way to generate insight and practice social interest simultaneously.

Grand Canyon Exercise

Divide the class into groups of 8 to 10 students. Explain to each group that they have been hiking in the Grand Canyon and are now lost. Within the group, however, exists all the expertise necessary to help the group survive for the 3 days it will take to return to civilization. The tasks of the group are: (a) to identify what knowledge, skills, and talents will be necessary to survive the ordeal and (b) to discover who in the group has the expertise necessary to make survival possible. The special conditions are:

1. Everyone must identify a skill he or she possesses that can assist the group to survive.
2. The members of each group cannot play roles or make up skills. They must draw on their *real* talents and/or experiences as *themselves*.
3. The group must unanimously agree that a talent is valuable; and, if someone in the group has no contribution to make, the group is "stuck" in the canyon until a crucial talent is found for that person.

Several levels of insight can be drawn from this exercise, and there are specific outcomes, not the least of which is the cohesion a group who struggles to solve a problem and reach a goal can achieve. In addition, an appreciation of genuine talents can result. Also, the group is placed in a structured setting where cooperation, not competition, is a prerequisite to success. Transferring that condition to real-world settings, such as parent-child conflicts or husband-wife misunderstandings, is evident to the students as they generate discussion.

Additional Concepts

Numerous Adlerian concepts and assumptions can provide the foundation for functional classes in marriage preparation, personal development, or personality. A sample of ideas to be taught follows.

1. Your family of origin has contributed to your personality development, and both family structure (constellations) and family atmosphere (linked to parental values) help contribute to your uniqueness.
2. Regardless of your past experience, you are responsible for and the governor of your current attitudes and behavior.
3. Your past experience does not determine the way you are today, rather your definition of the future "determines" your present behavior.

4. All behavior is purposive, and your relationships with others help you achieve goals.
5. Social interest is the key to "mental health" and to fulfillment in relationships.
6. Inferiority feelings are universal and can be beneficial.
7. Your current patterns of interactions, including your attitudes toward men, women, the world, and yourself, are reflections of assumptions learned in your family of origin that may be mistaken.
8. Your earliest recollections are selective perceptions consistent with your basic goals in life.
9. Your two basic goals of belonging and superiority can be pursued with or without social interest, with attending consequences of fulfillment or frustration.
10. Courage is the willingness to the tasks of life.
11. Relationships with others are fundamental to fulfillment. We are inherently social beings.
12. Any love relationship you pursue will reflect in microcosm your more general attitudes toward others, including the way you handle conflict, give of yourself, receive from others, or cooperate.

Summary

Three specific classroom strategies have been illustrated that are beneficial in teaching Adlerian concepts, such as family constellation, inferiority feelings, social interest, etc. First, class atmosphere and here-and-now behavior in a classroom can be pointed out as representative of the concepts being introduced. Second, structured class exercises can be assigned to provide a common experience from which discussion and insight can be generated. Although the "Grand Canyon Exercise" is an original, Pfeiffer and Jones (1969–1977) have compiled exercises that could be modified for use as teaching tools for specific teleoanalytic concepts. Finally, outside-of-class exercises that require interpersonal involvement in the real world have been suggested. The purpose of this method is to link psychological concepts to classroom examples to actual experience.

It has been proposed that teleoanalytic theory and practice can be used in educational situations to achieve goals identical with those typically thought of in clinical settings. Gaining insight into personal lifestyle, choosing healthier behaviors and goals, increasing courage, and developing social interest are stated goals of education, especially "functional" marriage education. This article has illustrated specific methods of presentation that link concepts with real-life experiences

References

Ansbacher, H. L., and Ansbacher, R. R. (Eds.). *The individual psychology of Alfred Adler.* New York: Harper Torchbooks, Harper and Row, 1967.

Papenek, H. The use of early recollections in psychotherapy. *Journal of Individual Psychology.* 1972, 169–176

Pfeiffer, J. and Jones, J. *A handbook of structured experiences for human relations training* (6 vols.) La Jolla, California: University Associates Press, 1969–1977.

Changing the Sibling Rating
for the Lifestyle Inventory
to Family Rating

Adele Thomas

The Lifestyle Inventory, developed by Mosak and Schulman, includes the section, Sibling Rating. I have converted this into a Family Rating. In the ratings of most to least I now include the parents as well as the siblings.

I am a college counselor, working with students. We spend as much as two sessions on this part of the Inventory, and with the insights that occur. My clients range in age from seventeen to seventy, with older, returning students, generally women, less than a quarter of my caseload. All students come in voluntarily and no fees are charged. We deal with short and longer term therapy, of necessity delimited by semesters and the school year. Generally clients come in with a stated problem which may be, but usually is not, the actual one. Counselor and client then make a somewhat contract, dealing with the time period and issues to be discussed. The contract is renegotiable. I find that certain basic problems underlie everyone's presentation of their difficulties. At some point, everyone shares the feeling that had their parents done a better job, handled things in another more favorable way, their lives would be different.

Consequently, the more quickly the client perceives the parents as lacking omnipotence and perceives them as human, frail and as ordinary as the student him/herself, the sooner he/she accepts the responsibility of choice for change.

A part of any lifestyle is the perception of one's parents. If one chooses to accept parents in the Sullivanian model (Sullivan, 1953) of Good Mother (Father), Bad Mother (Father), the grown child is still hampered by these omnipotent but unreal "Important People." They don't actually exist and can possibly only be excised as ghosts from the biased apperception of the past.

Several years ago, I worked with a young woman of twenty-five whose father had divorced her mother when my client was twelve. She had hated her father for doing this and had shared the sense of rejection and lack of desirability that her mother had experienced. This was particularly difficult for her because the mother was a very neurotic woman who did not get along well with her daughter. The father intellectualized emotions and wouldn't deal with hurtful situations. It took a long time for the client to be able to offer and accept a less intense relationship with her father. I feel we could have worked faster and clarified the parents in her own mind if we'd used the Family Rating. Initially, she had experienced a series of disappointing love affairs where she tried so hard to be the loving supportive partner that her own needs were submerged. She seemed to choose men who didn't experience her as having particular value or importance. When she started to relate to her father on realistic terms (accepting him as not capable of great warmth or caring) she became more able to assess her own style and needs. Her work improved to the point of Special Honors at graduation and the love affairs became fewer, less frantic and more enduring and satisfying.

Another reason for the success of using the Family Rating is not clearly defined in my mind. It would take indepth studies to prove but, television in the 1960s could be partly responsible for troubled young adults being dissatisfied with their home and family lives. The Donna Reed Show, Father Knows Best, and Leave it to Beaver, for instance, brought "perfect" families right into one's own home and one's own perspective. Occasionally and ruefully, clients bring up these kind of programs as proof positive that maybe their families really were pretty awful. And, indeed, whose family could measure up?

Whatever the influences of the media might be, there is a need to clarify role models with clients who are disappointed with their own parents. Who

Adele Thomas, "Changing the Sibling Rating for the Lifestyle Inventory to Family Rating, "*The Individual Psychologist*, March 1979, pp. 27–32. Reprinted by permission of the publisher.

is to say what a really great and masculine father is really like? The reality is, there is no guarantee that parents will turn out to be great if getting to know them promotes understanding. The following brief case, using the Family Rating illustrates this point.

One twenty year old male came in with the problem of not wanting to be alone with his father, afraid that he would be disappointed if he really knew his father. This was precipitated by a proposed week-long fishing trip involving just the two of them. He, Joe, also felt that his mother was stronger and brighter than his father. This was the family evaluation and the father agreed with it. In doing the Family Rating, this was the first time I decided to include the parents. There were only two siblings, Joe and a sister two years older. I wondered if in some way the children had modeled themselves after the same sex parents. They had.

Mostly Joe placed himself next to the father in the ratings. There were, however, some important exceptions. Joe was more daring than his father, second only to his sister. Father was the most feminine, Joe the least. Mother and Joe were the most masculine. Father was the most obedient, Joe the least. Joe's standards of right and wrong were among the highest, father's the lowest. Father and Joe were the most easy going, charming and pleasing but father was the most cheerful, sociable, had the best sense of humor and was the most considerate. On these Joe ranked all the way down with his mother. Joe got his way almost as much as mother, father the least. Joe sees himself as more sensitive and idealistic and more of an excitement seeker.

Father then, appeared to be the most sociable and had the greatest need to be liked and accepted. Father is seen to be more willing to adapt and conform as the price of peace. Joe found that he could accept this as his father's style.

However, it was clear that mother had the more traditional masculine role, father the feminine. Most important, Joe was accepting this in a nonjudgmental way. Then, when his terminally ill grandmother lay dying of cancer, and this was the first important person in Joe's life to die, he spoke to the family. He pointed out the need to make plans for funeral and burial. He accepted mother's decision to make arrangements for a family burial plot. He was distressed, but conceded the father's need to be sure there was enough food for the mourners after the funeral.

There are many issues still to be worked on, but Joe has come to realize how closely he identifies with the father. Recently, he brought in a dream. In it his parents were sitting in the living room of their home when Joe was a child. There was a great deal of tension in the atmosphere. Suddenly father looked at mother and said, "I don't like you." Inasmuch as father has never said such a thing to mother, and is very affectionate and loving to her, Joe was perplexed. I suggested that Joe was actually the father figure in the dream. Joe accepted this and wondered if his father didn't sometimes feel this way too.

Sometimes the Family Rating simply gives a jumping off point, a chance to relieve some of the pressure a client feels and the opportunity to offer some encouragement. The following case is like that. There is much work to be done, ground to be covered. But at least she doesn't feel so alone.

A young woman of nineteen came in feeling that no one really cared about her, at school or at home. Her mother was described as apathetic, uncaring and the father simply yelled a lot. She was the youngest of three children with a sister five years older and brother three years older. What seemed to set the father off was his children not helping mother with the housework. Mother was a careless housekeeper and the children were sloppy. But mother never defended the children, she simply withdrew from any interaction.

The Family Rating produced nothing unpredictable about the father, but mother was the most easy going, charming, pleasing and cheerful. She was the most considerate and the least bossy, got her way the least, had the lowest rating in temper, as fighter and the next to last with a chip on her shoulder and stubborn. She was shy, sensitive and easily hurt. She was also most idealistic and least materialistic. At this point, my client, Kate, started to act with interest and enthusiasm which belied her initial dull, depressed affect. She remembered that her mother had a birthday party for her favorite doll when Kate, age three, had declared it was her doll's birthday. Mother had even made the doll a special, very tiny cake. Sister was remembered, with great pleasure, to be jealous. She also told me that though she had always brought home the lowest school marks, mother had encouraged her drawing which she enjoyed. On the Christmas she was ten, her gift was private art lessons. Kate is an art major now, and art was the only area of personal success that she experienced through high school. Kate is starting to realize that she chose to use her socially more adept sister as a role model, and couldn't overtake her in the area she felt so important. But the first breakthrough occurred when she accepted her mother as loving and caring and somewhat sloppy.

Sometimes nothing has really happened. In the following case, a man was stalemated with real and imagined hurts within his family. It was necessary to make him see how his anger and stereotyping were working against him. He needed a shove to get moving and this worked.

A homosexual male started to consider his family as more than either tormenters or faceless bodies when he applied the Rating to his five siblings and his parents. We have a long way to go in his therapy but on the basis of our work in this area he chose to test his new insights and go home for dinner for the first time in eight months (since he had openly declared his homosexuality). He discovered, with his new understanding and limitation of unrealistic expectations, he could at least have a reasonably pleasant evening. Real reconciliation with his father probably won't ever happen. He likes the rest of the family and they like him. He has been able to get to some unfinished business that he had found disturbing.

Sometimes I'm as surprised as my client at what comes out in the Rating and where it takes us, as in the following case.

Susan is eighteen and a freshman. She's a bright student and has always had more responsible jobs, at a higher pay than you might expect for her age. She works well and with confidence. The oldest of three children, she has a brother three years younger and a sister five years younger. She describes her family as being isolated from each other, uncooperative and uncaring.

She's angry at her parents and particularly with her father who she finds is inconsistent in meeting out punishment and in his response to infractions. She seems to feel that not being punished for wrong doings is as serious as being punished unfairly. Susan appears to have written off her mother as uncaring and disinterested.

On the Rating she places her father and herself together as most intelligent, most mischievous, openly rebellious, least critical of self and least pleasing. They're the most bossy, get their way the most and are the most materialistic. However, mother and Susan have the highest standards of right and wrong, are the most charming, sociable, have the best senses of humor, sulk the least, and

are the most sensitive and easily hurt. They're the most idealistic and responsible; they're also the excitement seekers.

Susan was surprised to see how closely she identified with her parents and defended the traits she had in common with her father as important and needed in order to be successful. However, she liked the warm and sociable "feminine" traits she shared with mother. Most important, some of the barriers of isolation started to topple. Inasmuch as her presenting problem was painful genital sex with a dearly loved boyfriend, gynecologically unexplainable, this started to take on a new significance. She was able to say that she didn't want sex at this time, only closeness.

Sometimes the Family Rating gives the therapist an expected confirmation, and serves the purpose of getting the client to start thinking and changing some long held ideas. The final case illustrates this.

A woman in her late thirties has come to me to help deal with the pain and anger of the break up of her second marriage. Her father, now dead, was an alcoholic and remembered as brutal when drunk, to Mary, the client, and her mother, also dead.

Mary was an only child and her memories of her childhood were mostly of fear and terror. She felt threatened and sided with her mother, as the two victims of the father's tyranny. She had few friends from high school on because she became increasingly embarrassed to bring them home, particularly boys. She escaped into an early marriage at eighteen. This marriage produced three children and lasted nine years. She divorced her husband who had become an alcoholic. Her second husband didn't drink excessively but turned out to be childish and irresponsible.

The Family Rating made Mary aware of the predictable pattern. She felt mother and father were the least intelligent, least industrious and had the lowest standards of achievement. That father made the most mischief, was the most openly rebellious, but mother was the most covertly rebellious. Father's standards of right and wrong were high, and right next to Mary's but mother's were way down. Father and mother were both critical of others, but surprisingly, father was easy going. Mary and mother were the most pleasing, sociable and considerate. Father and mother were the most bossy (with mother into "shoulds"). Father demanded his way the most and mother the least, the same with temper. Father was the fighter, but father and mother both had a chip on their shoulder and both were stubborn, but mother sulked.

Mary and father were the most sensitive and easily hurt, and both were excitement seekers. Both parents were responsible but father was the most withdrawn.

The memories and feelings this elicited prompted Mary to realize that father often was goaded by mother, who enjoyed her victim's role. Mother emerged as a controller. Mary is starting to see that she shares that priority with her mother. Her two marriages were to weak men, who chose different methods of escape.

Including the parents into the Family Rating gives the client a chance to see the parent in simple everyday terms, rather than someone larger than life, either great or awful. It allows the parent to become an ordinary human being and ordinary human beings can be dealt with more easily.

"It fits the holistic construct of the nature of the social environment and seems to promise additional information in keeping with what Danica Deutsch referred to as family lifestyle" (Gold, 1977).

References

Mosak, H., and Shulman, B. *The life style inventory.* Chicago: Alfred Adler Institute, 1971.

Sullivan, H. S. *The interpersonal theory of psychiatry.* New York: W. W. Norton & Company, 1953.

Gold, L. Private correspondence, 1977.

PART III: RESEARCH

The Technique, Utility, and Validity of Life Style Analysis
R. S. Gushurst

The term "life style" has a dual meaning. On the one hand, it refers to a complex construct deeply embedded in the Adlerian theory of personality; on the other, it describes a very concrete formulation made by a particular psychologist, using a particular individual's answers to a standardized set of questions. In the first sense, like the term "ego" in psychoanalytic theory, which can be fully understood only in relation to a number of interdependent constructs such as "repression," "id," "superego," and so forth, a full comprehension of the term "life style" requires a grasp of such related constructs as "social embeddedness," "teleological functioning," "phenomenological perspective," and so forth. Consequently, to discuss life style in the first sense is really to outline the basic structure of Adlerian theory—a task which has previously been accomplished by Allen (earlier in this issue) and others (Ansbacher and Ansbacher, 1964; Dreikurs, 1950). This paper will therefore assume that the reader is already familiar with this theoretical material, and it will define the term "life style" rather briefly and abstractly as: the totality of system principles which account for the consistency and directionality of an individual's life-movements.

The following paper, while concentrating on the practical dimension of life style, will also assume that the reader is somewhat familiar with the literature in this area. It will attempt to contribute to this work in three ways: first, by analyzing the procedure commonly used by Adlerians in formulating an individual's life style; second, by describing and illustrating some of the prominent uses of such formulations, and their agreement with other schools of thought; and third, by discussing the validity of the whole procedure. At the same time, even if the reader is not highly conversant with the literature in this area, the following remarks will hopefully be helpful in their own right.

The Formulation of a Life Style

Summarizing the Family Constellation

Adlerians characteristically collect two types of information: the individual's answers to a family constellation questionnaire (Dreikurs, 1954; Shulman, 1962) and his early recollections (Dreikurs, 1954; Mosak, 1958). However, since the analytic procedures used with these types of information are quite different, they will be discussed separately.

The family constellation questionnaire, when fully interpreted, provides a brief portrait of the individual's early social world—the influential forces to which he reacted, and the raw material from which he selected, in creating an apperceptive framework to assist his survival and progress through life. The questions are designed to elicit those factors which Adlerians have most frequently found to be important—such things as birth order, comparative sibling characteristics and interactions, parental characteristics and interactions with both themselves and their children, adjustments to physical development, schooling, peers, family values, socio-economic status, and so forth.

The task of the diagnostician is to integrate this wealth of information, and to extract from it a few central features: a brief description of the individual's *role* within his family (either alone, or in comparison

Robin Gushurst, Technique, Utility, and Validity of Life Style Analysis, *The Counseling Psychologist*, 3(1), 1971, 30–39. Copyright © 1971 by *The Counseling Psychologist*. Used by permission.

with the roles played by the other members of the family); his *major areas of success and failure; the major influences* which seem to have affected his decision to adopt the role that he did; and perhaps also an inferential statement about his apparent *major goals and/or conceptions* of himself, others, life in general, or of some particular aspect of life, such as sexuality, physical handicaps, religion, and so forth. Once accomplished, such an integration should provide a picture somewhat similar to that given by playwrights when introducing their characters: the individual should be able to recognize himself and his family, and the diagnostician should have a "bird's eye view of the personality in its nascent state" (Shulman, 1962).

The question, however, is how to achieve the synthesis: the questions are fairly ordinary and straightforward, but the integration appears to most people, especially to beginners, as an act of magic. Also, in spite of several articles on the subject, there is little discussion of what the diagnostician actually *does*; and as long as this technique remains mysterious and inexplicit, the door is left open for both ungoverned subjectivity and for the criticism of non-replicable, unscientific procedures. The following notes are therefore presented as an early attempt at explication, for both the assistance of the inexperienced, and for the potential, if only partial, objectification in psychological research.

The starting point is naturally Adlerian theory, in the broad sense, including not only the writings of Adler, but also the many refinements and elaborations of his disciples. The theory both identifies and emphasizes certain *factors which are felt to have a significant influence on personality development*—such as organ inferiorities, pampering, abuse, sibling rivalry, and so forth—and indicates *what certain types of phenomena imply* about the individual with whom they occur. For example, Mosak and Shulman[1] note that poor penmanship can sometimes be a sign of covert rebellion, especially when it appears in a person who strives to conform and "look good." A girl's refusal to wear a bra and girdle can also be associated with rebellion, for here too the person may seek to avoid restrictions—either in regard to her expected sexual role, or simply to restrictions in general. In this sense, outside of illustration, the major aim of most of the articles on family constellation and family atmosphere—especially those by Shulman (1962), Shulman and Nikelly (1971), and Dewey (1971)—is to aid the diagnostician by specifying, as comprehensively as possible, both the major influences that are commonly found in different types of families and the implications of different types of phenomena. The hope of these articles is that the diagnostician, guided by a broad familiarity with these factors and implications, will be able to identify them quickly and accurately when they appear in a given individual's description of himself and his family.

Secondly, the diagnostician must be able to *recognize patterns:* that is, he must learn to note that *certain traits, because of an inner logic or necessity, tend to cohere;* that if two or more traits of a certain kind are present in a given personality, certain other traits are likely to appear; and if these other traits do not appear, some explanation must be found for their absence. For example, if a person is demanding and always wants his own way, it can be anticipated that he will use various procedures, active and/or passive, to get others to give him what he wants. It can therefore be anticipated that such a person may have a temper (to intimidate), may sulk and feel sorry for himself (to make others feel guilty and give in to him), and may perhaps also know how to charm and please (in order to manipulate).

The reasons for such coherences seem to lie in the basic unity and self-consistency of personality; and because of this, as Mosak (1971) points out, it is possible to specify a number of common types of life styles and their correlated traits.[2] In describing these life styles, Mosak contributes to the resource presented in the articles on family constellation and family atmosphere: he too is providing the diagnostician with a set of *templates* that can facilitate the analysis of a large amount of information by permitting the rapid identification of common personality syndromes. Thus, taken together, these several articles afford the diagnostician a kind of training similar to that of a botanist who learns that certain configurations of leaves and stems identify certain species of plants; and that if certain configurations are present, certain other configurations are likely to be present as well, even if the available sample is not large enough to immediately confirm their presence.

At the same time, however, the diagnostician must develop in himself the ability to *ferret out new patterns* whenever the available templates do not seem

---

1. Personal Communication.
2. Mosak identifies 14 different lifestyle themes. There is, for example, "the controller" who is

> "either a person who wishes to control life or one who wishes to insure that life will not control him. He generally dislikes surprises, controls his spontaneity and his feelings. Since all of these may lessen his control. . . . he favors intellectualization, rightness, orderliness, and neatness. In his godlike striving for perfection, he depreciates other (p. 78)."

Then, there is also the "getter," the "driver," the "gooder than thou," the "victim," the "martyr," the "baby," among others. (Ed.)

to fit the data. To some extent, he can rely at this point on his entire experience of life, and perhaps especially his knowledge of literature, for additional templates; a particular pattern, though unmentioned in Adlerian writings, or in other theories of personality, may nevertheless resemble someone he has met or read about—such as the local postman or Shakespeare's Othello. When this supply is exhausted, he is finally left to his own devices for the problems will then be new, and new solutions, by definition, are necessarily creative. As a result, any objectification of life style analysis must stop at this point, for truly creative procedures are not fully explicable; their essential novelty precludes description or prediction.

On the other hand, once the diagnostician has identified certain patterns within a given family, his next task is to *compare these patterns for similarities and differences.* Suct comparison is required by at least two assumptions in Adlerian theory: first, areas of *contrast* are thought to reflect either competition (especially when this occurs between siblings) or oppositional role-modeling (which has been identified, in at least one of its aspects, by the psychoanalytic definition of "identification with the aggressor"); second, areas of *similarity* are thought to indicate either the presence of alliances between the siblings, the common adoption of important family values, or the effect of imitation and positive role-modeling (Dreikurs, 1954; Shulman, 1962). Furthermore, such comparison permits the diagnostician to assess the nature of an individual's relative success or failure, especially as this relates to the important family values. For example, a child who is quite successful (i.e., accomplished) at being the family rebel might nevertheless feel like quite a failure in relation to a sibling who is the successful "good boy," especially if proper behavior is an important family value. On the other hand, the relative feeling of success experienced by these siblings could easily be reversed in a family that values rebellion and rugged individualism rather than proper behavior.

Finally, if the diagnostician is willing to gamble somewhat, he can make *inferences* about the feelings, attitudes, and goals that seem to accompany a particular personality pattern and familial role. To some extent such inferences can be facilitated by descriptions of common life styles, such as those presented by Mosak (1971); for in these cases the diagnostician can merely include probable correlates of an already identified coherence. For example, if one identifies the pattern of a "driver," one can easily infer that such a person will "nurse the fear that he is a 'nothing.'" In other cases, however, the diagnosti-

cian may have to empathize with the apparent position and personality of the individual, and ask himself how he would feel, think, act, and believe if he were such a person in such a family. To successfully accomplish this requires both a broad experience of life and a flexible imagination—and even then it remains risky (Sullivan, 1953; Bakan, 1956). But such inferences are not essential for a life style analysis; and when they are made, their accuracy can often be checked by the recognition or the disbelief of the individual himself.

Thus, in summary, the analysis of a family constellation requires four things: first, a solid and comprehensive familiarity with the factors that Adlerian theory considers most influential in personality development, the implications that Adlerians find in certain types of phenomena, and the common life styles identified by Adlerians; second, the ability to recognize, discover and characterize patterns; third, the ability to compare patterns for the presence of similarities and differences; and fourth, the ability to make accurate inferences, either by extrapolation within an already identified coherence, or through an intuitive, emphathic grasp of a particular phenomenal world.

Interpreting the Early Recollections

Early recollections (ER's) are the second type of information commonly collected by Adlerians. An individual's ER's are the specific incidents which he remembers from his early childhood—incidents which happened only once, preferably before the age of nine or ten years, which he can remember clearly and in detail, genuinely with visual recall, and including one's thoughts and feelings at the time of the incident. Memories of this kind are distinguished from "reports" which seemingly detail the infinite number of facts and recurrent events that constitute the context of one's early life. ER's are considered especially valuable, in contrast to reports, because of their uniqueness, clarity, specificity, and general scarcity—all of which, according to the projective theory of memory and recent thinking about the relationship between perception and motivation, make them likely *indices of contemporary attitudes and desires* (Mosak, 1958; Gushurst, 1971). That is, they provide a brief picture of how an individual views himself, other people, and life in general, what he strives for in life, and what he anticipates as likely to occur in life.

Most of the articles on ER's either discuss the projective theory of memory, provide illustrative interpretations, or discuss their various uses in therapy, vocational guidance, and so forth (Adler, 1958;

Dreikurs, 1954; Mosak, 1958; Nikelly & Verger, 1971). In other words, the state of the literature is very similar to the work on family constellation; no one describes what the diagnostician actually *does* when he interprets an ER; and the same problems, of subjectivity and non-replicable procedures, are present once again. Gushurst (1970; 1971) has attempted to modify this situation by providing an early analysis of a possible, reliable, and replicable interpretive strategy. However, since this analysis is rather complex and lengthy, the reader will simply be referred to this work, and the present paper will merely note some of the suggestions made by other writers:

(ER's) are first interpreted thematically and second with respect to specific details. . . The characters incorporated in the recollection are not treated in interpretation as specific individuals but as prototypes. They represent people or women in general or authority figures rather than the specific individuals mentioned. While the content of the recollection is given primary consideration, a sequential analysis provides a more rounded picture of the individual. The characteristic outlook rather than the characteristic behavior is portrayed. (Mosak, 1958, p. 107–108.)

The main theme or pattern is to be interpreted in a manner similar with the TAT theme or the figure drawings, and are not to be broken into separate fragments. Starting with hunches, individual themes are brought together and their unity and pattern spells out a message—the client's feelings and emotions provide the main interpretive clue. (Nikelly and Verger, 1971, p. 57–58.)

Identifying the Basic Mistakes

Once the Adlerian diagnostician has summarized the major elements of the subject's family constellation and interpreted his early recollections, he then seeks to specify some of the prominent "mistakes" in the subject's approach to life—especially if the information has been collected in the context of psychotherapy, where the aim of the diagnosis is to establish a point of departure for therapeutic efforts.[3] At this point, the diagnostician turns his attention largely to the individual's early recollections for the summary of the family constellation, as indicated earlier, is primarily a picture of the individual's personality in its "nascent state." However, in cases where the individual is unable to produce any early recollections, or where there is clear contemporary evidence that the individual's current life continues the patterns of his early life, the family constellation material can be used in itself, though it should definitely be used with caution.

At any rate, to locate "basic mistakes," it is obviously necessary for the diagnostician to have a conception of what is "right"—that is, a normative guideline or perspective from which to assess the presence and character of deviations. This guideline, at least in part, is provided by Adlerian theory, largely through its concepts of "social interest" and "the ironclad logic of social living" (Ansbacher & Ansbacher, 1956; Dreikurs, 1950). These concepts emphasize the importance of sharing, equality, interest in others, responsibility, and contribution—all of which are considered essential for harmonious social living. Thus, if an individual's early recollections, or his role in his family constellation, indicate an undue interest in having his own way, in being superior to others, in avoiding responsibility, or in having power over others, the diagnostician familiar with Adlerian theory can easily identify these approaches as mistaken. In this sense, the norms spelled out by Adlerian theory can be used in much the same fashion as the "major influences on personality," or the "common life styles" that were mentioned earlier—in this case, as templates for the rapid identification of mistaken approaches to life.

The difficulty, however, is that Adlerian theory—while clearly, thoroughly, and explicitly normative in its basic postulates—is not always sufficiently differentiated or specific to provide clear guidelines for the multitude of different personalities one is likely to encounter in everyday therapeutic practice; indeed, it seems improbable that any theory could provide such specificity. Consequently, the diagnostician is sometimes thrown back on his own "common sense," on his intuitive grasp of "the logic of social living," for elaborations that will handle the novel. For example, if an individual remembers, in an ER, his attempt to make friends by offering his playmates some cookies, his "mistake" might not be in his desire to approach or please others, but in his conviction that he has to "buy" his way to friendship. Thus, there is often a risk in specifying basic mistakes, similar to that noted earlier in the discovery of new patterns or in the formulation of intuitive inferences in a family constellation: it presents a demand for creative accuracy. But there is also the dual consolation that interpretive errors can often be noted by the subject himself, and that most of the major mistakes in life—such as mistrust, selfishness, lack of confidence, over-ambition, and so forth—are not only fairly simple, but well known and easily recognizable.

In summary, the Adlerian diagnostician proceeds by extracting the major features that appear in an individual's answers to the family constellation questionnaire, thereby obtaining a brief picture of his nascent personality; the individual's current outlook on

3. These "basic mistakes" are of the same order as discussed by Ellis (1962). They are, as well, vividly portrayed in Mosak's descriptions of troublesome life styles. (Ed.)

life is then obtained by interpreting his early recollections; and the mistaken elements in his approach to life are then specified by comparing his contemporary convictions with those which seem to be required by the "logic of social living." Most importantly, when these diagnostic procedures have been completed, the individual has before him some very specific problem areas on which to focus, should he decide to change his life.

The Uses of Life Style Analysis and Its Relation to Other Schools of Thought

The information provided by a life style analysis is primarily useful in two ways. First, it not only helps the therapist or counselor to understand his client, but it also helps the client to feel understood—both of which commonly serve to solidify rapport and start the therapeutic relationship on an optimistic foundation. Second, it helps the therapist, in at least four different ways, to formulate a course of treatment: it provides a number of issues of "mistakes" on which to focus (Dreikurs, 1957); it permits a tentative prediction of possible problems in treatment, especially as these concern the relationship between the client and therapist (Mosak, 1965); it may offer suggestions about the optimal kind of treatment for a particular client—for example, group or individual therapy (Mosak, 1958); and it may provide clues for vocational guidance, largely by identifying major skills and areas of interest (Mosak, 1958).

The following examples will attempt to illustrate all of these different uses; but to accomplish this, it will not be possible to present complete and detailed summaries of either family constellations or early recollections, for this would require too much space. However, by presenting brief summaries of different types of life styles it will not only be possible to indicate some of the great *diversity* in life styles as well as some of the very different types of *symptoms* that accompany different life styles in trouble, but it will also be possible to demonstrate that *different aspects of a given life style are often of differential utility* in a given case. Furthermore, it will also be shown that the features Adlerians observe in different life styles have been *observed by other writers*—a consideration that would seem to give Adlerian practice a certain degree of *consensual validity*.

Example 1: A young man was referred by the police for embezzling funds from his employer. He was considered efficient and hard working, was well liked by other employees, and seemingly had good relationships with his superiors. He did not need or use the money he stole; he simply took it and kept it hidden. A life style analysis revealed good relationships with both parents and siblings,

successful achievement in both social and academic areas, and no discouraging handicaps. In several of his early recollections the young man remembered committing various infractions of school regulations; but since his father was principal of the school, his teachers had simply spoken to him and let the matter drop; also, on each occasion he felt unusually powerful and invulnerable. In time he began to develop a sense of immunity and superiority: he enjoyed his exemption and would sometimes practice it merely for "kicks."

The major symptom here is a form of delinquent "acting out," and the key factor behind it is clearly traceable to the young man's early *position in his community,* and to the way he chose to exploit this position. The focal issue for therapy would be his desire for exemption; and group therapy might be preferable to individual therapy, not only because one of his major life goals is blatantly anti-social, but also because the influence of peers might be far more effective than that of an authority figure. Vocational counseling is not an issue here; but in therapy one might anticipate that this person would seek to fracture or circumvent the "rules" of the group. Sullivan (1953) called attention to this syndrome when he wrote:

Occasionally some figure in the home is of such great social importance that the new authority figures are intimidated, and treat the child as exceptional. For example, the psychiatrist may see an adult in treatment who is the son of an important politician, and may discover that the potency of this politician-father had so altered the freedom with which corrective authority could be imposed on his son that to an extraordinary extent the person as an adult continues to suffer from the warp acquired at home as a child. (p. 229)

Example 2: A middle aged spinster complained of alcoholism, nervous tension, and social isolation. She was physically unattractive: her front teeth were noticeably protrudant, her hair was rather stringy and unkempt, and she wore very thick glasses that gave her eyes a beady, globular appearance, like those of an insect. A life style analysis disclosed that she had been severely near-sighted from early childhood and had worn glasses from the age of three. She was an only child, had always felt ugly, and had sucked her thumb until the age of six. She had a good relationship with her parents and did fairly well in school; but she had never felt confident enough to date, and when her parents died in a car accident when she was seventeen, she became a chronic "loner."

The symptoms here are related to social insecurity and the attempt to find relief through alcohol. The problem is clearly related to a long-standing and deeply felt *organ inferiority* for which the client was never able to successfully compensate. Vocational guidance does not seem needed here; but improvement of her self-image, and modification of her probably exaggerated social expectations would be the major focus of therapy. Group therapy would perhaps be the treatment of choice, for in a group she could discover acceptance, not in spite of her disability, but almost because of it (Dreikurs, 1960). The predicted problems might include irregular attendance and additional drinking, both due to an increase of anxiety related to greater social contact. Robert White (1964), who has re-identified contemporary ego-psychologists as belated Adlerians, noted this general pattern when he wrote:

The body, including both its competence and its attractiveness, takes a significant place in the development of self-esteem, especially between the ages of five and twenty. Any marked deviations from the norm, unless they are on the side of athletic ability in boys and beauty in girls, are likely to create sharp feelings of inferiority. (p. 155)

Example 3: A shipping clerk expressed a feeling of utter emptiness, as if he were dead. He did not feel depressed; it was more a profound and unshakable apathy. His daily routine was very barren: he ate, went to work, ate again, and went to sleep. His friends had drifted slowly away, along with his interests and activities; and when asked what he wanted to do, he expressed no desire to do anything. A life style analysis revealed that he was raised largely by his mother; his father was a salesman and frequently absent on trips. His mother, feeling lonely would often confide in him and rely on him for comfort; at other times, feeling angry and frustrated, she would unpredictably beat him for some minor negligence. He eventually came to dread any kind of closeness, experiencing it as either a demand or as something basically uncertain and dangerous. At the same time, he never ceased to desire closeness and found life meaningless and empty without it.

This person, like Camus' anti-hero in *The Stranger*, experiences life as shallow and impoverished. His early *parent-child relationships* were either non-existent or painful; and later, when he had the opportunity to form new relationships, he chose to re-institute the former, preferring emptiness to pain. Vocational guidance is not an issue here, but therapy would be essential—perhaps especially group therapy, where intimacy could be approached more slowly, and where the diversity of people and problems might reveal a similar diversity of solutions. The predicted problems would include fear and avoidance reactions to gestures of caring, with perhaps also a pervasive resistance to change in general. Karen Horney (1950) identified a syndrome very similar to this, calling it the "appeal to freedom." She described the origins of this syndrome by noting:

(The individual) may have received affection, but in a way that more repelled than warmed him. There may have been, for instance, a parent who was too egocentric to have any understanding of the child's needs yet made great demands on the child to understand him or give him emo-

tional support. Or he may have had a parent so erratic in his mood swings that he gave effusive demonstrative affection at one time and at others could scold or beat him in a fit of temper without any reason that the child could understand (p. 275).

Example 4: An adolescent was referred by the Department of Children and Family Services. He was described as "schizoid, paranoid, and potentially violent." He was unable to complete any type of training program, and was chronically suspicious and hostile, and had a history of aggressive behavior. A life style analysis showed that he had been raised in a number of different orphanages, for his parents had abandoned him when he was still an infant. He never established any close relationships with adults, for there were always so many other children that he felt lost and unwanted. With his peers he tried to be friendly, but he always felt like the scapegoat, as if others sought him out deliberately to abuse him. His early recollections depicted scenes of unprovoked maliciousness, with himself as an innocent and helpless victim.

The symptoms in this case identify a person who feels surrounded by enemies, and the origins of this conviction are straightforwardly related to an early failure in *social relationships*. Satisfactory parental and adult relationships were obviated by unfortunate circumstances; and good peer relationships were apparently handicapped by extreme discouragement. Vocational guidance would be an important aspect here; but individual therapy, with the focus on establishment of a solid, trusting relationship, would assume predominant importance. The predicted problems would include suspiciousness, veiled provocations, as well as self-defeating endeavors. Sullivan (1953) described some of the origins of this problem when he wrote:

In any large group of school children habitually in contact with each other, some of the juveniles will definitely suffer from ostracism by a considerable number of others—and insofar as (their) associations with other unfortunate juveniles fail, this experience is not tributary to good self-esteem. . . (They) usually show pretty durable evidence of having been in an inferior position with respect to other compeers (p. 236).

Taken together, the above examples now only show some of the diversity of problems that can be illuminated by a life style analysis, but also indicate that different aspects of a given life style are sometimes more relevant than others. An example of *sibling rivalry* was not included, for such a case will be described later, in a further example. Also, because the above examples were chosen for their simplicity and unidimensional character, they should not be considered either common or representative. It is more typical for a life style to reflect a complex interaction of several different factors, thereby requiring a more intricate analysis. The examples presented in the following section, while illustrating different issues, should make this evident.

The Validity of Life Style Analysis

The validity of life style analysis is still an open question, for there has been no direct or systematic investigation of this procedure. At the same time, it is not only possible to indicate how such research might be constructed, but also how to present some tentative, indirect, and non-systematic evidence that at least points in the direction of validity. The following remarks will therefore discuss both of these issues, as a preliminary approach to a much larger problem.

In the first case, it is important to remember that "validity" is always a relative finding—relative to either a particular utility in a particular context, or relative to another instrument of already established practical and contextural validity (Mischel, 1970). This means that the validity of life style analysis would have to be assessed in relation to either a particular *use* (such as screening police candidates, or differentiating between successful and non-successful bank managers), or through comparison with *another assessment procedure* (such as an MMPI, a Rorschach, or ratings by peers). In many respects the former would be easier to execute, for it would simply require the transformation of life style information into variables relevant to the discrimination being considered. (Whether or not such a transformation could be made successfully is of course a completely different question.) The latter, however, would necessitate the selection of a *truly comparative instrument*; for if the two procedures were assessing different dimensions of personality, or assessing the same dimension in different ways, no agreement or "concurrent validity" would be established (Gushurst, 1971). For example, consider the following comparison between an interpreted TAT story and a life style summary, both of which were collected from the same subject and interpreted "blind" by two different psychologists.

TAT Story (Card 17BM)
This is a boy in gym class. He's very muscular—extremely—the star of his class. He's in a contest to see who can climb the fastest. There are a lot of people watching. He wants to impress them. He's a little scared, but he throws himself into it. He climbs faster than he's ever climbed before, breaks his own record. The crowd is amazed. He feels proud and happy.

TAT Interpretation
This person wants to impress himself and others with outstanding performances and achievements. There is also a potential fear of failure and/or overdriven strivings in this area.

Life Style Summary
The first born son in a family with very ambitious and professionally successful parents, J stayed ahead of his younger brother by adopting and fulfilling the parental values in almost all areas—social, academic, moral, and physical. At the same time, his success was never complete, for two reasons. First, he felt compelled to be the best; and if he wasn't, he felt like a "nothing." The threat of failure hung over him like a cloud, and even small setbacks were experienced as major shocks. Secondly, his brother, as the "baby" of the family, seemed to get the attention and affection of the parents without having to work for it. J not only came to resent this, but attempted to establish equality by intensifying his demands through open complaints, tantrums, and displays of hurt feelings. The parents responded to his behavior with condemnation and demands for "mature" behavior. As a result, J felt cheated and defeated: he could *not* achieve; but even his victories were hollow, for they never brought him what he most wanted, the affection of his parents.

It is fairly clear that the above TAT interpretation captures a large part of this person's life style—namely, his intense interest in achievement. On the other hand, it completely misses J's equally fundamental feelings of being "left out" and having "the cards stacked against him." Granted, if more TAT stories were collected and interpreted, these other issues might appear more clearly. But they might also not appear—either because the scenes depicted on the cards were not relevant to these other concerns, or because the subject chose to represent only one of his concerns. Thus, while the TAT can *potentially* be used as an instrument with which to assess the concurrent validity of life style analysis—as, for example, in a matching study, it would be unrealistic to anticipate a high degree of correspondence between the two procedures. In fact, there is even some research to support this caution, for Hedvig (1960) found that TAT stories are more effected by contemporary experiences than are early recollections; and since early recollections contribute in large measure to a life style analysis, it can be anticipated that such an analysis will contain a kind of stability that is not found in TAT interpretations. Furthermore, this same argument can be used in relation to the Rorschach and other projective tests; for most of these tests are "time sensitive" and tend to reflect contemporary moods and mental operations more frequently and clearly than long-range issues (Lindzey, 1961).

A comparison, on the other hand, between a life style analysis and either peer ratings, autobiographical statements, or systematic observations of a subject's behavior in a structured setting (such as a therapy group) might be far more fruitful. All of these procedures not only make use of larger samples of data, but they also more readily permit the observation of long-range behavior patterns—and often in naturalistic settings, rather than through the restricted stimulus conditions provided by a particular psychological test. Furthermore, as the following remarks will indicate, there is some indirect, but substantial research evidence that both demonstrate the utility of these procedures, and argues strongly for the validity of life style analysis.

In a large research study of college students, Madison (1966; 1969) used students' autobiographies and diaries as a major source of in-depth information concerning his subjects' past and present behavior. The autobiographies included descriptions of parents and siblings, neighborhoods and schools, ethnic backgrounds, family values, and so forth—in other words, they included most of the information that Adlerians collect when they ask for the answers to a family constellation questionnaire. The diaries on the other hand, contained extensive descriptions of the subjects' current inter-personal transactions, together with their thoughts and feelings about these transactions. What Madison did, among other things, was to compare the *patterns* observable in a given subject's autobiography with the patterns observable in the transaction described in his diary. The results, as most Adlerians would anticipate, showed multiple and obvious correlations, in the sense that major aspects of the students' contemporary lives seemed to be continuations of the patterns established in their early interactions with their families to the extent that Madison (1969) was led to remark that "neither the undergraduate or the psychologist seems to be sufficiently aware of the extent to which the student's response to college is dominated by the past."

As an example of this, consider the following statement in which Madison (1969) summarizes the major patterns apparent in the autobiography of one of his students:

As a child, Trixie perceived her father as intelligent, attractive, selfish, teasing, active, authoritarian, stubborn, defensive about masculinity, unresponsive to her interest in him, and religiously dogmatic. She saw him as a father who did not show his feelings for her and as rather retiring socially except in his professional role. Trixie perceived her mother as passive, accepting, loving, and conciliatory. As a child Trixie both modeled herself after her father and furiously rebelled against him, while perceiving mother and femininity as weak and beneath consideration. A younger sister Lucy, exaggerated these trends by taking on a passive, model-child role with infuriating success, driving Trixie into an even more extensive rebellious independence to differentiate herself from Lucy, whom she both opposed and wanted as a friend (p. 225).

In this passage, Madison writes what any Adlerian would identify as a summary of a family constellation: the concern is with personality traits, types of role modeling, and patterns of interpersonal transactions within the family. Following this, Madison quotes extensive passages from the diary of this student, extracting a number of very simple and straightforward conclusions:

In her response to roommates, Trixie found herself attracted to Lucy-like girls (feminine or model-student types) but then ended up treating them in ways that came to resemble her childhood rivalry with Lucy (1969, p. 226).

Trixie responded to boys in whom she perceived certain father qualities: selfishness, teasingness, being hard to get, and "defensive about masculinity." Her strongly rebellious and angry reaction to a summer resort manager and later, a landlady, reminds one of her fights with her father over her insistence on being independent of his surveillance (1969, p. 288-299).

It should be clear from the above example that Madison's study not only utilizes the same type of information that Adlerians consider most valuable for comprehending personality, but it also demonstrates the tremendous utility of this information as a tool for understanding contemporary behavior—which is precisely the use that Adlerians make of such material. Furthermore, while Madison's study is only a single study, and hardly affords a solid base for generalization, it is also a completely *independent* study, and therefore free of any suggestion of experimenter bias. In fact, Madison seems to be completely unaware of Adlerian thinking, because he does not include a single Adlerian reference in his bibliography. Moreover, since this study was not only carefully planned and executed, but also carried out in great depth over a period of several years, its findings can perhaps be given a degree of credibility much beyond the usual. It is therefore possible to see in this research both an early indication of the potential validity and utility of life style analysis and a guideline for future research in this area.

In summary, this paper has discussed a number of issues that concern life style analysis, presenting some early attempts at analysis, some illustrative examples, and some suggestions for future research. Since all of these issues are complex, they can all benefit from additional study, and the above remarks should be considered exploratory and provocative rather than definitive.

References

Adler, A. *What life should mean to you.* New York: Capricorn Books, 1958.

Ansbacher, H. L. & Ansbacher, R. *The individual psychology of Alfred Adler.* New York: Harper Torchbooks, 1964.

Bakan, D. Clinical psychology and logic. *American Psychologist*, 1956, 11, 655–662.

Dewey, E. Family atmosphere. In A. G. Nikelly (Ed.), *Techniques for behavior change.* Springfield, Illinois: Charles C. Thomas, 1971.

Dreikurs, R. *Fundamentals of Adlerian psychology.* Chicago: Alfred Adler Institute, 1950.

Dreikurs, R. The psychological interview in medicine. *American Journal of Individual Psychology,* 1954, 10, 99–102.

Dreikurs, R. Psychotherapy as correction of faulty social values. *American Journal of Individual Psychology,* 1957, 13, 150–158.

Dreikurs, R. *Group psychotherapy and group approaches.* Chicago: Alfred Adler Institute, 1960.

Ellis, A. *Reason and emotion in psychotherapy.* New York: Lyle Stuart, 1962.

Gushurst, R. S. *The interpretation of early recollections.* Unpublished Doctoral Proposal, University of Chicago, 1970.

Gushurst, R. S. *The reliability and concurrent validity of an idiographic approach to the interpretation of early recollections.* Unpublished Doctoral Dissertation, University of Chicago, 1971.

Hedvig, E. H. *A study of the effects of immediately preceding experiences upon early childhood recollections.* Unpublished Doctoral Dissertation, Northwestern University, 1960.

Horney, K. *Neurosis and human growth.* New York: Norton, 1950.

Lindzey, G. *Projective techniques and cross cultural research.* New York: Appleton-Century Crofts, Inc., 1964.

Madison, P. Complex behavior in natural settings. In T. Mischel (Ed.), *Human action: Conceptual and empirical issues.* New York: Academic Press, 1966.

REALIBILITY OF LIFE STYLE INTERPRETATIONS

Jacqueline Magner-Harris
Richard J. Riordan
Roy M. Kern
William L. Curlette

Despite the increasing number of clincial reports which support the value of Adlerian psychology, far too few studies have been generated which explore the theoretical validation of its basic tenets. Such a state of affairs can seriously undermine the theory's widespread adoption by practitioners in the field (Thorne, 1975). Certainly the idiographic nature of Adlerian psychology has hampered this type of research, especially those dealing with life style analysis (Mosak & Dreikurs, 1973). However, as Allen (1971) has pointed out, the day of "faith validity" is past. Allen himself drew from the works of a variety of theorists in order to demonstrate how their theoretical and empirical efforts confirmed basic Adlerian notions; yet he admitted that the need still existed for "more systematic research support" (p. 23). Gushurst (1971) also contended that the validity of life style analysis was still an open question, "for there has been no direct or systematic investigation of this procedure" (p. 37). He, too, proceeded to generate support for the validity of the life style analysis technique by comparing it to other widely used "nonobjective" assessment procedures.

While these studies further the theoretical basis of Adlerian psychology, their results have limited practical significance unless Adlerians can agree among themselves on an individual's dominant life style type. In this sense, consideration of life style validity before assessing interjudge agreement on life style types is putting the methodological cart before the horse.

Typically, individual Adlerian clinicians first analyze life style data about a client and then draw their conclusions. These conclusions about a client's life style may differ widely if several clinicians were to interpret one client's life style. The reliability of such clinical analyses can thus be questioned because no interjudge agreement data presently exists concerning this technique, which lies so vitally at the heart of Adlerian theory and therapy. The only study to date which addresses the existence of interjudge reliability in life style analysis was conducted by Ferguson (1964). She was able to demonstrate that summaries of life style protocols made from early recollections of 30 subjects diagnosed as psychotic, neurotic, and normal could be recognized and reliably matched to their owner's original protocols by clinicians. While her research lends some preliminary support for the reliability of clinical judgments on individuals' life styles, this support was limited to the area of interjudge agreements on early recollections alone.

Fortunately, two major developments, one theoretical and the other methodological, have enhanced the possibility of testing the reliability of a total life style assessment, despite its idiographic underpinnings. While Adler emphasized the uniqueness of the individual, he also contended that similarities exist among individuals and their life styles (Ansbacher & Ansbacher, 1956). Building on this notion, several Adlerians have posited the existence of certain commonly observed life style types and have described associated behaviors (Kefir & Corsini, 1974; Mosak, 1971). Thus it appears that the practical difficulty of categorizing idiographic behavior into nomothetic units has the potential of being accomplished without damaging the theoretical spirit of Adlerian thought.

Another stumbling block which has hindered the research on life style analysis has been the lack of a written instrument for the collection of life style data. Based on the conceptual work of Dreikurs (1950), Allen (1971), and Mosak (1971), Kern (1976) operationalized questions from interview guides into a written Life Style Questionnaire Inventory (LSQI). An "only child" form of the regular LSQI was also constructed. The LSQI facilitates

Magner-Harris, et al., "Reliability of Life Style Interpretations," *Journal of Individual Psychology*, November 1979, pp. 196–201. Reprinted by permission of the authors and publisher.

the study of interjudge agreement by gathering life style data which can then be given to several judges to make their independent assessments of an individual's life style.

The present study examined the interjudge agreement on life style types using 13 of Mosak's types (all except Superior One). The purpose of the study was to assess the reliability of three trained Adlerian judges' interpretations of subjects' life styles based on information contained in the LSQI.

Method

Experimental Procedure

The sample consisted of 60 male graduate students at two large urban universities who were randomly selected from a larger population of volunteer subjects. Each subject responded to the written LSQI. The 60 LSQIs were evaluated by three Adlerian judges who had completed graduate level course work in Adlerian theory and practice and who had used the life style analysis approach with clients within their particular clinical settings. Each judge was asked to analyze the data independently and then choose a dominant Adlerian life style from a list of Mosak's 13 types. Each judge had the further option of stating that the subject could not be typed.

Statistical Procedure

Interjudge agreement was defined as at least two out of three Adlerian judges selecting the same life style type for a subject. The number of agreements was divided by the total number of subjects (60) to obtain the proportion of times the judges agreed. This observed proportion of agreement was statistically tested with a binomial test for proportions to determine if it exceeded the proportion of agreement which would be expected by chance. In addition, an index which indicates agreement corrected for chance and the proportion of times all three judges agreed was also calculated.

The observed proportion of agreement was tested against two different proportions representing chance agreement. In statistical analyses of this type it is frequently assumed that each category (e.g., life style type) is equally likely in the population and then, based on this assumption, the probability that at least two out of three judges agree by chance is calculated. Calculation of the other proportion of agreement expected by chance was based on surveys of three practicing Adlerian psychologists to obtain their judgments concerning the frequency with which different life style types occur in the general population. The responses of the Adlerian psychologists were averaged to obtain a mean proportion for each life style type, and these means were used to calculate the proportion of agreement expected by chance.

Results

At least two out of three judges agreed on one of Mosak's 13 life style types for a subject in 41 out of 60 cases. This result was statistically significant with both approaches to determining the probability of agreement by chance. To describe the agreement among the judges corrected for agreement expected by chance, the M(I) index (Fleiss, 1975) was applied to the aforementioned analysis. For example, when chance agreement is based on assuming the types are equally likely, the M(I) index was .59, indicating that the agreement was 59% better than chance agreement. In addition to these findings, the results for agreement defined as all three judges selecting the same life style type and the corresponding M(I) indices are reported in Table 1.[1] In all situations, the results were statistically significant.

Discussion and Conclusions

This study found that the interjudge reliability of the written LSQI was moderately high. This implies that the life style data of a subject was not idiosyncratically interpreted by the judges. Instead, each judge's analysis of the subject's life style data agreed with the other judge's interpretations of the same data at a probability much greater than expected by chance.

1. For all four statistical tests, the experimentwise error rate is less than .05 based on the Bonferroni Inequality.

TABLE 1
Binomial Test for Proportions of Agreements on Life Style Types

Analysis	Definition of Interjudge Agreement	Observed Proportion	Chance Agreement	M(I) Index
Analysis I (assuming each life style is equally likely in population)	At least 2 out of 3 judges agree	.68* (41/60)	.22	.59
	3 out of 3 judges agree	.30* (18/60)	.006	.30
Analysis II (based on life style proportions from Adlerian psychologists)	At least 2 out of 3 judges agree	.68* (41/60)	.27	.56
	3 out of 3 judges agree	.30* (18/60)	0.12	.29

*Each proportion is statistically significant with $p < .01$.

Other implications based on these results are important both theoretically and methodologically. Because the agreement among the Adlerian judges was statistically significant, this supports the Adlerian contention that certain traits tend to cohere because of the basic unity and self-consistency of personality. In other words, the conceptual pool of Mosak's 13 types contains sufficient information to allow Adlerians to make consistent life style decisions with clients. This is not to say that Mosak's is the superior classification system; it only says that it appears to function adequately in terms of facilitating consistent decisions. Furthermore, the agreement among the judges also supports the procedure used for collecting the data—the LSQI. Hence, data from the LSQI may be used to identify patterns of behavior associated with particular life styles, which facilitates describing, comparing, and contrasting the behavior associated with each type.

There may be some who claim that a written procedure limits the conceptualization process in viewing life style data. Gushurst, however, reminds Adlerians that, by not attempting to remove the "mysterious and inexplicit" in the process of interpreting life style data, we are leaving "the door open for both ungoverned subjectivity and for criticisms of non-replicable, unscientific procedure" (1971, p. 31). Resolving the issue of interjudge reliability of life style interpretations is a necessary first step in the validation of one of the most potent constructs of Adlerian theory and practice.

References

Allen, T. W. The individual psychology of Alfred Adler: An item of history and a promise of a revolution. *The Counseling Psychologist*, 1971, *3*, 3–24.

Ansbacher, H. L., & Ansbacher, R. R. *The Individual Psychology of Alfred Adler*. New York: Basic Books, Inc., 1956.

Dreikurs, R. *Fundamentals of Adlerian psychology*. Chicago: Alfred Adler Institute, 1950.

Ferguson, E. D. The use of early recollections for assessing life style and diagnosing psychopathology. *Journal of Projective Techniques and Personality Assessment*, 1964, *28*, 403–412.

Fleiss, J. L. Measuring agreement between two judges on the presence or absence of a trait. *Biometrics*, 1975, *31*, 651–659.

Gushurst, R. S. The technique, utility, and validity of life style analysis. *The Counseling Psychologist*, 1971, *3*, 30–40.

Kefir, N., and Corsini, R. J. Dispositional acts: A contribution to typology. *Journal of Individual Psychology*, 1974, *30*, 163–178.

Kern, R. M. *Life style inventory questionnaire*. Georgia State University, 1976. (mimeo)

Mosak, H. H. Lifestyle. In A. G. NIkelly (Ed.), *Techniques for behavior change*. Springfield, Ill.: Charles C. Thomas, 1971.

Mosak, H. H., & Dreikurs, R. Adlerian psychotherapy. In R. J. Corsini (Ed.), *Current psychotherapies*. Itasca, Ill.: F. E. Peacock, 1973.

Thorne, F. *The Life Style Analysis Journal of Clinical Psychology*, 1975, *31*, 236–240.

The Early Recollections Rating Scale: Development and Applicability in Research

John Zarski

While a review of the literature indicates that early recollections have been of interest to counselors, psychologists, and other mental health practitioners for many years (Adler, 1931; Mosak, 1958, 1969; Nikelly, 1971; Papanek, 1972; Sonstegard, 1973; Ansbacher, 1973: Schrecker, 1973), only recently has an effort been made to develop instruments for objectively utilizing the data provided by early recollections for statistical research purposes. The purpose of this article is to discuss the development of two rating scales, utilizing early recollections, for the measurement of social interest from a research viewpoint. The emphasis in this paper is upon the development and refinement of an instrument for rating early recollections and reporting the results of studies which have been conducted utilizing this instrument. The reader is referred to the bibliography for additional readings on the theory of social interests and early recollections per se.

Support for this movement is provided by Mosak's (1958) belief that perception and memory are both related to the individual's frame of reference or attitudinal set; therefore, the early recollections of a person are seen as reflecting the person's perceptual framework within which he interprets life's experiences.

One of the earliest studies cited by Mosak (1969) in his review of research on early recollections was a study conducted by Langs and several colleagues (Langs, 1965 a; Langs, 1965 b, Langs, 1967; Langs, Rothenberg, Fishman, and Reiser, 1960). While these studies were psychoanalytic in orientation, the results suggested that early recollections were predictive of current functioning and personality. Since several of the hypotheses in this investigation focused on a facet of the predictive validity of early recollections, a contribution was made in terms of early recollections being a potentially useful technique. In a review of relevant research on the relationship between manifest content in early recollections and an individual's present life view (Brodsky, 1952; Eisenstein and Ryerson, 1951; Friedmann, 1950; Feichtinger, 1943; McCarter, 1961; Hedvig, 1965; Jackson and Sechrest, 1962), Altman (1973) found support for the conclusion that early recollections furnish important clues in the study of character and personality structure.

While some of these researchers may differ regarding a definition of early recollections, the basis for the development of the ERRS rests upon that provided by Ansbacher and Ansbacher (1956) where early recollections are seen as selections, distortions or inventions of past events to fit the underlying mood, purpose and interests of the person. It is not deemed necessary to determine the factual nature of the individual's early recollection since the actual occurrence of the incident is irrelevant to the Adlerian viewpoint of early recollections.

The following is a description of the Early Recollections Questionnaire, the Early Recollections Rating Scale, and a modified form of the instruments incorporating results from research studies conducted using the former named instruments.

The Early Recollections Questionnaire, developed by Rule (1972) and Altman (1973), consists of a page of instructions plus the questionnaire asking for six early recollections. The instructions stress the following directions: (1) the importance of recording only true recollections (not reports) and only those recollections which occurred before age eight (Dreikurs, 1967; Mosak, 1958; Verger and Camp, 1970); (2) the importance of including details, emotions, seemingly insignificant recollections and of disregarding the true chronological occurrence of remembered events (Dreikurs, 1967); and the request that six recollections be given, which is the number falling between the minimum and maximum suggested by Verger and Camp (1970) (see Appendix B, p. 135).

Reprinted by permission of the author.

The Early Recollections Rating Scale (Altman, 1973) consists of a bipolar seven-point scale developed to obtain a rating on nine continua thought to be indicative of the degree of social interest reflected in the early recollections (see Appendix C, p. 137).

The nine words of phrases (as selected by Altman in consultation with Adlerian psychology experts) were employed as possibly having value for each early recollection in determining degree of social interest as ascertained by rating the person's early recollections (see Appendix D, p. 139). Antonyms or opposites were selected for the opposing end of the bipolar scale. Each continuum contained seven points with seven being the number associated with the highest degree of social interest and one being associated with the lowest.

The nine continua are divided into two groupings: those reflective of the recollector's behavior and those reflective of the recollector's perception of the environment. The four continua rated according to the behavior exhibited in the early recollections were: withdrawn vs. gregarious; passive vs. active; aggressive/hostile vs. benevolent/kind; mistreated vs. befriended/treated well. The five continua rated according to the perception of the environment reflected in the early recollection were: threatening/frustrating vs. friendly/nurturing; rejecting vs. accepting; inferiority vs. self-confidence; depressing vs. cheerful; dependent vs. independent. Using this instrument, the author obtained mean ratings for each of the nine continua and a global rating. Utilizing a Pearson Product moment correlation, Altman reported inter-rated reliabilities on the ERRS for the nine bipolar variables ranging from .56 to .79, all significant beyond the .001 level of confidence. The six raters who participated in her study were all experienced in analyzing early recollections within the Adlerian framework; five of the raters had completed Adlerian-oriented counseling practicums, and the sixth had engaged in post-doctoral study at the Alfred Adler Institute.

Using a sample of 48 counselors participating in a six weeks guidance institute, Altman found that empathy, the dependent variable, correlated significantly with the early recollections global score and five of the nine social interest scores: benevolence, befriended, friendly, acceptance, and cheerful. A stepwise regression performed using empathy as the dependent variable and the nine social interest characteristics as independent variables led to the formulation of an equation which would predict empathy using the three variables: benevolence, friendly, and self-confidence.

Using Altman's ERRS, Zarski, Sweeney, and Barcikowski (1977) studied the relationship between counselor social interest and three dimensions of counseling effectiveness as measured by client satisfaction, client self-acceptance, and client sociability. The authors' strategy was to relate outcomes in counseling to a theoretical position on the qualities of the helping person rather than to the helping person's methodology. Adler (1938) indirectly referred to this strategy when he expounded upon the qualities of a person high in social interest; such a person has subsequently been described by others as fully functioning, self-actualizing, or exemplifying similar constructs (Allen, 1971; Mosak and Dreikurs, 1973).

In this study, the counselor's level of social interest was positively correlated with the client's satisfaction with counseling, and more importantly, with attitudinal measurements of the client's self-acceptance and sociability. Based upon Adler's concept of social interest, it may be reasoned that person's with higher social interest would facilitate the development of social interest (e.g., self-confidence, self-acceptance) in others by being effective models (Dowling and Frantz, 1975). Though this finding is only tentatively indicated by the validation of one aspect of Adler's theory, it would seem to merit consideration as a source of further study.

The present investigation also supported Altman's (1973) findings and seemed to demonstrate the potential usefulness of early recollections as tools for studying the counselor as an important variable in counseling process and outcome.

Accepting the premise that Adler's ideas are widely used by various social psychologies popular in practice today, the author believes that determining a person's social interest through an analysis of that individual's early recollections has wide applicability for research by persons of various orientations. Unlike other studies appearing in the literature (Crandall, 1975; Crandall and Reimanis, 1976; Reimanis, 1974), the intention is to transcend the issue of which measure is most effective and focus on which instrument might be more useful for a researcher, dependent upon which specific characteristics or constructs one desires to investigate. A review of the literature at this time provides a selection of four instruments for measuring social interest (Crandall, 1975; Greever, 1973; Reimanis, 1966; Altman, 1973), all purporting validity. Preliminary results of a recent study conducted by the present author, incorporating Crandall's, Greever's, and Altman's measures, call into question the findings of other studies.

Naturally it will be necessary to continue this type of analysis and the present author is currently analyzing data using a revised form of Altman's ERRS incorporating concepts/traits which more accurately represent the measureable "multidimensional" nature of social interest (see Appendices E, p. 140, and F, p. 141).

References

Adler, A. *What Life Should Mean To You.* Boston: Little, Brown, and Co., 1931.

Adler, A. *Social Interest.* London: Farber & Farber, 1938.

Allen, T. W. The Individual Psychology of Alfred Adler: An Item of History and Promise of a Revolution. *Counseling Psychologist,* 1971, *3,* 3–24.

Altman, K. E. The Relationship Between Social Interest Dimensions of Early Recollections and Selected Counselor Variables. Unpublished doctoral dissertation, University of South Carolina, 1973.

Ansbacher, H. L. & Ansbacher, R. R. (Eds.). *The Individual Psychology of Alfred Adler.* New York: Basic Books, 1956.

Ansbacher, H. L. Adler's Interpretation of Early Recollections: Historical Account. *Journal of Individual Psychology,* 1973, *29,* 135–145.

Brodsky, P. The Diagnostic Importance of Early Recollections. *American Journal of Psychotherapy,* 1952, 6, 484–493.

Crandall, J. E. A Scale for Social Interest. *Journal of Individual Psychology,* 1975, *30,* 187–195.

Crandall, J. E. & Reimanis, G. Social Interest and Time Orientation, Childhood Memories, Adjustment and Crime. *Journal of Individual Psychology,* 1976, *32,* 203–211.

Dowling, T. H. & Frantz, T. T. The influence of Facilitative Relationship on Imitative Learning. *Journal of Counseling Psychology,* 1975, *22,* 259–263.

Dreikurs, R. *Psychodynamics, Psychotherapy, and Counseling.* Chicago: Alfred Adler Institute, 1967.

Eisenstein, V. W. & Ryerson, R. Psychodynamic Significance of the First Conscious Memory. *Bulletin of the Menninger Clinic,* 1951, *15,* 213–220.

Feichtinger, F. Early Recollections in Neurotic Disturbances. *Individual Psychology Bulletin,* 1943, *3,* 44–49.

Friedmann, A. Early Childhood Memories of Mental Patients. *Individual Psychology Bulletin,* 1950, *8,* 1–1–116.

Greever, K. B., Tseng, M. S., & Friedland, B. U. Development of the Social Interest Index. *Journal of Consulting and Clinical Psychology,* 1973, *41,* 454–458.

Hedvig, E. B. Children's Early Recollections as Basis for Diagnosis. *Journal of Individual Psychology,* 1965, *21,* 187–188.

Jackson, M. & Sechrest, L. Early Recollections in Four Diagnostic Groups. *Journal of Individual Psychology,* 1962, *18,* 52–56.

Langs, R. J. Earliest Memories and Personality. *Archives of General Psychiatry,* 1965, *12,* 379–390 (a).

Langs, R. J. First Memories and Characterologic Diagnosis. *Journal of Nervous and Mental Disease,* 1965, *141,* 318–320 (b).

Langs, R. J. Stability of Earliest Memories Under LSD–25 and Placebo. *Journal of Nervous and Mental Disorders,* 1967, *144,* 171–184.

Langs, R. J., Rothenberg, M. B., Fishman, J. R., & Reiser, M. F. A Method for Clinical and Theoretical Study of the Earliest Memory. *Archives of General Psychiatry,* 1960, *3,* 523–534.

McCarter, R. E. Affective Components of Early Recollections. *Dissertation Abstracts,* 1961, *22,* 2090.

Mosak, H. H. Early Recollections as a Projective Technique. *Journal of Projective Techniques,* 1958, *22,* 302–311.

Mosak, H. H. Early Recollections: Evaluation of Some Recent Research. *Journal of Individual Psychology,* 1969, *2,* 56–59.

Mosak, H. H. & Dreikurs, R. Adlerian Psychotherapy. In R. Corsini (Ed.), *Current Psychotherapies.* Itasca, Illinois: F. E. Peacock, 1973.

Nikelly, A. (Ed.). *Techniques for Behavior Change.* Springfield, Illinois: Charles C. Thomas, 1971.

Papanek, H. The Use of Early Recollections in Psychotherapy. *Journal of Individual Psychology,* 1972, *28,* 169.

Quinn, J. Predicting Recidivism and Type of Crime From the Early Recollections of Prison Inmates. Unpublished doctoral dissertation, University of South Carolina, 1973.

Reimanis, G. Childhood Experience Memories and Anomie in Adults and College Students. *Journal of Individual Psychology,* 1966, *22,* 56–64.

Rule, W. R. The Relationship Between Early Recollections and Selected Counselor and Life Style Characteristics. Unpublished doctoral dissertation, University of South Carolina, 1972.

Schrecker, P. Individual Psychological Significance of First Childhood Recollections. *Journal of Individual Psychology,* 1973, *29,* 146–156.

Sonstegard, M. Life Style Identification and Assessment. *The Individual Psychologist,* 1973, *10,* 1–4.

Verger, D. M. & Camp, W. L. Early Recollections: Reflections of the Present. *Journal of Counseling Psychology,* 1970, *17,* 510–515.

Zarski, J. J., Sweeney, T. J., & Barcikowski, R. J. Counseling Effectiveness as a Function of Counselor Social Interest. *Journal of Counseling Psychology,* 1977, *24,* 1–5.

Early Recollections and Social Interest in Psychology Students

Daniel G. Eckstein
Thomas P. Springer

The significance of early recollections (ER's) is one of the most important discoveries of Individual Psychology (Adler, 1931; Mosak, 1958, 1969; Nikelly, 1971; Sonstegard, 1973; Taylor, 1975, Eckstein, 1976). Early recollections help provide insights regarding one's social interest, values, goals, self-esteem, conflicts, and basic attitudes toward self, others, and life in general.

The purpose of the present study is to investigate group ER differences relative to social interest between four different psychology classes. A specific hypothesis is that upper division psychology majors will demonstrate higher social interest than non-psychology majors.

The four classes represent various degrees of exposure to psychological principles.

Method

Two introductory psychology classes (N = 45 and 43) contained approximately 10% declared psychology majors; other students were taking the course as a requirement in various university curriculums. 80% of the students were freshmen. The third class was an upper division course on human growth and development (N = 23). Approximately 25% of the students were senior psychology majors, the remaining students evenly divided among undergraduate nurses, graduate counselors, and graduate elementary education teachers. The final class was a dynamics of adjustment seminar (N = 41). 50% of the class were undergraduate psychology majors, 40% were graduate counseling students, and 10% were miscellaneous undergraduate students enrolled as an elective. The course focused on a variety of experiential personal growth exercises and journals in addition to traditional class content.

Two weeks prior to the end of the semester all students were asked to record two early memories using the standard request to "Think back as far as you can, and describe the first incident that you remember. Describe what feeling you had at that time. Make sure it is a specific situation and not a generalization."

The Early Recollections Rating Scale (Altman, 1973) was used to blindly rate all ER's. The Ers consists of a bipolar seven-point scale developed to obtain a rating on nine social interest continua. Each continuum contained antonyms with a score of seven representing maximum social interest.

The nine continua are divided into two groupings: those reflective of the person's actual behavior and those indicating the individual's subjective perception of the environment. The four continua rated in the behavior category consists of withdrawn vs. gregarious; passive vs. active, aggressive/hostile vs. benevolent/kind; and mistreat vs. befriended/treated well. The subjective perception variables are: threatening/frustrating vs. friendly/nurturing; rejecting vs. accepting; inferiority vs. self confidence; depressing vs. cheerful and dependent vs. independent. Specific studies investigating social interest, empathy and counseling psychology can be found in Altman, 1973; Eckstein, 1976; Zarski, Sweeney and Barcikowski, 1977; and Baruth and Eckstein, 1978.

Results

Because of dispropriate sex-distributions of the 52 males and the 100 females in the four classes, an analysis of variance investigated differences between class, sex, and the interaction of class and sex. Of the 19 total variables in both ER's, four of the differences (22%) were significant by sex. In the first ER men felt more self-confident than women ($p < .01$) whereas in the second ER women were more cooperative, friendly, and befriended than men (all $p < .05$).

Reprinted by permission of the authors.

Table 1

Class Means and F Ratios for First Early Recollections

Class	1 Withdrawn/ Gregarious	2 Passive/ Active	3 Competitive/ Cooperative	4 Dependent/ Independent	5 Hostile/ Friendly	6 Rejected/ Accepted	7 Discouraged/ Self-confident	8 Depressed/ Cheerful	9 Mistreated/ Befriended
Intro Psy (N = 45)	3.62	3.33	3.93	3.26	3.44	3.71	3.20	3.35	3.91
Intro Psy (N = 43)	3.25	4.04	3.62	3.86	3.09	3.37	3.09	3.13	3.58
Human Growth & Develop. (N = 23)	2.91	4.56	3.30	3.73	3.08	3.13	3.34	3.04	3.34
Dynamics of Adjustment (N = 41)	4.78	4.31	4.34	3.93	4.24	4.54	4.12	4.12	4.61
F Ratios	7.50	2.60	2.77	1.88	3.27	4.74	2.36	2.77	3.73
Level of Significance	.0001	.05	.05	NS	.05	.01	NS	.05	.01

Table 2

Class Means and F Ratios for Second Early Recollections

Class	1 Withdrawn/ Gregarious	2 Passive/ Active	3 Competitive/ Cooperative	4 Dependent/ Independent	5 Hostile/ Friendly	6 Rejected/ Accepted	7 Discouraged/ Self-confident	8 Depressed/ Cheerful	9 Mistreated/ Befriended
Intro Psy (N = 45)	3.97	3.79	4.13	3.79	3.84	3.81	3.70	3.90	4.04
Intro Psy (N = 43)	4.25	4.60	3.86	4.23	4.16	4.39	4.23	4.32	4.60
Human Growth & Develop. (N = 23)	2.86	3.40	3.63	3.18	3.31	3.45	3.00	3.31	3.50
Dynamics of Adjustment (N = 41)	4.61	4.85	4.24	4.14	4.34	4.70	4.27	4.37	4.69
F Ratios	3.76	4.15	.85	3.92	1.51	2.94	2.41	1.63	2.43
Level of Significance	.01	.01	NS	.01	NS	.05	NS	NS	NS

Class mean differences are presented in Table 1 and Table 2. Results indicate that 11 of the 18 (61%) were significantly different, with students in the dynamics of adjustment class demonstrating higher social interest on all measures. The variables of gregarious, active, cooperative, and accepted were significantly higher on both ER's for the adjustment students.

Only one variable (6%) showed a significant interaction between class and sex. Male students in the human growth and development class were significantly more dependent than females.

Implications

A major finding of the study is that students enrolled in the dynamics of adjustment course demonstrate higher levels of social interest than students having had fewer hours in psychology. Additional research is recommended to empirically identify the specific factors responsible for such results. Having completed an experiential personal growth course could have been one factor. Age was not, as both the human growth and adjustment classes were upper division courses. Exposure to psychological principles may have contributed, but the most obvious conclusion is that students who major in psychology have higher social interest than people in general. Such apparent self-selection process should be viewed optimistically in relation to future mental health service providers.

Based upon Adler's concept of social interest, it may be reasoned that persons with higher social interest will facilitate the development of social interest in others by being effective models (Dowling, and Frantz, 1975).

Some ER sex differences were found and are being furthered explored through such journals as *Sex Roles*. Lastly, the utility and validity of ER's as an important measure of counseling effectiveness, individual and group differences, mental health, and social interest appears to be further established in behavioral science research.

Bibliography

Adler, A. *What Life Should Mean To You.* Boston: Little, Brown, and Co. 1931.

Altman, K. E. *The Relationship Between Social Interest Dimensions of Early Recollections and Selected Counselor Variables.* Unpublished doctoral dissertation. University of South Carolina, 1973.

Baruth, L. and Eckstein, D. *Life Style: Theory, Practice and Research.* Dubuque, Iowa: Kendall Hunt, 1978.

Dowling, T. H. and Frantz, T. T. The influence of facilitative relationship on imitative learning. *Journal of Counseling Psychology.* 1975, 22, 259–263.

Eckstein, D. Early recollection changes after counseling: A case study. *Journal of Individual Psychology,* 32 (2), 1976, 212–223.

Mosak, H. H. Early recollections as a projective technique. *Journal of Projective Techniques.* 1958, 22, 302–311.

Mosak, H. H. Early recollections: Evaluation of some recent research. *Journal of Individual Psychology.* 1969, 2, 56–69.

Nikelly, A. (Ed). *Techniques for Behavior Change.* Springfield, Illinois, Charles C. Thomas, 1971.

Sonstegard, M. Life style identification and assessment. *The Individual Psychologist.* 1973, 10, 1–4.

Taylor, J. Early recollections as a projective technique: A review of some recent validation studies, *Journal of Individual Psychology,* 31 (2), 1975, 213–218.

Zarski, J. J., Sweeney, T. J. and Barcikowshi, R. J. Counseling effectiveness as a function of counselor social interest. *Journal of Counseling Psychology.* 1977. 24, 1–5.

Early Recollection Changes After Counseling: A Case Study[1]

Daniel G. Eckstein

The significance of early recollections is one of the most important discoveries of Individual Psychology (Adler, 1931; Mosak, 1969; Nikelly, 1971; Sonstegard, 1973). Adler (1931) described the significance of such recollections:

Among the psychological expressions, some of the most revealing are individual memories. His memories are reminders he carries about with him of his own limits and of the meaning of circumstances. There are no 'chance memories'; out of the incalculable number of impressions which meet an individual, he chooses to remember only those which he feels, however darkly, to have a bearing on his situation. Thus, the memories represent his 'story of my life,' a story he repeats to himself to warm him or comfort him, to keep him concentrated on his goal, and to prepare him by means of past experience, so that he will meet the future with an already tested style of action. (p. 73)

A crucial Adlerian theoretical notion regarding ERs is that during the course of therapy either an entirely new set of memories will be recalled or the same "objective" recollection will be accompanied by a different "subjective" personal reaction. Dreikurs (1967) writes:

The final proof of the patient's satisfactory reorientation is the change in his basic mistakes, indicated by a change in his early recollections. If a significant improvement has taken place, new incidents are recollected, reported recollections show significant changes or are in some cases completely forgotten. (p. 71)

In a similar manner, Nikelly (1971) has noted that "ERs will often change before and after therapy in the same way the client's attitudes about himself and toward life are altered after treatment or following an unusual phase in his life" (p. 59).

This report is an effort to critically evaluate ER changes in one individual following nine months of counseling. The author's "subjective" case notes will be complemented by "objective" naive expert ER ratings in researching changes. Thus clinical impressions will be contrasted with a psychometric approach in examining ER changes.

Method

Jane, a 19 year old freshman at a women's college, requested counseling in her second week of school. Since a specific concern involved conflicts with her roommate, the counselor suggested that a life style analysis might be beneficial in providing some insights. After an exploratory relationship-building introductory session, life style data (including ERs) was obtained. Upon sharing with her the life style summary, the counselor met weekly with Jane for the balance of the nine month academic year. At the final counseling session, Jane was asked to report her earliest childhood memories again. No reference was made to previous ERs.

Standardized pre- and post-ER instructions were: "Think back as far as you can, and tell me your earliest childhood memories." Jane reported eight recollections and one recurring dream on the pretest, and five recollections on the posttest nine months later.

The 14 pre- and post ERs were randomly presented to raters with the following written instructions:

"Enclosed you will find the following:

—1 Early Recollections Rating Scale
—14 ER sheets containing either a dream or an ER
—A folded and stapled envelope to be opened *after* you have completed the 14 ER sheets

Daniel Eckstein, Early Recollection Changes After Counseling: A Case Study, *Journal of Individual Psychology*, 32(2), 1976, 212-223. Reprinted from the *Journal of Individual Psychology* with permission of the author and publishers.

1. The author gratefully acknowledges the permission of Catherine Altman and James Quinn to use the Early Recollections Rating Scale. The statistical assistance of Martha Bayes of the University of South Carolina was also invaluable.

Would you please follow this standardized procedure in rating?

1. Read and review the 'Instructions to Rater' sheet defining and describing the nine bi-polar variables.
2. Rate each sheet containing an ER on the 1–7 scale. Consider each ER *independently*; they are *not* to be considered together.
3. After completing your ratings, open the folded envelope and follow the appropriate directions."

The second sealed envelope contained both sets of ERs from the pre- and posttest. The raters received the following instructions: "Please read the entire set of early recollections and then make one general, global rating based on your total impression of all recollections. There is one sheet for each set of recollections. Please do not consult your previous ratings."

There was no indication that the ERs were from the same subject. It was thus possible to compare separate, isolated ratings with a general, global rating on all pre- and post-recollections.

Instrument

The Early Recollections Rating Scale (ERRS) was originally developed by Altman (1973) and later modified by Quinn (1973). It rates nine different basic attitudes, each variable being on a bi-polar scale containing seven numerical categories. A score of 4 indicates a "neutral" or "average" rating. Higher scores reflect greater social interest. The nine bi-polar ratings consisted of: A. Subject's Behavior Toward the Environment: (1) withdrawn-gregarious; (2) passive-active; (3) competitive-cooperative; (4) dependent-independent; and B. The Individual's Subjective Affect or Feeling of the Environment: (5) hostile-friendly; (6) rejected-accepted; (7) discouraged-self-confident; (8) depressed-cheerful; and (9) mistreated-befriended.

Altman (1973) obtained inter-rater reliabilities on the ERRS for the nine bi-polar variables ranging from .56 to .79, all significant beyond the .001 level of confidence. Six of eight raters in the present study had participated in the Quinn and Altman studies. All eight raters were experienced practicing Adlerian psychologists.

In her study, Altman found five social interest scores significantly correlated with measures of empathy, including: benevolence-aggression, befriended-mistreated, friendly-threatening, acceptance-rejection, and cheerful-depressing. She also found that three attitudes, benevolence, befriended, and self-confidence, were the best predictors of empathy.

Using a modified version of the ERRS which had a revised definition for the competitive-cooperative scale, Quinn studied relationships between ERs, recidivism and type of crime with prison inmates. He found no significant relationships between the ERs of recidivists and non-recidivists who had committed crimes against people. Conversely, in crimes against property, recidivists scored significantly lower than non-recidivists on the competitive-cooperative scale.

The present study utilized the modified Altman ERRS variables as used to investigate single ERs, and also included global ratings.

Statistical Procedure

Rater mean scores on all nine bi-polar ERRS variables were obtained for each individual pre- and post-ER. Mean scores of the global ERs were computed as were the sum of all Behavior and Affect variables. Two-tailed parametric T-tests evaluated mean differences between the pre- and post-counseling ERs.

Case Study

Although neither the subject's life style nor a comprehensive case history is considered necessary, a brief summary of the counseling follows. The counselor sought initially to *develop the relationship* including the Carkhuff (1969) core "rapport" dimensions of genuineness, empathy, positive regard, understanding, etc. The second phase of the relationship consisted of a *psychological investigation*, including the completion of the life style summary. The Kuder Occupational Interest Survey, the Tennessee Self-Concept Scale, the 16 Personality Factors and the Edwards Personal Preference Schedule were also administered. The third phase, the *interpretation*, disclosed results of the psychometric instruments coupled with clinical observations to provide some insight for the client.

Jane, the youngest of five children (sister nine years older, three brothers eight, five, and three years old, respectively), described her childhood in the parodoxical way of "unhappy, but happy"—"I often got frustrated when I tied knots in my shoes, always wanting to do what my brothers and sisters were doing; I was always younger, and couldn't keep up physically or emotionally. I liked ballet, played with dolls a lot, and liked to dance. I enjoyed drawing, but often got frustrated because I couldn't do it well enough, so I quit drawing completely until high school. I've always felt like the baby."

In relation to her siblings, Jane found her place by being a hard worker, helping around the house, being a "pleaser," critical of self and others, wanting and receiving her own way, sensitive and easily hurt, throwing temper tantrums, and by being idealistic and materialistic. She was also the sibling most spoiled by her parents, obtaining special attention, love, and material possessions from them. Her main sibling competitors appeared to be her sister and second brother who was five years older than Jane.

The following life style summary, what Dreikurs (1953) called the "theme of life, with its endless variations" (p. 43) was shared with Jane:

Life is a mixture of happiness and fun (i.e., when I'm playing or receiving special attention and material possessions) coupled with equally frightening experiences (i.e., when I encounter a new, unknown situation or am forced to rely on my own abilities).

Others should provide me help or comfort in crisis situations. I enjoy being with other people.

I want to be grown-up, but often find new experiences both challenging and frightening, especially when I must rely on myself. At such times I have a tendency to give up and become discouraged.

It is important for me to gain special attention, and be number one, especially with males, and to have special things provided me. I expect to have things to my own way.

I enjoy having fun mischievously, especially at the expense of bending the rules a bit.

Much time was spent discussing and revising the implications of the above life style summary with Jane. The counselor explained the life style summary as a general outline which Jane was encouraged to apply to specific situations supporting or rejecting basic notions about life, others, and self. Much to Jane's surprise, the life style did provide important insights, and a commitment for long-term weekly counseling was obtained.

The final phase of counseling provided a *reorientation* based upon insight and encouragement. After Jane and the counselor agreed upon her basic life style, she was led to become aware that her unique style worked to her advantage as well as to her disadvantage. By gaining insight and seeing her life style in action, Jane realized not only what was happening, but also began to understand that *she* had the *choice* of whether to continue specific behaviors or to act in new ways. Specific "conflict" situations included Jane's trouble with her roommate, her dependency upon male approval, plus her tendency to lean upon others in crises.

Throughout the counseling sessions, Jane experienced growth and renewed confidence in her ability to cope with problems. There were several disappointing setbacks—times in which she felt that no progress was being made. Jane was particularly concerned about her in tolerant attitude which frequently resulted in peer conflicts. Specific goals for her Thanksgiving and Christmas holidays focused on becoming more self-sufficient at home and in coping with her dependency on her boyfriend's approval. She was encouraged to "get in touch" and "ride-with" the frequent periods of depression, including writing detailed diaries about her feelings in such situations. Her "bullheaded intolerance" was also discussed, including role-playing specific desired behavioral changes.

In the spring Jane continued to expand her interests and began feeling better about her art abilities, her creativity, and herself as a woman. She became intensely involved in the women's rights movement and was more active in campus activities. Jane also moved from an "inward" self-exploration to an "outward" concern for others which culminated in volunteer work at a telephone crisis center. During the final two months of counseling, Jane's bi-weekly appointments focused mainly upon the continuing changes she was initiating spontaneously. The post-test life style data collection was conducted during the last visit, nine months after her intial counseling session. In a letter written during the summer she stated a new interest in personal meditation and reflection, a desire to work with others, and her improving self-concept.

Specific Early Recollections

The following pre- and post-counseling ERs were evaluated by the eight raters.

Pre-Counseling ERs

1. Had a nap—mom put us in smock dresses—man behind us had been painting—I sat down in bucket of paint—he was nice about it, didn't get mad—took me to mom; she and dad laughed. He took turpentine and got it out. Felt: in shock—didn't realize what had done, put on other dress—better dread being brought back by Mr. French.

2. My father put me on my sister's 2 wheeler—I didn't trust him—I was terrified—felt I was too young to do it. He then took me off, knew I was too scared. Later went back and pretended I was riding. Felt: scared—relieved when got off—most vivid—screaming and hanging onto Dad—he didn't understand how scared I was.

3. My sis dressed me up in costume—she took me into back yard: took pictures. I liked it because my hair was fixed like grandmothers. My sister then put her jewelry on me. Felt: in my glory—neat.

4. Suzie's birthday. Mother telling me I got my way with sister—there were two skirts; my sister

wanted to wear the crinoline: didn't want to wear apron—I ended up in crinoline, I didn't have to threaten her—used reason; put on for picture. She was irked, but she never said anything. Felt: slick that I had been able to reason with her and weird: had gotten my way outside home—in a social aspect.

5. Mom said could take ballet or go to kindergarten. I figured kindergarten would end in year. First day—had been downtown with mom. She said could start but I didn't have a ballet outfit. The teacher said I could dance on my feet. I walked into room—it was the biggest had ever seen. It scared and thrilled me—unbelievably big. Felt: like it—thought neat—knew would like ballet. But scared me because new and didn't know other girls.

6. Remember playing in crib—sis sang "Itsy Bitsy Yellow Polka Dot Bikini" stood up and "danced" to music—thought it was fun. I was supposed to be sleeping, but wasn't. Content to be there in room—content and playing. Felt: happy, having good time.

7. Laying in crib—had mobile over head—had favorite mobile—colors red, black, blue. Used to watch it. Thought: pretty, tried to reach them.

8. Scared in dark-bathroom—one time Mother told me if I'd go upstairs by myself—would be candy behind toilet. Didn't believe it—got aunt to go up—she said there was candy up there. I went up there—was sacred, but bold—two (Three Muskateers) were there. From then on not afriad. Proud of Mother—hadn't told me lie.

9. Dreams:—witch came into my room—woke up screaming and crying. Mother said lot of times new house causes bad dreams. Felt: safe—went back to sleep.

Post-Counseling ERs

1. Me and brother Allan—I was interior decorator—he was drunk—while mom decorating Christmas tree, we were playing. Hilarious—mom laughing at us; had to quit decorating just to watch us. She would decorate top half and let us decorate bottom half of tree. While she decorated top we entertained ourselves. Felt: Happy, having fun.

2. Playing Monopoly with brothers—got caught for cheating—they threw me out of game—but I wasn't mad—thought it was funny. Felt: didn't

really want to play; was bored, so that was my way of getting out of it.

3. When moved out of old house—sitting in back of stationwagon—we were taking last things out of house—remember being glad moving, but didn't know why. Felt: alone, but not in bad way.

4. Had white sandals; wasn't supposed to go barefooted. Put plug in sink to wash feet. Must have left plug in sink and left water running. She came home—there was water all over. It was a mess. She cleaned it up, but didn't get mad at me. I was upset. She knew why I had been up there, but she never said anything. The next day the lady next door bought me pink flip-flops to wear and mom didn't say anything. Felt: Okay, happy—had wanted flip-flops all along.

5. Father was teaching me to ride a two-wheeler—screamed at top of lungs—he was trying to teach me to ride—I should have been more cooperative. Felt: knew wasn't hurting me, should have been more cooperative.

Results

Table 1 shows the mean rater differences based on global ratings of the nine pre-counseling ERs compared to the five post-counseling ERs. Mean pre- and post-ratings for each of the specific ERRS bi-polar variables are compared, as are the sums of the four Behavior and the five Affect scales. There are significant differences for eight of the eleven variables. Mean scores improved on the posttest for all variables, the most significant change occurring on the depressed-cheerful scale ($p < .001$). Significant ($p < .01$) improvements were noted on the ER total score associated with behavior. Similar growth ($p < .01$) was noted on the total affect score.

Table 2 compares the ERRS variables for individual ERs on both pre- and posttests. The mean of the nine specific ERs comprised the pre-test score, while the posttest averages were based on the five concluding ERs. The Primary difference between Table 1 and Table 2 is that the former results are based on global ratings of all ERs, whereas the latter scores are determined by specific ERs. Results of Table 2 indicate that the separate ratings were less significant and more variable than global comparisons. Two of the four Behavior variables were significant ($p < .05$), while none of the five Affect variables differed significantly.

TABLE 1
Mean Pre and Post Global Early Recollection Ratings

Variable	Mean (n=8)	Standard Deviation	T Value	2-Tail Probability Level of Significance (df=7)
1. Withdrawn-Gregarious				
Pre	4.13	1.13	−2.38	.05
Post	5.38	0.74		
2. Passive-Active				
Pre	3.88	1.55	−2.11	NS
Post	5.25	0.71		
3. Competitive-Cooperative				
Pre	3.38	0.92	−2.37	.05
Post	4.38	1.20		
4. Dependent-Independent				
Pre	2.38	1.60	−3.63	.01
Post	4.63	1.51		
5. Hostile-Friendly				
Pre	3.13	0.64	−3.86	.01
Post	4.88	0.99		
6. Rejected-Accepted				
Pre	4.00	1.20	−1.93	NS
Post	5.25	1.17		
7. Discouraged-Self-confident				
Pre	3.25	0.89	−3.23	.01
Post	5.13	0.99		
8. Depressed-Cheerful				
Pre	3.38	0.92	−5.29	.001
Post	5.38	0.74		
9. Mistreated-Befriended				
Pre	4.12	1.25	−1.76	NS
Post	5.13	0.99		
Total Behavior (Variables 1-4)				
Pre	3.44	0.72	−4.10	.01
Post	4.91	0.76		
Total Affect (Variables 5-9)				
Pre	3.58	0.82	−3.23	.01
Post	5.15	0.93		

TABLE 2
Mean Pre and Post Individual Early Recollection Ratings

Variable	Mean (n=9)	Standard Deviation	T Value	2-Tail Probability Level of Significance (df=8)
1. Withdrawn-Gregarious				
Pre	3.96	0.49	−1.79	NS
Post	4.36	0.68		
2. Passive-Active				
Pre	4.64	0.74	−0.46	NS
Post	4.76	0.30		
3. Competitive-Cooperative				
Pre	4.02	0.12	3.06	.05
Post	3.82	0.19		
4. Dependent-Independent				
Pre	3.70	1.11	−2.97	.05
Post	4.64	0.60		
5. Hostile-Friendly				
Pre	4.25	0.44	1.24	NS
Post	4.07	0.38		
6. Rejected-Accepted				
Pre	4.49	0.56	1.14	NS
Post	4.22	0.47		
7. Discouraged-Self-confident				
Pre	4.21	0.59	−1.33	NS
Post	4.56	0.88		
8. Depressed-Cheerful				
Pre	4.62	0.47	−0.33	NS
Post	4.69	0.78		
9. Mistreated-Befriended				
Pre	4.63	0.67	0.04	NS
Post	4.62	0.54		
Total Behavior (Variables 1-4)				
Pre	4.58	0.70	1.83	NS
Post	4.11	0.57		
Total Affect (Variables 5-9)				
Pre	4.69	0.84	2.02	NS
Post	4.27	0.66		

Discussion

The major finding of this case study is that early recollections do appear to change significantly as a result of long-term counseling or therapy. This finding should be viewed optimistically by members of the helping profession who are committed to the belief that attitudes and behaviors *can* and *do* change.

The significant differences between the two sets of early recollections should also lend additional validity to the use of early recollections in assessing counseling changes. The high inter-rater reliabilities lend support for the use of the Early Recollections Rating Scale in evaluating significant content themes. However, additional validity studies are recommended.

Another important finding is that global ratings appear to be more uniform and more significant than individual ER evaluations. Such results are consistent with the belief that "the whole is more than the sum of the parts."

Adler stressed that specific events must be considered with reference to the total context (Zusammenhang) of the whole individual. In 1930 he wrote:

To deny the context (Zusammenhang) is like picking single notes to examine them for their significance, their meaning. A better understanding of this coherence is shown by Gestalt psychology which uses this metaphor frequently, as we do. The difference is only that we are not satisfied with the 'Gestalt,' as we prefer to say, with the 'whole,' when we refer all the notes to the melody. We are satisfied only when we have recognized in the melody the originator and his attitudes as well, for example Bach, "Bach's Life Style." (p. 205).

The results of this study would appear to confirm Adler's "global" emphasis.

It is also interesting to note the raters' reactions at the conclusion of the ER evaluations. Not realizing that the global recollections had been based upon the same subject, a frequent response was: "I thought the ERs were from two different people—one set was definitely more positive."

This pilot study attempted to validate empirically the notion that ERs do change as a result of counseling or therapy. This intensive single-individual case study gives evidence in the expected direction, and provides support for future multi-subject research with control groups.

References

Adler, A. Nochmals-die Einheit der Neurosne. *International Journal of Psychology*, 1930, 8, 201–216.

―――. *What life should mean to you.* Boston: Little, Brown, and Co., 1931.

―――. Significance of early recollections. *International Journal of Individual Psychology*, 1937, 3, 283–287.

Altman, K. The relationship between social interest dimensions of early recollections and selected counselor variables. Unpublished doctoral dissertation, University of South Carolina, 1973.

Carkhuff, R. *Helping & human relations.* New York: Holt, Rinehart and Winston, Inc., 1969.

Dreikurs, R. *Fundamentals of Adlerian psychology.* Chicago: Alfred Adler Institute, 1953.

―――. *Psychodynamics, psychotherapy and counseling.* Chicago: Alfred Adler Institute, 1967.

Mosak, H. Early recollections: Evaluation of some recent research. *Journal of Individual Psychology*, 1969, 2, 56–59.

Nikelly, A. (Ed.). *Techniques for behavior change.* Springfield, Ill: Charles C. Thomas, 1971.

Quinn, J. Predicting recidivism and type of crime from the early recollections of prison inmates. Unpublished doctoral dissertation, University of South Carolina, 1973.

Sonstegard, M. Life style identification and assessment, *The Individual Psychologist*, 1973, 10, 1–4.

Two Interpretations of Birth Order Position

John Nield, Donald Ward and
Thomas Edgar

One of the key concepts of Adlerian theory is that of birth order as it relates to family constellation. A great deal of the research on the Adlerian model has attempted to examine the relationships between birth order and various psychological and behavioral attributes. These numerous investigations have not resulted in consistent findings. The frequency of contradictory results in the literature could be interpreted as indicating that birth order is an inappropriate or insufficient organizing concept for human behavior. It is evident that those committed to the Adlerian model must respond to the challenge presented by these contradictory findings.

The vast amount of research on birth order is an accurate reflection of the importance of this concept to the model. In fact, the contradictory research findings may lead to the conclusion that the use of birth order as a psychological variable is a mistaken assumption of many practicing Adlerians. In order to resolve the dilemma and meet the challenge presented by the contradictory research findings, a careful analysis of the literature was undertaken to ascertain whether or not a different perspective could lead to a redefinition of the foundation on which the concept of birth order rests.

Two psychological variables which researchers have frequently investigated as correlates to birth order are intellectual attainment and antisocial behavior. Ansbacher and Ansbacher quote Adler as saying, "In my experience the greatest proportion of problem children are the oldest; and close behind is the youngest" (Ansbacher and Ansbacher p. 379, 1956). An apparent contradiction of this statement by Adler is the conclusion drawn by Pepper that, from her observations, the middle child is the most likely to be discouraged and thus become a problem child (Nikelly, 1976, p. 53). Adler himself states that the middle child is characterized as being rebellious and envious, but he goes on to say that the middle child is usually better adjusted than the older or younger sibling (Hall and Lindzey, 1967, p. 125). However, Adler does not define what he means by rebellious. Rosen (1961) and Rosenow and Whyte (1931) found first-borns to be over represented among problem children. However, Sletto (1934) and Altus (1966b) found the first-born to be under represented among problem children. Sletto found an inverse relationship between oldest children and delinquency (1934). A study by Toman (1969) indicated that middle children are under represented both at child guidance clinics and in the ranks of the adjudicated juvenile delinquent. It is evident that the literature is inconsistent in terms of assumptions and findings on the relationship between birth order and antisocial behavior in children.

The same kinds of inconsistencies have been found in theoretical and experimental works attempting to relate birth order to intellectual attainment. First-borns have been consistently characterized as demonstrating a higher degree of intellectual attainment than laterborns (Altus, 1966a; Breland, 1973). However, in a recent review of birth order effects, Schooler (1973) questioned the existence of birth order effects in both personality attributes and intellectual attainment. The primary factors upon which he based his position were that differences between first-borns and latter-borns have not been consistently found and that the differences that have been found could be explained by the changing cultural trend toward smaller average family size. However, Breland (1973) found that, even with controls for population trends, first-borns are still over represented among National Merit Finalists. In another study Nichols (1966) found a preponderance of first-borns among 1,618 finalists in the National Merit Scholarship Competition.

A number of researchers have found that ordinal family position shows a relationship to college matriculation (Altus, 1966a; Capra and Dittes, 1962;

John Nield, Donald Ward, and Thomas Edgar, Two Interpretations of Birth Order Position, *Individual Psychologist*, 14(2), 1977, 46–53. Reprinted from the *Individual Psychologist* by permission of the publisher.

Dankin, 1964; Hall and Barger, 1964; Schachter, 1963; Warren, 1966). Bradley (1968) listed a number of psychological attributes in an attempt to explain this preponderance of first-borns on college campuses found by these researchers. Bradley also found that this tendency toward over representation of first-borns on measures of intellectual attainment begins at least as early as grade school. The first-born children included in his study of Minneapolis grade schools tended to excel in academics in excess of their proportion of the total school population and also had the most extensive vocabularies.

Although the literature appears to be contradictory as it pertains to birth order and antisocial behavior and intellectual attainment, Dreikurs (1968) attempted to explain the inconsistencies as adjustments to dethronement within the family pattern. Pepper (Nikelly, 1976), emphasizing the concept of birth order as a dynamic explanation, states that child development is not so much a result of factors which converge on the child, but the result of the child's own interpretation of these factors. What seems to be more important than chronological birth order is the interpretation the person makes of birth circumstances. Thus, at times authors seem to be referring to psychological definitions of birth order, while the researcher is investigating chronological ordinal birth position.

Method

Subjects included 54 delinquent boys from a state youth training center and 44 honor roll boys from the high school in the community at which the training center was located. The delinquent sample consisted of 15 to 18 year old males who had been adjudicated juvenile delinquent by the courts and who had been placed in the residential institution. The honor roll sample included 15 to 18 year old males who had maintained a composite grade point average of 3.5 or above on a 4.0 system at the local high school. It was decided a priori not to include subjects from single-child families. Only one delinquent male met this criterion and was not included in the study, no honor roll subject was an only child, and all other males who met the respective requirements in each setting were included in the study.

The instrument used in the study was adapted from the "Family Constellation" section of the "Guide for Initial Interviews establishing the Life Style" developed by Dreikurs (1967, p. 138). This adapted questionnaire contains questions concerning the family constellation and the description and rating of siblings and self on a ten-trait adjective checklist. Each subject completed the questionnaire,

and chronological birth order positions were determined from the subject's listing of siblings and self. Because the birth order data were neither interval in nature nor normally-distributed nonparametric statistical procedures were applied.

Results

The results of a chi square analysis of the combined chronological birth order data indicated that either delinquency or honor-roll categorization or both were not independent of chronological birth order, (2) = 9.16, p. .01. Scheffe's method of multiple contrasts for nonparametric data was applied to the data and indicated that, while honor roll categorization was independent of chronological birth order, delinquency categorization was not. Middle-born delinquent males were found to be over represented in the sample, (2) = 24, p. .01.

The second major emphasis of the study was an investigation of the relationship between honor roll and delinquent categorization and psychological birth order. A method for determining psychological birth order from the ratings of siblings and self on the ten-trait adjective checklist from the adapted instrument was devised. The definitions of psychological oldest-, middle-, and youngest-born were:

1. The psychologically oldest child is the sibling who tends to be rule-, authority-, and past-oriented. These children are protective of others and tend to be responsible for others. They may be conservative, bossy, nosy high achievers, dependable, ambitious, and have a dislike for change.
2. The psychologically second or middle child is very active, rebellious, subtle, liberally oriented, and a martyr. They are often sensitive to injustices, unfairness, feelings of being slighted, and having no place in the group.
3. The psychologically youngest child is the sibling who tends to be spoiled and is used to having their own way. They often are manipulative and may cry, have temper tantrums in order to obtain their objectives or get special service. Often the psychologically youngest children are charmers.

Two post-master's degree students, trained in both Adlerian theory and life style assessment, were trained by the principal investigator to use this method to identify the psychological birth order of each subject. The two raters had no knowledge of the honor roll or delinquent categorization of the subjects. Their initial independent ratings of the 98 sub-

TABLE 1
Comparison of Chronological and Psychological Birth Order
in Relation to Delinquent and Honor Roll Categorization

	Chronological				Psychological			
	Observed		Expected		Observed		Expected	
	n	%	n	%	n	%	n	%
Delinquent								
Oldest	10	18.5	18	33.33	6	11.1	18	33.33
Middle	35	64.8*	18	33.33	43	79.6*	18	33.33
Youngest	9	16.7	18	33.33	5	9.3	18	33.33
Honor Roll								
Oldest	17	38.6	14.7	33.33	26	59.0*	14.7	33.33
Middle	17	38.6	14.7	33.33	10	22.7	14.7	33.33
Youngest	10	22.8	14.7	33.33	8	18.2	14.7	33.33

*p .01

jects resulted in 79 agreements, 38 of the 44 honor roll subjects, r = .93, p. .01, and 44 of 54 delinquent subjects, r = .84, p. .01. The raters were then asked again to rate independently each of the subjects on which there had not been initial agreement. This second rating resulted in total agreement by both raters on all 98 subjects. A chi square analysis was then applied to the combined psychological birth order data. As with the chronological birth order data, it was found that either delinquency or honor roll categorization or both were not independent of psychological birth order, (2) = 31.54, p .01. The Scheffe method of multiple contrasts for nonparametric data indicated that there were specific differences between psychological middle-born and other two birth order positions among delinquents and between psychological oldest-borns and the other two birth order positions among honor roll students. Psychological middle-born delinquents were over represented among delinquents, (2) = 52.15, p .01, and psychological oldest-borns were over represented among honor roll students, (2) = 13.33, p .01.

Table 1 presents a visual display of the results of the chi square analyses for both chronological and psychological definitions of birth order for both delinquent and honor roll subjects. An inspection of the table reveals that, although the data did follow Adlerian theoretical assumptions for the delinquents, using chronological birth order definitions, they did not for honor roll subjects. However, both delinquent and honor roll subjects' data followed Adlerian theoretical assumptions.

Discussion and Implications

An interpretation of the results of the data from this study seems to support Adlerian theoretical assumptions, when psychological definitions of birth order are used. The psychological first-born was over represented on the intellectual attainment variable, honor roll categorization, whereas the psychological middle-born was over represented on the antisocial behavior variable, adjudicated juvenile delinquent categorization. However, the use of a chronological interpretation of birth order yielded inconsistent findings. Although a chronological interpretation of birth order effects would suggest that chronological first-borns would be over represented on the intellectual attainment variable, first borns in the study were not found to be over represented on the honor roll. Nonetheless, the chronological middle-born was over represented on the antisocial variable, adjudicated juvenile delinquent categorization, which is consistent with a chronological interpretation of the effects of birth order.

An important methodological contribution of this study was the use of two distinct psychological attributes, intellectual attainment and antisocial behavior, as dependent variables in the same quasi-experimental design. Most of the studies in the literature investigated only one dependent variable as a correlate of birth order. Thus, it has been difficult to identify the source of the inconsistent and sometimes contradictory findings, because the inconsistency could have been due to methodological differences, differences in experimenter operational definitions of birth order, or empirically valid inconsistencies in the theory.

Another important methodological contribution resulted from the consistent findings of the investigation of the relationship between birth order, using psychological definitions, and both psychological attribute variables, intellectual attainment and antisocial behavior. These findings lend support to the hypothesis that the concept of psychological birth order is a valid concept within Adlerian theory.

It was demonstrated that the use of psychological definitions of birth order is a parsimonious, reliable, and valid procedure for translating Adlerian theory into both research and practice. Graduate students were trained in the accurate and reliable use of the procedure with a minimum of time and difficulty.

Thus, the results of the study indicate that the reason for the inconsistency and contradiction in the literature on the effects of birth order on psychological variables has not been an inadequacy in the Adlerian theory nor in methodological differences among researchers. Rather, the confusion has resulted from the differences in the definitions of birth order which have been used.

Adler himself found contradictions in his observations of human behavior as it relates to birth order (Hall and Lindzey, 1967, p. 125). It is ironic that, although the major reason for Adler's break from Freud was his rejection of a biological and deterministic interpretation of human behavior and personality development, some Adlerians have continued to use a deterministic and biological factor such as chronological birth order as a major construct in their work. It is apparent that some people have not recognized the importance of Adler's statement that a person must be trained to use birth order as a psychological tool, because it is not a simple chronological definition of birth order that is important:

We have often drawn attention to the fact that before we can judge a human being we must know the situation in which he grew up. An important moment is the position which a child occupied in his family constellation. Frequently we can catalogue human beings according to this view point after we have gained sufficient expertness, and can recognize whether an individual is a first-born, an only child, the youngest child, or the like. (Adler, 1949, p. 149)

The results of the study indicate that the Adlerian construct of birth order is a valid and reliable organizing concept for understanding human behavior. It was also found that the use of a psychological interpretation of birth order is perhaps the most viable and valid way in which to operationalize the concept into practical terms. This finding is consistent with Adler's own work and recommendations and provides an explanation and solution for the past difficulties in using birth order as a research and therapeutic tool.

References

Adler, Alfred. *Understanding Human Nature.* New York: Perma Books, 1949.

Altus, W. D. Birth order and achievement. *Science,* 1966a, *152,* 1177–1184.

———. Birth order and its sequelael, *Science,* 1966b, *151,* 44–49.

Ansbacher, Heinz, L., & Ansbacher, R. R. *The Individual Psychology of Alfred Adler.* New York: Harper & Row, 1956.

Bradley, R. W. Birth order and school related behavior. *Psychological Bulletin,* 1968, *70,* 45–51.

Breland, H. M. Birth order effects: A reply to Schooler. *Psychological Bulletin,* 1973, *80,* 210–212.

Capra, P. C., & Dittes, J. E. Birth order as a selective factor among volunteer subjects. *Journal of Abnormal and Social Psychology,* 1962, *64,* 302.

Dankin, D. G. *An Introduction to KSU Students.* Unpublished report, Kansas State University, Student Counseling Center, September, 1964.

Dreikurs, Rudolf. *Psychology in the Classroom* (2nd ed.). New York: Harper & Row, 1968.

Hall, E., & Barger, B. Background data and expected activities of entering lower division students. *Mental Health Project Bulletin,* 7, University of Florida, May, 1964.

Hall, Calvin S., & Lindzey, Gardner. *Theories of Personality* (2nd ed.). New York: John Wiley & Sons, Inc., 1967.

Nichols, R. C. The origin and development of talent. *National Merit Scholarship Reports,* 1966, *2,* No. 10, Evanston, Illinois: National Merit Scholarship Corporation (Mimeo).

Nikelly, Arthur G. *Techniques for Behavior Change.* Springfield: Charles P. Thomas, 1976.

Rosen, B. C. Family struction and achievement motivation. *American Sociological Review,* August 1961, *30,* 574–584.

Rosenow, C. & Whyte, Anne H. The ordinal position of problem children. *American Journal of Orthopsychiatry,* 1931, *1,* 430–444.

Schachter, S. Birth order, eminence, and higher education. *American Sociological Review,* October, 1963, *2,* 757–768.

Schooler, C. Birth order effects: Not here, not now! *Psychological Bulletin,* 1972, *78,* 161–175.

Sletto, R. F. Sibling position and juvenile delinquency. *American Journal of Sociology,* 1934, *39,* 687–699.

Toman, W. *Family Constellations.* New York: Springer, 1969.

Warren, J. R. Birth order and social behavior. *Psychological Bulletin,* 1966, *65,* 38–49.

Early Recollections as a Projective Technique: A Review of Some Recent Validation Studies

Jane A. Taylor

Mosak (1958) reviewed much of the literature dealing with early childhood recollections (ERs) and discussed the interpretation and application of ERs as a projective technique according to the theory of Adler's Individual Psychology. This article examines some of the more recent research directly related to the projective use of ERs.

According to Adler (1937) a person's

early recollections are found always to have a bearing on the central interests of that person's life. Early recollections give us hints and clues which are most valuable to follow when attempting the task of finding the direction of a person's striving. They are most helpful in revealing what one regards as values to be aimed for and what one senses as dangers to be avoided. They help us to see the kind of world which a particular person feels he is living in, and the ways he really found of meeting that world. They illuminate the origins of the style of life. The basic attitudes which have guided an individual throughout his life and which prevail, likewise, in his present situation, are reflected in those fragments which he has selected to epitomize his feeling about life, and to cherish in his memory as reminders. He has preserved these as his early recollections (p. 287).

Thus, whatever a person may select to remember from his childhood is related to the individual's present fundamental view of life and can be used projectively to assist in understanding his repetitive behavior patterns, his evaluation of himself and his world, and his role in the world (Kadis, 1958; Mosak, 1958, 1965).

Since Adler first discussed his view of the significant role of ERs, little interest had been shown among therapists and counselors outside of Adlerian circles regarding the diagnostic/projective usefulness of ERs until the last fifteen years. Prior interest in ERs generally seemed to be according to Freud's (1956) beliefs about ERs being concealing memories rather than Adler's (1937) view that ERs are revealing memories—though both men felt that the memory is selective.

M. G. Lieberman (1957) reported a study designed to test the hypotheses that there is a significant correspondence between the material revealed in ERs and other projective data. Her sample was composed of eleven psychotic and eleven non-psychotic females who were each administered a full test battery consisting of the Wechsler-Bellevue, Rorschach, Bender-Gestalt, and House-Tree-Person drawings. Each subject's ERs were also solicited and the following questions asked: What is the earliest incident that you can remember in which your mother was involved?—your father?" The subject's ERs were then given to the experimenter along with the ages of the subjects. The experimenter wrote reports on each subject based only on her memories while the staff psychologist composed reports based on the findings of the test battery. The two reports for each subject were then compared using a checklist of descriptive items to evaluate personality traits (such as Perception of the Environment: Threatening Physically, Threatening Emotionally, or Friendly). Each item, according to Lieberman, was previously chosen and then specifically defined in order to eliminate as much ambiguity as possible. Though Lieberman's sample was small, she obtained significant results in terms of the presence of more agreement than disagreement in relation to the type of material revealed in the psychological reports based on a projective test battery as compared to the reports based on the ERs (t = .65, P < .001). She also found a significant correlation (R = .66, P < .001) between the amount of information elicited from ERs and that obtained from the psychological report though, of course, more information was obtained from the psychological report. Thus, Lieberman concluded that

Jane Taylor, Early Recollections as a Projective Technique: A Review of Some Recent Validation Studies, *Journal of Individual Psychology*, 31(2), 1975, 213–218. Reprinted from the *Journal of Individual Psychology* with permission of the author and publishers.

EKs may serve as a rapid valuable sample of the type of data likely to be obtained from the longer time consuming projective test battery examinations. Differences in memory content distribution between the psychotic and non-psychotic groups were noted though no statistical analysis was done because of the small sample size.

In another attempt to validate the projective use of the ER technique, McCarter, Tomkins, and Schiffman (1961) examined the use of ER characteristics to predict performance on a variety of the Tomkins-Horn Picture Arrangement Test scales. The Tomkins-Horn protocols of 75 male university students were compared to predicted Tomkins-Horn performances estimated from each subject's ER. The authors concluded that results obtained from the comparison, indicated ERs to be a valid method of personality appraisal specifically in the areas of degree of activity, including work, and social interest. The authors were not able to validate ER prediction of optimism-pessimism.

Based on the assumption that the ERs of a patient should bear some relationship to his current neurotic symptoms, the ERs should be of diagnostic value according to Jackson and Sechrest (1962). This assumption is essentially the same as the one on which the two preceding studies were based. In this study the authors examined the following hypotheses:

1. ERs of patients suffering from anxiety reaction will show obvious fear.
2. Depressed patients will give memories of abandonment.
3. Obsessive-compulsive patients will recall strong prohibitions.
4. The ERs of patients with gastrointestinal disorders, such as ulcers and colitis, will concern gastrointestinal distress.

The results reported by the authors indicate that though the absolute frequencies of the themes were too low to have import for differential diagnosis, more than the other groups the ERs of anxiety neurotics were characterized by themes of fear, depressed patients by themes of abandonment, and gastrointestinal sufferers by themes of gastrointestinal distress—these findings are in accord with hypotheses 1, 3, and 4. Jackson and Sechrest also reported finding that themes of sex were more frequent among the obsessive-compulsives, and themes of illness, accident, and trauma were more frequent among the anxiety neurotics and gastrointestinal sufferers and the group of normals who were included for comparison purposes. In conclusion, the authors found that the neurotics as a whole had more unpleasant ERs than the normal group; however, the four neurotic categories did not differ significantly among themselves in the pleasantness of their ERs.

Hypothesizing that (a) experiences of success and failure will not significantly influence ERs, although they will influence Thematic Apperception Test (TAT) stories, and (b) experiences of hostility and friendliness will not significantly influence ERs, although they will significantly influence TAT stories, Hedvig (1963) conducted two experiments and analyzed the results for thematic content of the ERs and TAT stories. In order to test the hypotheses, 360 subjects were randomly assigned to one of twelve experimental conditions which were: ERs or TAT stories written by subjects (1) after experience of success, failure, or neutral experience (a total of six conditions), or (2) after experience of friendliness, hostility, or neutral experience (a total of six conditions). Analyses of variance of pleasantness ratings assigned by subjects to TAT stories and ERs indicated no significant differences as a result of the major experimental conditions. The x^2 analysis of the thematic content for the success-failure experiment showed that only the need-achievement theme significantly differentiated the various experimental conditions for the TAT stories; the experimental conditions did not differentiate the ER groups. In the friendliness-hostility experiment, thematic analysis showed significant differences in the TAT groups for hostility and aggression, and unhappiness; no significant thematic differences were found between the ER groups. Hedvig concluded that she had at least partially confirmed her hypotheses that experiences of success-failure and friendliness-hostility significantly influence TAT stories but not ERs. She felt that this demonstrated greater stability of ERs than TAT stories.

E. D. Ferguson (1964) published an article dealing with her research on the use of ERs for assessing life styles and diagnosing psychopathology. She demonstrated that life style summaries based on ERs are reliably communicable to a wide range of professional workers by having ten clinicians (Adlerian, eclectic, Freudian) match life style summaries written by three of the Adlerian clinicians on the basis of ERs collected from 30 subjects (10 psychotics, 10 neurotics, 10 normals) to ER records. Of the total number of matchings attempted by the clinicians, all but one were found to be significantly better than chance. In terms of the ability of the clinicians to make valid diagnoses of psychopathology from ERs none were able to make diagnoses better than chance. Ferguson suggested this inability to make accurate diagnoses of psychopathology on the basis of

ERs can be explained by the fact that on the whole Adlerians consider knowledge of life style insufficient to make such predictions; that is, Adlerians feel that only the interaction of a given life style with a given set of environmental circumstances (a crises, for example) leads to psychopathology (p. 410), not the life style alone.

Hedvig (1965) reported a study investigating the extent to which three Adlerian clinicians could determine from the ERs of 51 elementary and high school students whether they had been diagnosed by a clinical team as cases of psychoneurosis or as cases of adjustment reaction, conduct disturbance. When the data were subjected to x^2 analysis, the combined results were significant at the .001 level of confidence, though taken separately, the abilities of the judges individually differed widely. When the diagnoses of the judges were correlated, the highest correlation was only .11, even though the correlations computed between the diagnoses of each of the three clinicians with those of the clinic were .70, .32, and .08, the first two of which were found to be significant at the .01 and .05 levels of confidence. Hedvig's results indicate that on the basis of ERs alone, experienced Adlerian clinicians can make accurate diagnostic judgments only to a limited extent—and that appears to be dependent upon the ability of the individual clinician. Her findings do suggest the usefulness of ERs as part of a battery of projective tests or as an aid in the formulation of an individual life style.

Summary

Since the publication of Mosak's (1958) article, interest in the projective usefulness of ERs has grown among therapists and counselors. Six articles specifically dealing with attempts to establish the validity and reliability of the diagnostic/projective use of ERs have been summarized here. The results of these articles lend support to the use of the ER as a diagnostic/projective technique in that:

1. ERs may serve as a rapid, valuable sample of the type of data likely to be obtained from the longer time consuming projective test battery examinations (Lieberman, 1957; Hedvig, 1965).
2. ERs may serve as a valid method of personality appraisal, specifically in the areas of degree of activity, including work, and social interest (McCarter, Tomkins & Schiffman, 1961).
3. There appear to be some thematic differences among ERs produced by subjects diagnosed as

belonging to several neurotic categories (Jackson & Sechrest, 1962).
4. There is evidence to suggest that ERs are not influenced by situations of success or failure, hostility or friendliness, and thus are more stable than TAT stories which do appear to be influenced by such situations (Hedvig, 1963).
5. Life style summaries based on ERs are reliably communicable to a wide range of professional workers (Ferguson, 1964). On the other hand however, information obtained from ERs only does not appear to be adequate for valid diagnosis of psychopathology for most clinicians (Ferguson, 1964; Hedvig, 1965) nor for the prediction of optimism-pessimism (McCarter, Tomkins & Schiffman, 1961).

The results of these studies are far from conclusive, but they are encouraging. It is hoped that during the next decade, we will see the appearance of more conclusive evidence in support of what seems to be a valuable clinical tool.

References

Adler, A. Significance of early recollections. *International Journal of Individual Psychology*, 1937, *3*, 283–287.

Ferguson, E. D. The use of early recollections for assessing life style and diagnosing psychopathology. *Journal of Projective Techniques and Personality Assessment*, 1964, *28*, 403–412.

Freud, S. *Psychopathology in everyday life.* (A. A. Brill, trans.). New York: The New American Library, 1956.

Hedvig, E. B. Stability of early recollections and thematic apperception stories. *Journal of Individual Psychology*, 1963, *19*, 49–54.

Hedvig, E. B, Childhood and early recollections as basis for diagnosis. *Journal of Individual Psychology*, 1965, *21*, 187–188.

Jackson, M., & Sechrest, L. Early recollections in four neurotic diagnostic categories. *Journal of Individual Psychology*, 1962, *18*, 52–56.

Kadis, A. L. Early childhood recollections as aids in group psychotherapy. *Journal of Individual Psychology*, 1958, *14*, 182–187.

Lieberman, M. G. Childhood memories as a projective technique. *Journal of Projective Techniques and Personality Assessment*, 1957, *21*, 32–36.

McCarter, R. E., Tomkins, S. S., & Schiffman, H. M. Early recollections as predictors of the Tomkins-Horn Picture Arrangement Test Performance. *Journal of Individual Psychology*, 1961, *17*, 177–180.

Mosak, H. Early recollections as a projective technique. *Journal of Projective Techniques and Personality Assessment*, 1958, *22*, 302–311.

Mosak, H. Predicting the relationship to the psychotherapist from early recollections. *Journal of Individual Psychology*, 1965, *21*, 77–81.

Statistical Evaluation of Attributes in Adlerian Life Style Forms

Mary Louise O'Phelan

Adler felt that one's lifestyle was formulated and established by 5 years of age and that, because of inexperience and lack of judgment, the child will make wrong assumptions of what the world of reality is all about. Man sees all his personal problems from a perspective that is his own creation—his own style of life (Beecher Beecher, 1971). Individuals differ in life style; each life style is characteristic for him alone. Apparent contradictions in the same person form part of a consistent mode of behavior which is apparent if we know their goal. With regard to man in particular, Alfred Adler (1958) declared that the way to understand one's behavior and actions is to know one's goal. Man does not merely react, rather he adopts an individual attitude based on the impressions formed in early childhood. The meaning given to life, goal pursued, style of approach, and emotional disposition are all fixed. They can be changed only if one becomes free from the mistakes involved in childhood perceptions of the surrounding world.

What is a life style? It has been postulated by Adler as being the sum total of attitudes, goals and beliefs the child develops in his attempt to find a place for himself. For Adler, life style represented the organismic idea of the individual as an actor rather than a *reactor*; of the purposiveness, goal directedness, unity, self-consistency and uniqueness of the individual, and of the ultimately subjective determinaton of his actions (Ansbacher, 1967).

On the other hand, life style inventories refer to a format of questions used by the Adlerian counselor which enable him to see the client's "central convictions which, to oversimplify, describe how he views himself in relation to his view of life" (Mosak, 1972, p. 232). Gushurst (1971) seems to summarize the dual meaning of life style when he comments that,

on the one hand, it refers to the complex construct deeply embedded in the Adlerian theory of personality, on the other, it describes a very concrete formulation made by a particular psychologist, using a particular individual's answers to a standardized set of questions. (p. 30)

Some Adlerians who do a formal analysis of a client's life style collect information concerning his family constellation—birth order, sibling relationships, achievements and deficiencies, parent-child relationships, and family climate. To understand his current outlooks and goals, the client's early recollections are interpreted. The goal of the projective diagnostic activity is to elicit the pattern of living—the life style (Mosak, 1972).

The client's whole life plan and pattern of behavior is founded on his private logic. It is within the private logic that the client forms his goals and it is these goals that explain his behavior. The client's private logic is not based on a psychological cause-and-effect relationship, rather it is primarily dependent upon and consistent with his goals and intentions. Maladjustment in individuals is often understood through their goals of which they are unaware (Nikelly, 1971). The information obtained while doing a formal life style inventory helps the counselor recognize the goal toward which the client is moving and understand the private logic which motivates the client to act. To understand a person is to recognize the goals he has set for himself. All movement in the psychic life is goal directed. This is the teleological stand of Individual Psychology (Wexberg, 1929/1970).

As early as 1907, Alfred Adler published a format of life style questions designed for therapeutic interview. This questionnaire was written in German

Mary Louise O'Phelan, "Statistical Evaluation of Attributes in Adlerian Life Style Forms," *Journal of Individual Psychology,* November 1977, pp. 203–212. Reprinted by permission of the author and publisher.

and translated into English in 1917. Other English translations of Adler's life style questionnaire appear in his book *Social Interest* (1939/1964, pp. 299–307) and is later reprinted by his daughter Alexandra Adler in *Guiding Human Misfits* (1948, pp. 83–85). Erwin Wexberg (1929/1970) who was associated with Adler at least as early as 1914 also published a set of questions relating to life style which was revised and annotated by Bernard Shulman (Wexburg, 1929/1970, p. 33). In 1954 Dreikurs published a parsimonious life style format which is similar to one used by many Adlerians. Harold Mosak and Bernard Shulman were associated with Dreikurs at this time, and later a hypothesis was set forth by Mosak and Shulman (1971) stating that the self-ratings or attribute section of the life style format could be placed in six separate categories, i.e., *achievement, social proprieties, gender, interpersonal mechanics, right-wrong* and *posture.* Categories can be helpful in evaluation rather than treating each of 37 attributes separately. These categories are useful, yet there is no published statistical evaluation of their validity. However, it must be recognized that this information is evaluated in the context of the total life style form which includes questions concerning family constellation, attributes (self and sibling ratings), sibling interrelationships, description of parents, physical development, social development, sexual development, school and career, dreams and early recollections. It must also be noted that the subject compares self to siblings rather than using self as an absolute standard.

This research was designed to test statistically Mosak and Shulman's hypothesis with the hope of opening the door to further statistical analysis of the life style format. The following hypotheses were formulated by the author to serve as the basis of this research:

1. Mosak's assumption that the life style instrument's "attributes" tend to cluster together to compromise specific "syndromes"; i.e., achievement, social proprieties, gender, right-wrong, personal mechanics and posture, may be statistically validated with factor analysis.
2. Males and females show categorical differences which may reflect the distinctive socialization process of each sex in America.
3. Birth order groups (using only first and second children) perceive themselves in the family atmosphere according to their position in the family. People in each birth order group view themselves differently, and this is reflected in their self ratings.

4. A victim typology was compared to a control group of other Adlerian typologies. (This form of typing was developed by Mosak and Shulman *after* Dreikurs and Adler.) It was hypothesized that victims perceive themselves in a manner which is congruent with their goals and this is reflected in self ratings.

Method

Subjects. 315 subjects were randomly obtained from a clinician's files which contained the Minnesota form of life style inventory, Twenty were discarded because the attribute *height* was not filled in; 21 were discarded because they were given the new form which lacked the word *competitive*, making 36 attributes instead of 37 listed on the other form. In addition, the order was not the same, making it impossible to use these data. Thirty more life styles were discarded because two or more attributes were not filled in, leaving a sample of 144 (68 males and 76 females).

From ths pool of subjects, three birth order groups were obtained: only child (6 males, 12 females), first child (14 males, 12 females), and second child (8 males, 10 females). First and second children had no more than a 3-year maximum age difference between sibings, which is suggested by Mosak (1972) as the criteria to be used to evaluate characteristics associated with each birth order group, i.e., if there is a 5-year span between first and second child, we can assume that the first child will most likely have the characteristics of an only child. This same pool of subjects provided a selection of typologies using *victim* as a group (12 males, 9 females) and a control group (11 males, 10 females) consisting of other typologies including: the getter, the person who must be superior, the person who needs to be liked, the baby, the person who craves excitement, the pleasure seeker, and the martyr. (The martyr can be distinguished from the victim in his moral righteousness. His goal is to suffer and thus enable himself and evaluate himself above all others. On the other hand, the victim sees life as abusive and full of suffering but does not realize that he often provokes his own downfall.) The experimental and control groups used in this study were obtained by the life style interpretation of the clinician who had provided the files which were used for this project. The early recollection section of the life style questionnaire, rather than the attributes, were used as the basis of analysis since questioning for early recollections is a standard procedure used for determining life style.

Instruments. The first two pages of the Minnesota life style evaluation forms were used. The first page contained information regarding the family constellation, including birth order and number of brothers and sisters. The second page asked for ratings of self and siblings on 37 attributes. The order and number of attributes listed by the Adlerian Institute of Minnesota may differ slightly from other forms.

Data Analysis. A priniciple components analysis with a Varimax rotation was run on the 144 pieces of data asking for six factors in keeping with Mosak and Shulman's original hypothesis of six categories. The items were keyed in the following order; High = 3, Medium = 2, Low = 1. Scores were obtained for each clustering of attributes which characterized the six factors by using the sum of the ratings across all of the items in each of the factors. The data was then analyzed for hypothesized differences between male and female, birth order groups, and typologies.

Results

Hypothesis 1. Hypothesis 1 states that Mosak and Shulman's assumption of six categories of attributes will cluster into six factors. This hypothesis was statistically analyzed and supported. Tables 1 and 2 indicate that Mosak and Shulman's original hypothesis and six factors obtained are similar. Factor 1 corresponds to Mosak and Shulman's achievement category. Factor 2 is similar to social proprieties, factor 3 conforms to the gender category and indicates a masculine definition (i.e., positive weightings for masculine, physical strength, athletic, and height). Factor 4 resembles the right-wrong category which keyed to socially unacceptable behavior. Factor 5 parallels interpersonal mechanics, and factor 6 conforms to the final category of posture.

Hypothesis 2. Hypothesis 2 states that males and females show categorical differences which may reflect the distinctive socialization process in America. The findings were not in the expected direction. Table 3 represents means and standard deviations of factor scores for males and females. A two-tailed analysis of variance for each group indicates that Hypothesis 2 is supported. On Factor 1 (achievement) females scored higher than males ($P<.05$). Females scored higher on the attributes included in Factor 1: intelligence, grades in school, competitive, standards of achievements, standards of right-wrong, conformed, and idealistic. On Factor 3 (gender) females scored higher than males

TABLE 1

Six Categories of Attributes Proposed by Mosak and Shulman (1971)

Achievement	Right-Wrong
Intelligence	Obedient
Grades	Made mischief
Industrious	Openly rebellious
Standards of achievement	Covertly rebellious
Lived up to standards	Standards of right-wrong
Helpful at home	Proper
Looks	Fair
Talents	Critical of others
Handicaps	Critical of self

Social Proprieties	Posture
Charm	Idealistic
Pleasing	Materialistic
Cheerful	Loner
Considerate	Persistent
Selfish	Gave up
Sociable	Methodical
Cheerful	Neat
	Excitement maker
Interpersonal Mechanics	Complainer
	Responsible
Assertive	Got others to do it
Bossy	Did it himself
Demanded way	Withdrawn
Got way	Chip on shoulder
Sense of humor	Punished
Temper	
Started fights	**Gender**
Shy	
Sulks	Athletic
Stubborn	Feminine
Sensitive — easily hurt	Masculine
	Looks
	Daring

($P<.05$). This factor is masculine and indicates that these female clinical subjects scored higher than males on the following attributes: physical strength, masculine, athletic, and height. They scored lower than males on the attribute feminine. On Factor 4 (right-wrong) females tended to score higher than males ($P<.10$), although it is keyed toward misbehavior. The females' higher score on Factor 4 indicates that they rated themselves higher than males on the attributes: openly rebelled, selfish, complained, temper tantrums, demanded way, and mischievous. They scored lower

TABLE 2
"Attributes"—Varimax Rotated Factor Matric after Rotation with Kaiser Normalization

Factor 1 (Achievement)

+ intelligence	.75
+ grades in school	.72
+ competitive	.52
+ standards of achievement	.71
+ stds of right and wrong	.55
+ conformed	.41
+ idealistic	.46

Factor 2 (Social Proprieties)

+ used charm	.61
+ demanded way	.62
+ got way	.76
+ spoiled	.67
+ looks	.45
− punished	.41

Factor 3 (Gender)

+ physical strength	.63
+ masculine	.81
− feminine	.80
+ athletic	.48
+ height	.40

Factor 4 (Right-Wrong)

− conformed	.55
+ openly rebelled	.61
+ selfish	.53
+ complained	.56
+ temper tantrums	.67
− standards of behavior	.57
+ demanded way	.48
− tried to please others	.40
+ mischievous	.43

Factor 5 (Personal Mechanics)

+ sensitive − easily hurt	.65
+ felt sorry for self	.75
− sense of humor	.58
+ tried to please others	.49
− number of friends	.43

Factor 6 (Posture)

+ hard worker	.62
+ helped around the house	.71
+ considerate	.56
+ materialistic	.56
+ standards of achievement	.40

The attribute *critical of others* did not show up with a .40 or more loading in any category.

than males on: conformed, standards of behavior, and tried to please others (attributes with a negative loading on Factor 4).

Hypothesis 3. Hypothesis 3, stating that people in different birth order groups view themselves differently and will therefore respond differently to self-ratings, received some support. A one-way analysis of variance was run on birth order data using *only* child, first child, and second child groups with six factors. Factor 4 (right-wrong) indicated that *only* children were scoring higher in this category than first or second children (P<.05). This finding is in keeping with the factor attributed to *only* children as stated by Pepper (1971, p. 50). The *only* child answered higher than first and second children to the attributes included in Factor 4, which include: openly rebelled, selfish, complained, temper tantrums, demanded way, and mischievous. The *only* child scored lower in the following charateristics: conformed, standards of behavior, and tried to please others (attributes which had negative loadings on Factor 4).

Hypothesis 4. Hypothesis 4, stating that individuals categorized into different Adlerian typologies perceive themselves in a manner which is congruent with their goals and is reflected in their self ratings, received slight support. The *victim* and control group of other Adlerian typologies were compared. A one-way analysis of variance run on these data indicated a .10 probability level approaching significance between the victim and control group on Factor 4 (personal mechanics). The attributes included in this category are said to be characteristic of the victim typology. The victim scored higher than the control group in sensitive-easily hurt, felt sorry for self, and tried to please others. They scored lower in sense of humor and number of friends.

Discussion

The results support Mosak and Sulman's hypothesis that the 37 attributes on Adlerian life style forms falls into six distinct categories. These categories can have value to the clinician for interpreting the attribute section of life style forms.

TABLE 3
Male-Female Differences on Factor Scores

Factor 1 (Achievement)

	X	Standard Deviation
male	15.544	1.904
female	15.145	1.703

F = 3.085 P < .05**

Factor 2 (Social Proprieties)

	X	Standard Deviation
male	15.559	1.856
female	15.645	1.944

F = .504 P < .47

Factor 3 (Gender)

	X	Standard Deviation
male	9.632	1.554
female	10.145	1.208

F = 4.395 P < .03**

Factor 4 (Right-Wrong)

	X	Standard Deviation
male	19.379	1.902
female	19.842	1.826

F = 3.572 P < .06

Factor 5 (Interpersonal Mechanics)

	X	Standard Deviation
male	12.412	1.261
female	12.276	1.694

F = .580 P < .44

Factor 6 (Posture)

	X	Standard Deviation
male	10.618	1.639
female	10.974	1.177

F = 1.928 P < .16

N — Male 68

Female 76

**significant P < .05

Instead of using 37 separate attributes as a basis of analysis in the self rating section of the life style form, we can observe categories of behavior which refer to certain aspects of personality.

Males and females in this sample exhibited differences in self ratings which were opposite of characteristics usually manifested in each sex. Males answered low in achievement; low on gender (which was masculine) and low in right-wrong, which is keyed to mischievous behavior, while the females scored high in these same categories. The fact that a clinical group was used for this evaluation might generate such questions as: Do we state that many who are going for clinical help have a sexual identity problem? Or, are they merely people who refuse to cooperate with the socialization process of each particular sex and feel guilty because they are not the "same" as others? Perhaps these differences depend on whether the subject rated self in comparison to a male or female. Nevertheless, questions such as these could form the basis of future hypotheses to be tested with this same set of self ratings using a nonclinical group.

One dimension showed differences which can be said to be a result of the child's place in the family. *Only* children differed on Factor 4 (right-wrong), which is in keeping with the characteristics attributed to only children. A profile emerged of a child who is pampered, enjoys his position as center of interest, wants his own way, and is interested only in himself, although we must consider the fact that these data were obtained from clinical files and these characteristics may not be so prevalent in the general population of only children. Perhaps larger groups of *each* child category should be observed on self ratings for more significant findings between groups. More work should be done in this area using a uniform spacing between children so that all research would refer to the same birth order groups. A defined set of characteristics, as stated by Mosak (1972), could enable birth order research to stabilize into consistent findings for each group.

The typology findings between victim and control group approach significance on Factor 4 (interpersonal mechanics), which would be an expected outcome, considering the probable behavior associated with this typology.

These findings only take into account the attribute section of the life style questionnaire. The entire life style form could be statistically evaluated for ease in analysis by the clinician. Since life style assessment is a holistic approach, the interaction of examiner administering the test to the client opens the door to different dynamics which provide clues to the examinee's personality. These clues do not manifest themselves in objective procedures. Nevertheless, statistically defined guidelines could be developed that would be an asset to basic interpretation of life style forms. Perhaps this type of research will stimulate more interest in this area that will result in providing the clinician an aid in the interpretation of life style forms.

References

Adler, A. *Guiding human misfits.* New York: Philosophical Library, 1948

Adler, A. [*Social interest: A challenge to mankind*] (J. Linton and R. Vaughn, Trans.). New York: Capricorn Books, 1964. (Originally published, 1939.)

Adler, A. *What life should mean to you.* New York: Capricorn Books, 1958.

Ansbacher, H. Lifestyle: A historical and systematic review. *Journal of Individual Psychology*, 1967, *23*, 191–212.

Beecher, M., and Beecher, W. *The mark of Cain: An anatomy of jealousy.* New York: Harper & Row, 1971.

Gushurst, R. S. The technique, utility and validity of lifestyle analysis. *The Counseling Psychologist*, 1971, *3*(1), 30–39.

Mosak, H. H. Life style assessment: A demonstration focused on family constellation. *Journal of Individual Psychology*, 1972, *28*, 232–247.

Mosak, H. H., and Shulman, B. H. *Life Style Inventory.* Chicago: Alfred Adler Institute of Chicago, 1971.

Nikelly, A. G. Private logic. In A. G. Nikelly (Ed.), *Techniques for behavior change.* Springfield, Ill.: Charles C. Thomas, 1971.

Pepper, F. C. Birth order. In A. G. Nikelly (Ed.), *Techniques for behavior change.* Springfield, Ill.: Charles C. Thomas, 1971.

Wexburg, E.[*Individual psychological treatment*] (Rev. and trans. by B. H. Shulman). Chicago: Alfred Adler Institute of Chicago, 1970. (Originally published, 1929.)

A Factor Analytic Consideration of Life Style Data

John D. West
Donald L. Bubenzer

Adlerian Psychology has been accused (Thorne, 1975) of having fewer studies concerned with theory validation than any other system of psychology. Thorne also submits that Adlerian theory has not received the research validation it deserves. This was suggested in light of growing clinical evidence indicating the value of Adlerian theory. The idiographic foundation of Adlerian Psychology has complicated research efforts (Mosak & Dreikurs, 1974).

Although Adler stressed the uniqueness of his patients, he nevertheless recognized similarities among individuals and their life styles (Ansbacher & Ansbacher, 1956). Mosak and Dreikurs (O'Phelan, Note 1) hypothesized that the self ratings on the attribute section of the life style format could be divided into six categories. Several Adlerians (Brown, 1976; Kefir & Corsini, 1974; Mosak, 1972) have, at a theoretical level, described behaviors associated with commonly observed life styles. Dewey (1972) also presented 13 examples of differing family atmospheres. Adlerians, in their consideration of personality variables, have searched for patterns, common themes or clusters. The present study focused on discerning those factors contributing to significant variance of life style data.

Method

The 400 subjects in this study, 200 males and 200 females, were students enrolled in undergraduate courses at Idaho State University. Approximately 75% of the subjects were enrolled in social science or education, while the remainder were students in a vocational technical program.

The Self-Administering Life Style Inventory (SALSI) developed for this study was administered to the subjects. Inventory construction utilized the following procedure:

1. Item selection attended to questions clinicians frequently asked during a life style assessment in that each item statement reflected one of the general categories outlined in Mosak and Shulman's *Life Style Inventory* (1971).

2. A large number of items relevant to the *Life Style Inventory* were initially considered. Through discussion with colleagues, the number of items was reduced prior to a pilot study.

3. Following the pilot study, which involved 31 Introduction to Education students, the SALSI was further reduced to 137 items. Six items related to physical development were sex biased and eliminated. After each item, bipolar distractors of "Most-Least," "Highest-Lowest" or "True-False" were presented.

4. The early recollections section of the inventory described a procedure for having subjects write three memories. Two trained judges then read the memories and responded to items on the inventory.

5. The reliability of the SALSI was established by a test/retest method involving 19 women and 13 men who consented to retake the instrument at the end of a 2-week interval. Test/retest reliability utilizing the Pearson r was .81. The Pearson r for interrater reliability for judgments of early recollections was .78. Both reliability coefficients were significant at the .01 level.

John D. West and Donald L. Bubenzer, "A Factor Analytic Consideration of Life Style Data," *Journal of Individual Psychology,* May 1978, pp. 48–55. Reprinted by permission of the authors and publisher.

Through the use of factor analysis, an attempt was made to delineate various themes which existed among self-reported data from the SALSI. In an exploratory study of this type, it seemed appropriate to specify the following questions as opposed to stating hypotheses:

1. Are factors obtained when data from the inventory are factor analyzed interpretable using Adlerian theory?

2. How many "Adlerian" factors does the factor analysis of the inventory specify?

An item-by-item matrix of phi coefficients (IBM, 1970) was established for the SALSI, the factor vectors were extracted, and a varimax rotation of the factor matrix described variable loadings on each factor. Eleven iterations were completed before the maximum change in communality estimates was less than 0.001. Cattell's scree test (Child, 1973) was used to decide how many factors should be extracted for analysis. In obtaining a criterion for significant factor loadings ±0.3 (Child, 1973) was used.

Results

The purpose of this study was to determine those factors contributing to significant variance of life style data. A factor analysis indicated the existence of seven factors contributing significantly to variance explained on the SALSI instrument. The seven factors accounted for the following percentages of SALSI variance: Factor I—6.1%, Factor II—5.24%, Factor III—3.95%, Factor IV—3.03%, Factor V—3.03%, Factor VI—2.04%, and Factor VII—1.83%. The seven factors and their cumulative variance are presented in Table 1

Discussion and Conclusion

Results of this study indicate added construct validity for Adlerian life style theory, as the following discussion of the factors attests:

Factor I lends support to the Adlerian (Shulman & Nikelly, 1972) emphasis on the parents' relationship. The accord or discord between the parents sets the atmosphere for the entire family, and it also gives the child his first and most vivid impression of the relations between the sexes

Table 1
Factors Found to Account for Significant Variance of Life Style Data on SALSI

Factor	No. Items	Cumulative Variance	Loading
1. Family Atmosphere As Presented By The Parents (06.1%)			
(101)	My father tried to please my mother.		.72154
(116)	My parents functioned smoothly together.		.69915
(113)	My parents discussed their work and interests together.		.66385
(112)	My parents did a number of fun things together.		.60708
(90)	My father showed interest in what I was doing.		.59952
(115)	My parents would encourage each other in individual interests.		.58063
(65)	My father spent quite a bit of time with the family.		.56826
(79)	My father was understanding.		.55576
(103)	My father tried to avoid having problems with my mother.		.51224
(114)	My parents were openly affectionate towards each other.		.50166
(109)	My parents agreed on child rearing procedures.		.49914
(88)	My father had a high sense of right and wrong.		.49482
(92)	My father trusted me.		.45062
(108)	My parents had the same ambitions for their children.		.36788
(77)	My father was a hard worker.		.36691
(105)	My father tried to put my mother down.		−.58469
(111)	My parents would argue rather often.		−.51168
(87)	My father was critical of others.		−.32319

Table 1.—*Continued*

2. Excitement Seeking (11.3%)

(12)	Openly rebellious.	.68975
(28)	Tended to get mad.	.62742
(11)	Made mischief.	.62435
(29)	Tended to get in fights.	.59272
(30)	Chip on shoulder.	.53082
(32)	Stubborn.	.50845
(14)	Punished.	.47715
(6)	Daring.	.45259
(26)	Demanded way.	.43432
(25)	Bossy.	.42663
(40)	Excitement seeker.	.34601
(31)	Sulked.	.30736
(10)	Obedient.	−.65103
(24)	Considerate.	−.38518
(20)	Pleasing.	−.37744

3. Involvement (15.3%)

(39)	Withdrawn.	.68313
(33)	Shy.	.62895
(54)	I tended not to jump into new social situations spontaneously.	.47609
(34)	Sensitive and easily hurt.	.39422
(56)	Among my friends, I was frequently a leader.	−.30120
(22)	Sociable.	−.57115
(51)	It was easy to make friends.	−.54946

4. Conformity In School (18.3%)

(46)	I usually do well in my school work.	.71097
(2)	Grades in school.	.65267
(1)	Intelligence.	.55410
(41)	I felt at ease and comfortable in my classes.	.46908
(50)	Spelling was one of my favorite subjects.	.39292
(47)	I often left my school work unfinished.	−.72161
(42)	I would often copy another student's work in order to do better.	−.38907
(43)	I frequently refused to do what my teachers wanted.	−.37415

5. Family Atmosphere As Presented By The Mother (20.9%)

(83)	My mother was understanding.	.68794
(98)	My mother was easygoing.	.47846
(93)	My mother trusted me.	.47954
(91)	My mother showed interest in what I was doing.	.46720
(82)	My mother had many friends.	.31847
(84)	My mother tended to get mad.	−.52067
(86)	My mother was critical of others.	−.45771

6. Gender (22.9%)

(8)	Feminine.	.63492
(9)	Masculine.	−.77992
(6)	Daring.	−.50452
(5)	Athletic.	−.47601
(40)	Excitement seeker.	−.43711
(18)	Easy going.	−43411
(23)	Sense of humor.	−.37114
(11)	Made mischief.	−.34195

7. Family Atmosphere As Presented By The Father (24.8%)

(95)	My mother punished me more than my father did.	.67395
(99)	My father was easygoing.	.52399
(94)	My father punished me more than my mother did.	−.75797
(61)	My father was strict.	−.47744
(85)	My father tended to get mad.	−.43721

(Dreikurs, 1958). Adler (1969) indicated the significant position of father as in Factor I, saying, "His mysterious comings and goings arouse the interest of the child much more than the constant presence of a mother" (p. 104).

Factors II, III and IV relate the subjects' perceptions of how they found their places in a group. The factors appear to represent different aspects of the subjects' characteristic approaches to life. One's characteristic manner of finding significance might be described as that point where the three vectors formed by Factors II, III and IV intersect.

The item grouping comprising Factor II looks like those personality characteristics that Mosak (1972) has termed excitement seeking. The factor points to the degree of commotion, danger, dullness and routine that one desires in life. One end of the continuum is characterized by items that might be checked by persons who wish to create excitement in their life through flirting with danger, creating excessive fears, breaking rules and sulking. The other end of the continuum is comprised of items indicating persons who wish to avoid excitement and commotion. In this factor there was a preponderance of items (12 vs. 3) that stressed commotion-seeking behavior rather than commotion-avoiding behavior.

Factor III is comprised of items that relate to degree of involvement in social situations. Thus, items on one end of the continuum are reflective of a gregarious approach to friendships, while items on the other end of the contiuum indicate a shy, hesitant, sensitive approach to social situations.

Factor IV consists of items relating to the subjects' choices concerning conformity in school. Adler (1970) stated, "A good way of finding out the degree of social feeling of a child is to observe him at the time he enters school" (p. 11). Subjects' selective perceptions support Adler's emphasis on school-related experiences. Items with positive correlations reflect a conforming approach to life, i.e., attitude toward spelling, doing well in school and being comfortable in the classroom, while items with negative correlations indicate a nonconforming approach to life.

Within Individual Psychology theory, one might posit that these three variables—excitement seeking, involvement and conformity—interact in a consistent manner, and speculate that it would be possible to plot the elements of a person's life style by establishing the degree to which each variable is present and by discovering the interactional patterns between the variables.

Factor V suggested, as does Adlerian theory, that mothers contribute significantly to life style development. This factor, preceding the family atmosphere as presented by the father, suggests that the traditional perception of mothers' effect on personality development is still valid. Dreikurs (1958) mentioned that even in earliest infancy, the child responds to the mother's behavior and that understanding, sympathy and a little tenderness gives the mother a permanent lease on her child's affection.

Factor VI was first hypothesized by Mosak and Dreikurs and later empirically supported by O'Phelan (Note 1). The factor contained four of the five postulated attributes of Mosak and Dreikurs: the feminine item, the masculine item, the daring item, and the athletic item. The factor also contained three of O'Phelan's five attributes: the feminine item, the masculine item, and the athletic item. Adler (1969) indicated, "Certain character traits count as masculine, others as feminine, albeit there is no basis to justify these valuations" (p. 107).

Factor VII indicated the importance of the father's influence. Adler (1958) mentioned that, "The father's influence on his children is so important that many of them look on him, throughout their lives, either as their ideal or as their greatest enemy" (p. 135). The positively loaded items describe the fathers as less punitive than the mothers and as easy going. The negatively loaded items describe the fathers as punitive, strict and tending to get mad. Adler (1958) also suggested, "It is unfortunately frequent that the father of the family is given the task of punishing the children" (p. 135). Factor V and Factor VII appear to strengthen the Adlerian emphasis on parenting style and its effects.

Adler (Ansbacher & Ansbacher, 1956) mentioned that the desire for typologies was associated with a limited conceptual capacity. A paper-and-pencil inventory places a large restriction on the conceptualization process. The above comments need to be considered exploratory and provocative rather than definitive. Data from this study adds to the needed statistical confirmation of theoretical assumptions.

Reference

1. O'Phelan, M. Statistical evaluation of attributes in Adlerian Life Style forms. Paper presented as an honors dissertation at Hamline University, St. Paul, Minnesota, 1975, and since published in *Journal of Individual Psychology*, 1977, 33(2), 203–212.

An Investigation of the Inter-Judge Agreement on a Subject's Vocational Choice and Life Style Type

Jacqueline Magner-Harris
Richard J. Riordan
Roy M. Kern

A continuing problem in the counseling field has been its lack of an adequate base in theory which bridges the gap between the rhetoric of guidance and the reality of practice in schools, colleges, and clinical settings (Berdie, 1972; Holland, 1974; Sprinthall, 1972). Vocational guidance services have been especially prone to be described as atheoretical, ineffective, and impractical by a host of writers who have observed the current situation (Cochran, Vinitsky & Warren, 1974; Holland, 1974; Ivey & Morrill, 1968; Morrill & Forrest, 1970; Warnath, 1971). More specifically, it appears counselors conduct their personal-social counseling using one counseling theory and another to address the problem of work and vocational development. And, in reality, vocational counseling approaches may actually have no articulated theory undergirding their efforts. Influential writers in the counseling field such as Ginzberg (1975) and Patterson (1971) have aggravated this split between personal-social and vocational counseling by emphasizing the importance of one and downplaying the importance of the other.

Warnath (1975) and Holland (1974) as well as other writers have suggested that counselors need to choose a theoretical model broader than the vocational choice or vocational development models, a move which would break down what Zaccaria (1970, p. ix) has called the "oversimplified educational/vocational/personal-social trichotomy" of counseling. The adoption of a theory which successfully bridges the gap between vocational and personal concerns and which addresses all aspects of life's problems and human development could, it seems, facilitate a client's growth in all dimensions of his life simultaneously.

Adler's Individual Psychology holds great potential for fulfilling just such a mission. Adlerians have always contended that an integration of the voca-

tional/educational/personal-social aspects of guidance and counseling theory and practice was possible under the Adlerian theoretical umbrella. Adler clearly addressed the question of a person's occupation in his theory by considering it to be one of the three major tasks of life. Over fifty years ago Adler stated that "none of these (life) problems can be solved separately; each of them demands the successful approach to the other two" (1958, p. 239). His position foreshadowed the current thrust of vocational theorists such as Bordin, Holland, Roe, Super, and Tiedeman, all of whom emphasized the interplay of psychology and work (Tiedeman, 1975).

Adler maintained that a person's choice of occupation was an expression of the person's style of life and that this choice made possible the observation of a person's whole style of life. "He is showing us the main direction of his striving and what he values most in life" (1958, p. 244). Adler's thoughts on occupation suggested the current emphasis on the developmental nature of vocational choice when he proposed that the child's choice of an occupation was preceded by some dominant interest influenced first by the mother in the early years and later by the total family environment. He stated, "If ever I am called on for vocational guidance, I always ask how the individual began and what he was interested in during his first years. His memories of this period show conclusively what he has trained himself for most continuously; they reveal his prototype and his underlying scheme of apperception" (1958, p. 242).

When asking a child what he will be when he grows up, Adler (1958) pointed out that most will have a ready answer. He stated that the task of the counselor then is to "recognize the underlying motives, to see the way they are striving, what is

Reprinted by permission of the authors.

pushing them forward, where they are placed, their goals of superiority, and how they feel they can make it concrete" (p. 243). He continued: "Through the way in which the child thinks, behaves, and characteristically perceives, his interest becomes specialized for his future occupation" (1929, p. 148).

When Adler spoke of this process of understanding the client and the later process of helping the client to make a satisfactory vocational adjustment he assumed that the counselor's accurate prediction of the client's vocational choice could beneficially affect the client's adjustment in his vocational sphere as well as other spheres of his life. He believed that the client's life style and occupational choice were intrinsically bound together and that an understanding of a person's life style could lead to the prediction of a person's occupation.

Adlerians routinely use life style analysis to understand the current behavior and predict the future behavior of their clients in the counseling process. Typically, a somewhat standardized life style interview is employed (Allen, 1971; Dreikurs, 1967; Eckstein, Baruth & Mahrer, 1978, see appendix G, p. 145) to gather information about the individual's life style. Such components as birth order, family atmosphere, comparative sibling and parental characteristics and interactions, adjustments to physical development, schooling, peers, family values and socio-economic status, and early recollections are explored by the clinician to determine the client's life style.

Adler and other Adlerians (Dreikurs, 1950; Mosak, 1958; Nikelly & Verger, 1971) have suggested that such an analysis provides clues for vocational guidance, since career choice is a reflection of the person's life style. Despite this theoretical basis for using the life style analysis technique to yield information, which correctly interpreted, could be indicative of an individual's vocational preferences as well as other personality traits, little use has been made of this technique as a tool in the vocational guidance process.

Reasons for the lack of use of the life style analysis in vocational guidance are understandable because there has been no empirical testing of the total concept of life style. To present most research conducted on the life style concept has attempted to use certain elements such as birth order, early recollections, or parental influence constructs to predict occupational choice. It is not surprising that the results of many of these studies have often been inconclusive and contradictory.

For example, a weighty body of literature indicates that first borns are more controlling, conforming, and intellectually oriented and have vocational interests which dovetail with their attributes, and second and later borns prefer occupations which are less intellectually demanding and require creative and social interaction skills. Gandy (1974), however, pointed out in his review of this literature that these studies as a whole were not well-controlled methodologically. Thus, it was impossible to state that the birth order, or birth order and sex variables alone, accounted for vocational interests. Two studies which attempted to control for the confounding variables yielded negative results (Gandy, 1974).

In studies which examined the differences in personality and vocational interests with siblings in the same family constellation, the results have been generally more positive (Croake & Hayden, 1975; Olson, 1973; Verger, 1968). That is, competition between the first and second siblings did appear to create some differences in personality dimensions and vocational interests.

Another vein of research involving early recollections has proven to be more fruitful and less complicated. "An individual's early recollections (ER's) are the specific incidents which he remembers from his early childhood—incidents which happened only once, preferably before the age of nine or ten years, which he can remember clearly and in detail, generally with visual recall, and including one's thoughts and feelings at the time of the incident" (Gushurst, 1971, p. 32). Because ERs are believed to reveal an individual's internal attitudes about himself, other people, the world he lives in, his goals, and his anticipation for the future or in other words, his life style, Adler recommended routinely asking for ERs from clients for use in vocational guidance. Several researchers have used early recollections to differentiate and/or predict individual's vocational preferences successfully (Holmes & Watson, 1965; Manaster & Perryman, 1974; Attarian, 1973). These studies offer preliminary evidence that the life style analysis technique could successfully predict vocational choices of clients.

In addition to the piecemeal approach of current research on life style, another stumbling block which may explain why few clinicians have used the life style analysis technique is the lack of concurrent validity studies. Not only has the predictive validity of the total life style analysis method not been investigated but neither has the technique's predictive efficacy been compared to that of vocational guidance instruments or tools currently available. Few clinicians will choose to use the life style analysis technique if they have no empirical evidence about the usefulness of this method in comparison to other, more accepted, vocational assessment instruments.

A third reason for the infrequent use of the life style analysis technique in vocational counseling has been the lack of an empirical test of the technique itself. Individual Alderian clinicians may analyze life style data of a given client and draw differing conclusions about the person's life style. The reliability of such an analysis can be questioned because no inter-judge agreement data exists at present. Probably the only study to date which supported the existence of inter-judge reliability in life style analysis was Ferguson's study (1964). She was able to demonstrate in her study that summaries of life style protocols made from the ERs of thirty subjects diagnosed as psychotic, neurotic, and normal could be recognized and reliably matched to their owners' original protocols by a wide range of clinicians. While her research lends some preliminary support for the reliability of Adlerian clinicians' judgments on individuals' life styles, this support is limited to the area of inter-judge agreements on ERs alone.

Possibly the major roadblock to the use of life style analysis in vocational counseling is the time requirement. Life style analysis is time consuming and may therefore be prohibitive for many clinicians.

In summary, from a theoretical standpoint, the life style analysis technique appears to be a promising tool to bridge the gap between the vocational and personal-social dimensions of the counseling process. However, to date it has lacked the empirically based validity and reliability studies to warrant its extensive use.

Purpose

The purpose of this study was to examine the issues of reliability and validity related to the use of a written life style analysis technique in counseling. Specifically, the study investigated the inter-judge agreement on a subject's vocational choice and Adlerian life style type. The predictive validity rates for each judge's assessment of the subjects' occupations were examined. The predictive validity rates of judges using the life style analysis technique to determine the subjects' occupations were compared to the predictive validity rate of a vocational instrument commonly employed by counselors, Holland's Self-Directed Search (SDS).

Method

Sample

Sixty male graduate students enrolled at two large urban universities who volunteered to participate and who were randomly selected from a larger population of volunteer subjects served as the sample. Each of the subjects was currently employed in an occupation which was representative of one of Holland's six occupational types: realistic, investigative, social, artistic, enterprising, and conventional. Each subject met certain requirements for participation in the study: (1) enrollment in a graduate degree program in a field compatible with his current occupation; (2) a present plan to complete his graduate program for a degree; (3) at least one year of self-described satisfactory experience in his occupation; and (4) no present plans to change his occupation to one not represented in those related to his Holland occupational type.

Procedure

Each subject completed a written Life Style Questionaire Inventory (LSQI); an information questionnaire, which was created to establish whether the subject met the above selection criteria; and the SDS. The written LSQI was developed from the conceptual work of Dreikurs (1950), Allen (1971), and Mosak (1971). From these interview guides, Kern and Curran operationalized the questions into a written inventory for research purposes. An "only child" form of the regular LSQI was devised for subjects who were without siblings. The LSQI was used in a preliminary study in order to compare its efficacy of vocational prediction to that of the standard "live" life style interview method of gathering life style data. Both methods of data gathering yielded high rates of prediction of subjects' occupations. This result, coupled with a favorable outcome of a test of the difference between the prediction rates of the two methods, supported the use of the written method of data collection in this study.

The LSQI's were given separately to three Adlerian judges who had completed at least one graduate level course in Adlerian theory and practice and who were experienced in the use of life style analysis. Each judge was asked to analyze the data and indicate what he thought each subject's occupation was from a list of six possible choices representing Holland's six occupational types. The judges were also told to choose a dominant Adlerian life style type from a list of Mosak's (1971) 13 types. After the judges had made their selections of subjects' dominant life style types, another, more generic typology system delineated by Kefir and Corsini (1974) from the work of eight personality theorists was also applied to the data by the researcher. The use of the two typology classification systems enabled the researcher to synthesize the idiographic data from the life style analysis into usable categories which could be examined for reliability.

The second predictive instrument, the SDS, was scored and a high letter code (dominant occupational type) was assigned to each subject. This letter was examined to determine if it matched the code letter assigned on the basis of the subject's actual occupation. The high point code was used so that the task of the SDS would be equivalent to the task of the Adlerian judge, namely selecting a vocational type for each subject, since the judges were in effect selecting a type when they chose an occupation representing a stereotype of that particular Holland type.

Results

An analysis of the data regarding the reliability of the Adlerian judges' selections of the subjects' occupations based on the written life style analysis inventory indicated that two out of three judges agreed on 46 out of the 60 experimental subjects' vocational choices. Using a binomial table, it was found that this result was significant ($p < .0001$) and is reported in Table 1.

TABLE 1
The Binomial Test of Proportion of
Agreement on Subjects' Occupations

# of Judges Agreeing	Chance Probability	Observed Proportions
At least 2 out of 3	.44	$\frac{46}{60}$

****$p < .0001$

In order to correct for agreement expected by chance, a general conceptualization based on Cohen's & Scott's indices, M(I), was applied to the results of the aforementioned data. The M(I) Index was .58, indicating that agreement by two out of the

three judges on the subjects' occupations was 58% better than chance agreement alone (Table 6).

The proportion of correct choices of the subjects' occupations by the judges was analyzed with the Cochran Q Test which yielded a chi square of 4.67, $p > .05$. This result, shown in Table 2, also indicated inter-judge agreement because there were no significant differences among the judges' observed proportions of agreement on the subjects' correctly identified occupations.

TABLE 2
Cochran Q Test of Difference of Proportions
of Correct Occupations by Judges

	Observed Proportions by Judge
4.67	p for judge 1 = 29/60
	p for judge 2 = 26/60
	p for judge 3 = 35/60

$p > .05$
$df = 2$

The agreement among the judges regarding the subjects' dominant life style types was examined also using the binomial table. At least two out of the three judges agreed on one of Mosak's 13 life style types for a subject in 41 out of 60 cases. This result was also statistically significant, $p < .0001$. The M(I) Index was .59, indicating that the agreement was 59% better than chance agreement. Table 3 shows that when the Kefir and Corsini typology was analyzed for judges' agreement and the Mosak typology was further examined for agreement, the observed proportions of agreement were statistically significant; hence there was support for the idea that the life style types can be reliably discerned. The M(I) Indices range from .30 to .86 and are reported in Table 6.

The three Adlerian judges were also able to predict successfully the occupations of the subjects in 29, 26, and 35 of the cases. In each case, $p < .0001$. These results are reported in Table 4.

TABLE 3
Binomial Test of Proportions of Agreements on Subjects' Types

Typology	# of Agreements on Type	Chance Agreement	Observed Proportions
Mosak—13 types	At least 2 out of 3	p = .22	41/60
Mosak—13 types	3 out of 3	p = .006	18/60
Kefir and Corsini—3 types	At least 2 out of 3	p = .78	58/60
Kefir and Corsini—3 types	3 out of 3	p = .11	38/60

**** $p < .0005$ in all cases

TABLE 4
Binomial Test of Proportions of the Correct Predictions of Subjects' Occupations by Each Judge

Judge	Prediction by Chance	Observed Proportions
1	.17	29/60
2	.17	26/60
3	.17	35/60

****$p > .0001$ for each judge

The M(I) Indices, shown in Table 6, for judges 1, 2, and 3 respectively were: .37, .31, and .49. Because all three judges were able to predict the subjects' correct occupations at a level significantly greater than the probability based on chance, it appeared that trained judges could predict subjects' occupations from their life style data.

The Mantel and Haenszel test (cited in Fleiss, 1973) was used to test whether the proportion of subjects who had their occupational types correctly predicted by the SDO was significantly different from the proportion of subjects who had their occupations correctly predicted by the three Adlerian judges. The result of this test was a chi square of 3.5, $p > .05$. This result is reported in Table 5. While the SDS yeilded 37 correct predictions of the subjects' occupational types as compared to the three judges' prediction rates of 29, 26, and 35, there was no significant difference between the proportion of correct predictions made by the two methods.

TABLE 5
Mantel and Haenszel Test for Difference in Proportions of Correct Predictions of Subjects' Occupations by Two Methods

	Observed Proportions by Judges/Procedure
3.5	p for judge 1 = 29/60
	p for judge 2 = 26/60
	p for judge 3 = 35/60
	p for SDS = 37/60

p .05
df = 1

Discussion and Implications

This study found that (a) the inter-judge reliability of the written LSQI was high; (b) the predictive validity of the written LSQI for the subjects' occupations was high; and (c) there was no significant difference between the occupational prediction rates associated with the SDS and the written life style analysis technique. The first implication which can be drawn from these results was that the life style data was not idiosyncratically interpreted by the judges. Instead each judge's analysis of the life style data in terms of occupational choice interfaced with the other judges' interpretations of the same data at a much greater probability than chance. The same can be said of the judges' agreements on the subjects' dominant Adlerian and generic types.

TABLE 6
M(I) Indices for Agreement on Life Style Types and Occupations Corrected for Chance

Agreements/ Judge	Agreement by Chance	Agreement Not Corrected for Chance	Outcome	M(I) Indices (Agreement Corrected for Chance)
At least 2 of 3 (H1)	.44	46/60 or .77	Any occupation	.58
At least 2 of 3	.22	41/60 or .68	13 Mosak types	.59
3 of 3	.006	18/60 or .30	13 Mosak types	.30
At least 2 of 3	.78	58/60 or .97	3 Kefir/Corsini types	.86
3 of 3 (H3)	.11	38/60 or .58	3 Kefir/Corsini types	.58
Judge 1	.17	29/60 or .48	Correct occupation	.37
Judge 2	.17	26/60 or .43	Correct occupation	.31
Judge 3 (H4)	.17	35/60 or .58	Correct occupation	.49

Other implications based on these results are both important theoretically and methodologically. Because the Adlerian judges were able to choose a type for each subject (each judge also having the option of stating that the subject could not be typed) and agreed among themselves on a dominant type for each subject at a probability rate significantly greater than the probability rate based on chance, it appeared that the Adlerian contention that certain traits tend to cohere because of the basic unity and self-consistency of personality was correct in this instance. Hence typologies can be used to categorize certain patterns of behavior associated with particular life styles and to construct a parsimonious way of describing, comparing, and contrasting the behavior associated with each type.

Secondly, not only was the usefulness of Mosak's typology supported by the data but the more generic types proposed by Kefir and Corsini were also supported. Thus it appears that more general, eclectic kind of typology could be used for future research to categorize personality and its dominant patterns of interaction which would be of a more manageable number. The lack of significant differences among the judges' vocational prediction rates also suggests that clinicians who wish to use Adlerian theory and practice to bridge the gap between their personal-social and educational/vocational counseling could become knowledgeable and skilled enough in the theory and use of the life style analysis technique after a graduate course comparable to that taken by the study's judges to begin the use of the method in their counseling practices.

The data further indicates that the predictive validity rates of the Adlerian judges were not only significantly greater than rates based on chance for the task of predicting subjects' occupations, but that the judges' combined ratings did not differ significantly from the prediction rate generated by the SDS. Drawing from these findings, the predictive validity of the life style analysis technique for vocational purposes was confirmed; the contention that the technique was as generally effective in predicting the subjects' occupational expressions as the SDS was supported; and the theoretical notion which buttressed these hypotheses—that occupational choice is an expression of life style—was supported. These results constituted the first empirical evidence that data which includes all the elements of life style can be used to predict one expression of a person's life style such as vocational choice.

Conclusions and Recommendations

While certain limitations of the study are evident, they also suggest future research possibilities. First,

due to the narrow sample used, there is a lack of generalizability of the study's results to other populations, a deficit which can be corrected by conducting the same study with female, high school age and lower level occupational groups. While recognizing the possible implications of the higher intelligence and achievement motivation among this study's sample of graduate students which could have affected the results, therefore limiting their generalizability, it is assumed that there existed a great deal of basic similarity between the subjects and other men satisfactorily employed in the same occupations.

In addition, no attempt was made to randomly select judges from those graduate students/-counselors who had a minimum of one course in Adlerian Psychology. Consequently, the successes of these judges on the task cannot be generalized to all counselors who have had similar training and experience. However, because the judges' training and experience with the technique happened to fall on a continuum from very little to a great deal of experience, they did appear to be representative of other counselors who might have been selected as judges.

Besides the need for future research with different samples of subjects, other tests of the validity of the life style analysis technique could further substantiate the results of this study. Predictions of subjects' scores on instruments such as the Strong Vocational Interest Blank, the 16PF, the MMPI, the FIRO-B, and so on and/or comparisons with these assessments procedures could contribute additional data about the life style analysis technique's predictive and concurrent validity.

Another similar line of research which needs to be undertaken is the empirical validation of the Adlerian typologies. At present there is no objective criteria measure available against which to validate the judges' selections of a life style type for a subject. It would be fruitful then to establish laboratory situations in which the dynamics were such that persons who had been previously "typed" by Adlerian judges would be expected to behave in ways characteristic of their types. The subjects' objective behavior then would be a measure of the concurrent validity of the judges' selection of a type for that subject.

Another possible method of assessing the criterion-based validity of types would be to use available, empirically-established instruments which appear to assess behaviors comparable to those associated with the person's type. Possible instruments for this purpose include the FIRO-B, Rotter's I–E scale, and the Crowne-Marlowe Social Desirability Scale.

While the process of interpreting life style data "remains mysterious and inexplicit, the door is left open for both ungoverned subjectivity and for criticisms of nonreplicable, unscientific procedures" (Gushurst, 1971, p. 31). Two ways of attacking this problem without violating the principle of "unique wholeness" of the individual which underlies the concept of life style are suggested. First, Adlerians could video-tape the process they go through in interpreting the life style data and later review the tape and explain the rationale that led to their conclusions. Secondly, a discriminant analysis of life style data might provide information concerning the relative weights of life style variables for distinguishing among various occupations. While this procedure would not replace the intuitive, subjective part of the life style analysis, it could help clinicians to key in more systematically and consciously on variables which appear to be especially significant in the development of certain life style types. Of course the inherent difficulty in understanding the life style analysis process is not only the need to quantify the data in some manner for research purposes but to capture what may be the major intangible—the individual's perception of his world and interactions in it. Yet this challenge must be attemped if some of the "mystery" of the life style analysis process is to be removed in a scientific and replicable manner.

References

Adler, A. *Problems of neurosis: A book of case-histories.* London: Kegan Paul, Trench, Truebner & Co., 1929.

———. *What life should mean to you.* New York: Capricorn Books, 1958.

Allen, T. W. A life style. *The Counseling Psychologist,* 1971, *3,* 25–29.

Attarian, D. J. Early recollections: Predictors of vocational preference (Doctoral dissertation, University of Arizona, 1973). *Dissertation Abstracts International,* 1973, *34,* 3049A. (University Microfilms No. 73-28, 790)

Berdie, R. F. 1980s counseling: Applied behavior scientist. *Personnel and Guidance Journal,* 1972, *50,* 451–456.

Cochran, D. J.; Vinitsky, M. H.; & Warren, P. M. Career counseling: Beyond "test and tell." *Personnel and Guidance Journal,* 1974, *52,* 657–664.

Croake, J. W. & Hayden, D. J. Trait oppositeness in siblings: Test of an Adlerian tenet. *Journal of Individual Psychology,* 1975, *30,* 175–178.

Dreikurs, R. *Fundamentals of Adlerian Psychology.* Chicago: Alfred Adler Institute, 1950.

———. *Psychodynamics, psychotherapy and counseling.* Chicago: Alfred Adler Institute, 1967.

Eckstein, D.; Baruth, L.; & Mahrer, D. *Life style: What it is and how to do it.* Dubuque, Iowa: Kendall/Hunt Publishing Company, 1978.

Ferguson, E. D. The use of early recollections for assessing life style and diagnosing psychopathology. *Journal of Projective Techniques and Personality Assessment,* 1964, *28,* 403–412.

Fleiss, J. L. *Statistical methods for rates and proportions.* New York: Wiley & Sons, 1973.

Gandy, G. L. Ordinal position research related to vocational interest. *Journal of Counseling Psychology,* 1974, *21,* 281–287.

Ginzberg, E. *The manpower connection: Education and work.* Cambridge, Mass.: Harvard University Press, 1975.

Gushurst, R. S. The technique, utility and validity of life style analysis. *The Counseling Psychologist,* 1971, *3,* 30–40.

Holland, J. L. Vocational guidance for everyone. *Educational Researcher,* 1974, *3,* 9–15.

Holmes, D. & Watson, R. I. Early recollection and vocational choice. *Journal of Consulting Psycology,* 1965, *29,* 486–488.

Ivey, A. E. & Morrill, W. H. Career process: A new concept for vocational behavior. *Personnel and Guidance Journal,* 1968, *47,* 644–649.

Kefir, N. & Corsini, R. J. Dispositional sets: A contribution to typology. *Journal of Individual Psychology,* 1974, *30,* 163–178.

Manaster, G. J. & Perryman, T. B. Early recollections and occupational choice. *Journal of Individual Psychology,* 1974, *30,* 232–237.

Morrill, W. H. & Forrest, D. J. Dimensions of counseling for career development. *Personnel and Guidance Journal,* 1970, *49,* 299–305.

Mosak, H. H. Early recollections as a projective technqiue. *Journal of Projective Techniques,* 1958, *22,* 302–311.

———. Lifestyle. In A. G. Nikelly (Ed.), *Techniques for behavior change.* Springfield, Ill.: Charles C. Thomas, 1971.

Olson, T. D. Family constellation as related to personality and achievement. (Doctoral dissertation, Flordia State University, 1973). *Dissertation Abstracts International,* 1973, *33,* 5000-B. (University Microfilms No. 73-10, 333)

Patterson, C. H. *An introduction to counseling in the school* (2nd ed.). New York: Harper & Row, 1971.

Sprinthall, N. A. Humanism: A new bag of virtues for guidance. *Personnel and Guidance Journal,* 1972, *50,* 349–356.

Tiedeman, D. V. Structuring personal integration into career education. *Personnel and Guidance Journal,* 1975, *53,* 706–711.

Verger, D. M. Birth order and sibling differences in interests. Journal of *Individual Psychology,* 1968, *24,* 56–59.

Warnath, C. F. *New myths and old realities: College counseling in transition.* San Francisco: Jossey-Boss, 1971.

———. Vocational theories: Direction to nowhere. *Personnel and Guidance Journal,* 1975, *53,* 422–428.

Zaccaria, J. S. *Theories of occupational choice and vocational development.* Boston: Houghton Mifflin Co., 1970.

Comparative Lifestyles in Two Sexually Homogeneous Environments

Daniel G. Eckstein
Judy Pettigrew Eckstein

One of Alfred Adler's most significant contributions was his unified, holistic notion of an individual's "lifestyle," the constant theme of life and its variations. Because the term *lifestyle* has become so commercialized, we need to recall Adler's definition.

As Ansbacher and Ansbacher (1967) note, Adler equated the "style of life" with the self or ego, one's own personality, the unity of personality, individuality, individual form of creative activity, the method of facing problems, opinion about oneself and the problems of life, and the whole attitude to life. Rudolf Dreikurs (1953) followed Adler's holistic notion by noting that "the lifestyle is comparable to a characteristic theme in a piece of music. It brings the rhythm of recurrence into our lives" (p. 44). Although each individual's own style is unique, Harold Mosak, contemporary Adlerian authority on lifestyles, has identified (in Nikelly, 1972) 14 different, commonly observed lifestyles. Particularly relevant to this article is Mosak's (1959) description of the following: "The 'getter' exploits and manipulates life and others by actively or passively putting others into his service. He tends to view life as unfair for denying him that to which he feels entitled. He may employ charm, shyness, temper, or intimidation as methods of operation. He is insatiable in his getting" (p. 194).

We have observed that both incarcerated male juveniles and college females often present pampered lifestyles. This view is consistent with Adlerian literature (Adler 1964a, 1964b, 1967, 1970; Rattner in Nikelly, 1972). Perhaps the crucial difference in the two populations relates to the passive or active nature of such pampered lifestyles. Incarcerated male juveniles are typically aggressive "getters" in exploiting others; conversely, many females from upper middle-class families have chosen a more passive, dependent role in getting

their way. Both populations contain many pampered lifestyles, but significant active-passive roles appear to have emerged.

Experiences in Juvenile Corrections

Several studies have been conducted concerning correctional populations (Ansbacher, Ansbacher, Shiverack, & Shiverack, 1967; Chaplin, 1967, 1970; Eckstein, 1978; Hillson & Worchel, 1958). Adler (1970) presented the following statements regarding delinquents and pampered lifestyles:

We assert that in criminals we invariably find evidence of the pampered lifestyle. Delinquents who have committed one or more crimes picture the world as a place where everyone else exists for their exploitation, where they have the right forcibly to take possession of the goods, health, or life of others and to set their own interest above the interest of others. In such cases we can always find a certain attitude which can be traced through the life history of the delinquent back to childhood. Delinquents are always individuals whose social interest suffered shipwreck in childhood, whose social interest did not attain full maturity. They begin very early to take forcibly anything which seems to them to belong to them. (p. 257)

At the risk of overgeneralization, we have found that many incarcerated males often feel unfairly treated by society, that they can break the rules and not have to suffer the "logical consequences," and that they are often discouraged. Having failed to gain attention in socially accepted ways, they resort instead to socially unacceptable, but personally enhancing, delinquent behavior.

Two specific Adlerian techniques found to be useful included what Nikelly (1972) described as "stroke-and-spit" tactics: "Stroking means that the

Daniel G. Eckstein and Judy Pettigrew Eckstein, "Comparative Lifestyles in Two Sexually Homogeneous Environments," *The Individual Psychologist*, September 1978, pp. 27–33. Reprinted by permission of the publisher.

therapist gives of his time and effort to help the client listen to himself and to cultivate an active, social interest. In *spitting* the therapist discloses the skillful maneuvers of the client, who may be seeking to avoid intimacy or who is directly hostile to others, and thereby exposes his ineffective ways of behaving (i.e., 'Look what you are actually doing'). Spitting implies that the disclosure is unpleasant enough so that the client no longer desires to continue this behavior" (p. 88). Thus, through encouragement, trust relationships between counselor and client are possible. A psychological investigation follows, including a lifestyle plus other relevant psychometric information. The crucial interpretation and reorientation phases involve sharing possible mistaken goals (i.e., undue attention, power, revenge, inadequacy), while encouraging the use of more socially appropriate ways of fulfilling the unique lifestyle.

Incarcerated juveniles appear to be sensitive to "society-oriented" counselors "unfairly" trying to change their lives; yet, they are often encouraged when they gain insights concerning possible explanations of their delinquent activities. A discussion of more socially appropriate methods of fulfilling the same needs is included. Adler's personal discussion exemplifying the useful and useless nature of lifestyles has been especially appreciated by these adolescents. As a child, Adler had a fear of death, resolving to overcome it by becoming a physician. However, another person with a similar fear of death may become a grave digger, triumphing over death at each burial rite. Just as the incarcerated males can realize the useful-useless side of the same need, they can similarly employ more socially appropriate means of attaining their goals. It seems futile to argue whether the incarceration is justified; rather, encouragement in fulfilling their goals through more useful ways has proven to be more effective.

In addition to the use of lifestyles as a perferred method of treatment, many Adlerian family counseling techniques are appropriate. Since 30 to 35 boys were housed together, group cooperation and consideration should be stressed. We also learned that regular family-type problems occurred; for example, a recurring problem was that larger, aggressive boys would attack smaller, passive students in the dorm. Of course, the smaller boys instantly sought protection and retaliation through the counselor. Preventing such activities proved futile and frustrating for the counselor; however, realizing his error, he began to withdraw from such disputes, encouraging the students to work

things out for themselves. Just as in normal family conflicts, the smaller boys often had provoked the wrath of the larger teenagers. By experiencing the natural consequences of their actions, such fighting became less prevalant.

As Dreikurs (1967) notes, many psychopathic personality types resist personal treatment, responding to group spirit instead: "It is easier to change the objectives and tendencies of the whole group than of an individual alone. New group values must be developed to increase and improve the social values of an individual" (p. 23). For this reason, group counseling is a preferred mode of treatment.

Developing social interest can also be encouraged through such activities as coeducational dances with incarcerated females. Eckstein (1978) has demonstrated that information obtained through sociometric techniques has been helpful in determining friends who desire to attend such functions together.

Maslow's (1954) hierarchy of needs is also an important consideration for correctional counselors. Often such basic needs as safety, clean sheets and towels, soap, and toothpaste must precede higher levels of honesty, self-esteem, and self-actualization. Counselors who are not willing to deal with such primary needs initially may experience difficulties in correctional institutions. Perhaps the founder of the Salvation Army, General William Booth, had the right philosophy in his "soup, soap, and salvation" approach to such individuals.

Another important function of correction counselors involves community consultation. Frequent conferences with parents, especially in relation to the fallacies of authoritarian and permissive techniques, may provide insights into how they often make the adolescent's delinquent behavior productive. Whenever possible, participation in ongoing parent study groups through family education centers can be an important educational experience for such individuals.

Experiences in a Women's College

Seemingly at the opposite extreme from the predominately lower middle-class, black-dominated, male juvenile correction facility would be a predominately upper middle-class, white-oriented, 4-year women's college. Yet, despite the apparent contrasts, some similarities should be noted. As previously mentioned, both environments contain many pampered lifestyles, the apparent difference being in the active-passive manner of approaching the environment. In the introduction to *Problems of Neurosis*, Ansbacher (Adler, 1964a) summarizes Adler's view of the pampered lifestyle: "All neurotic persons who have developed from a pampered prototype expect to be appreciated before they will do anything of social value instead of after having done it, thus expecting the natural course of things to be reversed in their own favor" (p. 77). Such people want "to take without giving" (p. 95), want "everything for nothing" (p. 94) and "all or nothing" (p. 55).

In one's early recollections, Adler (1964a) says that references to mother or to the birth of another child are often clues to a pampered lifestyle. Other references to aunts, uncles, or grandparents providing special gifts and favors also appear frequently in recollections of the students of a women's college. Although it appears that parents and close relatives are guilty of spoiling such children, Adler (1967) stresses the *personal responsibility* of each individual receiving preferred treatment:

It cannot be said that bad training given by the mother is the element which is responsible for producing the pampered lifestyle. The child stumbles into this mistaken way by himself when the mother is the only person with whom he makes contact. This attitude could not occur unless the child claimed for himself all the advantages to be had in such a relationship. In other words, the child, under the circumstances indicated, will always think of himself, will see only possibility of success in expecting everything from his mother, in contributing nothing, in always taking and never giving. (p. 257)

In discussing women's role from an Adlerian perspective, Deutsch (1970) stresses that equality between the sexes could be more readily achieved if women would try to make clear to men how cooperation, rather than competition for dominance (i.e., radical feminist groups), benefits both sexes. She aptly notes: "Many men are simply not aware that women still encounter social inequalities. If this is brought to their attention in a noncombative spirit, and if they are shown how equality is of benefit *to men as well as to women*, men would more willingly participate in correcting any existing injustices" (p. 123).

Important and needed changes for women have occurred in recent years. The increased options of combining motherhood and personality-fulfilling careers have crucial implications for women college students. But change does not come easily, and we have noted that many women still enjoy the benefits (support, chivalry, etc.) of being the "fairer sex." Somehow it seems that the contemporary women's rights movement has often been received by female college students as "tennis-shoe stomping, bra-burning" radicals. Thus, it often seems unfeminine to become liberated.

It also seems that many female college students put themselves in a double bind. On the one hand, they are sensitive to present sexual inequities, but they still are seeking a strong male figure for support and guidance. Dreikurs' *The Challenge of Marriage* (1946) is still relevant concerning Adler's "masculine protest," reflective of both male and female resentment of masculine superiority; the fallacy of glamour and chivalry (pp. 39–40); and the fallacy of beauty and sex appeal (p. 74). Although female students generally score in the equalitarian range on various sex role questionnaires, nany women still feel dependent on male approval for their own feelings of self-worth. And, when females are in a sexually homogenous environment with decreased opportunities to interact with males, increased feelings of unworthiness and loneliness often occur.

At the risk of overgeneralization, we have found several common concerns relating to students experiencing problems in a women's college. In addition to feeling dependent, of being pampered, and expecting other people to be of special assistance, it appears that many female students give lip service to eliminating sexism (especially in salaries) and having equalitarian male-female roles. But there also appear to be many feelings of inadequacy in such tasks as getting a job and supporting oneself. Traditionally, exclusive male privileges and responsibilities often seem very difficult and frightening to women who have learned to depend on others for their "OK" feelings. Thus, liberation involves shedding some antiquated, but nonetheless comfortable lifestyles. "Stroke-and-spit" tactics can insure that the needed transition will be faster and less painful. Confrontation regarding women's own sexist stereotypes plus encouragement to engage in emergent behaviors are needed for lasting liberation.

Summary

Two specific, sexually homogeneous situations are discussed from an Adlerian perspective. Implications regarding incarcerated male juvenile offenders along with the cultural need and significance of the current women's rights movement are presented. Despite vast cultural, sexual, and racial differences between the two populations, a central theme is that pampered lifestyles frequently occur in both groups. The major difference appears in an active versus passive pampered orientation, with male juveniles being more aggressive than female college students.

References

Adler, A. *Problems in neurosis: A book of case histories* (P. Mairet, Ed.). New York: Harper & Row, Publishers, 1964. (a)

Adler, A. *Social interest: A challenge to mankind.* (J. Linton & R. Vaughan, trans.). New York: Capricorn Books, 1964. (b)

Adler, A. *The individual psychology of Alfred Adler: A systematic presentation in selections from his writings* (H. L. Ansbacher & R. R. Ansbacher, Eds.). New York: Harper & Row, Publishers, 1967.

Adler, A. *The science of living* (H. L. Ansbacher, Ed.). New York: Doubleday & Co., Inc., 1969.

Adler, A. *Superiority and social interest: A collection of later writings* (H. L. Ansbacher & R. R. Ansbacher, Eds.). Evanston, Ill.: Northwestern University Press, 1970.

Ansbacher, H. L., Ansbacher, R. R., Shiverack, D., & Shiverack, K. Lee Harvey Oswald: An Adlerian interpretation. *Journal of Individual Psychology*, 1967, *23*, 24–34.

Chaplin, J. P. Commentary on three Oswald interpretations. *Journal of Individual Psychology*, 1967, *23*, 48–52.

Chaplin, J. P. The presidential assassins: A confirmation of Adlerian theory. *Journal of Individual Psychology*, 1970, *26*, 205–212.

Dreikurs, R. *The challenge of marriage.* New York: Hawthorn Books, Inc., 1946.

Dreikurs, R. *Fundamentals of Adlerian psychology.* Chicago: Alfred Adler Institute, 1953.

Dreikurs, R. *Psychodynamics, psychotherapy and counseling.* Chicago: Alfred Adler Institute, 1967.

Eckstein, D. G. Some racial differences in responses to a sociometric text involving institutionalized juvenile offenders. Journal of Humanics, 1978, *6*(1), 5–9.

Hillson, J. S., & Worchel, P. The self-concept in the criminal: An exploration of Adlerian theory. *Journal of Individual Psychology*, 1958, *14*, 173–181.

Maslow, A. *Motivation and personality.* New York: Harper & Row, Publishers, 1954.

Mosak, H. H. The getting type: A parsimonious social interpretation of the oral character. *Journal of Individual Psychology*, 1959, *15*, 193–198.

Nikelly, A. (Ed.). *Techniques for behavior change: Applications of Adlerian theory.* Springfield, Ill.: Charles C. Thomas, Publishers, 1976.

APPENDICES

Appendix A

Contributors

Alfred Adler was a pioneer in the field of psychology and, although he had a medical background, he became interested in mental health. Adler was a member of the Freudian psychoanalytical group, but withdrew from the group and developed his own theory which he first explained in *Practice and Theory of Individual Psychology.*

Thomas Allen is an associate professor of counseling psychology at Washington University (St. Louis, Mo.). His current research interests pertain to the effects of psychological barriers on physical health and also the importance of early recollections and dreams of imagery and roles in human life.

Heinz Ansbacher is emeritus professor of psychology at the University of Vermont. For seventeen years he and his wife (Rowena) were co-editors of the *Journal of Individual Psychology.* They also edited *The Individual Psychology of Alfred Adler* and Adler's later writings under the title *Superiority and Social Interest.*

Leroy Baruth is a licensed psychologist and Professor at the University of South Carolina. His primary interests are family counseling, classroom discipline, and parent and teacher study groups.

Donald L. Bubenzer received his doctoral training at Ohio University and is Director of the Counseling Program at West Virginia Institute of Graduate Studies. He also has a counseling practice in Charleston, West Virginia.

Jay Colker while working as a counselor with drug addicts, is finishing his Master's Degree at the Alfred Adler Institute in Chicago. In addition, Jay has a consulting business "Transitions," focusing on the art of job hunting in which he does individual counseling and workshops with groups.

William L. Curlette is an Associate Professor of Educational Foundations at Georgia State University where his teaching area is educational statistics with an emphasis on discriminant analysis and classification.

Don Dinkmeyer has a Certificate in Psychotherapy from the Alfred Adler Institute, Chicago. He is the author of ten books, eighty-five professional articles, the "Developing Understanding of Self and Others" (DUSO) kit, and the "Systematic Training for Effective Parenting" (STEP) kit.

Don Dinkmeyer, Jr. is currently a doctoral student in counselor education at the University of Florida and an associate of Communication and Motivation Training Institute, Inc., Coral Springs, Florida.

Rudolf Dreikurs received his M.D. in 1923 and started a private practice and several guidance centers in Vienna, Austria. After leaving Vienna, he went briefly to Brazil and then came to the United States where he eventually founded the Alfred Adler Institute of Chicago. His teaching and writing are having a dramatic impact on education and life in this country.

Daniel Eckstein is a licensed psychologist, Director of Clinical Training, and Assistant Professor in the School of Human Behavior at the U.S. International University in San Diego.

Judy Pettigrew Eckstein is Coordinator of Consultation and Educational Services at the Ruston (LA) Mental Health Center. She is a doctoral candidate at the U.S. International University with special interests in humanistic psychology and human relations training.

Thomas Edgar is a professor of counselor education at Idaho State University (Pocatello) and completed his doctoral study the University of Wyoming. He has received post-doctoral training at the Alfred Adler Institute of Chicago and has served as an officer in the American Society of Adlerian Psychology.

B. Udelle Friedland is associate professor in the Department of Rehabilitation Counseling at Coppin State College (Maryland). She is currently serving as editor of *The Individual Psychologist* and is a psychologist in private practice concentrating on vocational and family concerns.

Elaine Funk was a professor of Theater and Communication at Bowie (Maryland) State College and was Coordinator of all Communication and Theater at the college. She was a certified director of Psychodrama, Sociometry, and Group Therapy.

Leo Gold is Dean of the Alfred Adler Institute in New York and also has a private practice in South Orange, N.J. He is a past president of the North American Society of Adlerian Psychology.

R. S. Gushurst is in private practice in Fredericksburg, Va. He is involved in consulting with school districts and presents workshops for the Alfred Adler Institute. His current research deals with anxiety and emotion as they relate to individual psychology.

Charles Huber is Assistant Professor of Counseling and Human Resources at the University of Bridgeport. He has written numerous articles and is completing a Post-doctoral Fellowship at the Center for Rational-Emotive Therapy in New York.

Patty Jung is a doctoral candidate in Christian Ethics at Vanderbilt University currently writing her dissertation on the implications of human embodiment for the structures of character. She divides her time between diapers and Ricoeur.

L. Shannon Jung received his doctorate from Vanderbilt University and is presently teaching Sociology and Religion at Virginia Intermont College, Bristol, Va. His writings have been published in numerous journals including: *Dialog*, *Religion in Life*, and *Christianity and Crisis*.

Roy M. Kern is a professor within the Department of Counseling and Psychological Services at Georgia State University and is also Coordinator of the Elementary School Counseling Program as well as responsible for teaching the family therapy sequence within the department.

Richard Kopp is Coordinator of Theoretical Instruction and Curriculum at the California School of Professional Psychology (Los Agneles) where he has been a faculty member since 1973. He also maintains a private practice in Altadena, Ca.

Bill Kvols-Reidler is a therapist at Aurora (Colorado) Mental Health Center. He is co-director and co-founder of the Rudolf Dreikurs Institute of Colorado. Previously, Bill was president of the Alfred Adler Institute of Dayton and vice-president of the Ohio Association of Individual Psychology.

Kathy Kvols-Riedler is a co-founder of the Rudolf Dreikurs Institute of Colorado and a therapist at the Aurora Mental Health Center. Kathy has previously worked as a student volunteer service coordinator, a juvenile detention center counselor, and a pre-school teacher.

Donald Lombardi is professor of Clinical Psychology at Seton Hall University and also has a private practice. He is currently serving as Court Psychologist for the Essex County Juvenile Court and Youth House.

Betty Lowe is Associate Coordinator of the Parent-Teacher Education Center at the University of Oregon. She is very interested in Adlerian Psychology with an emphasis in lifestyle assessment.

Ray Lowe is Professor of Counseling Psychology at the University of Oregon. He has written numerous articles and was co-editor of *Adlerian Family Counseling: A Manual for Counseling Centers.*

Jacqueline Magner-Harris is Director of Counseling at St. Pius X High School in Atlanta where she does extensive group work and life skills training with students, counsels parents and families, and heads a peer counseling program.

William McKelvie is associate professor at Bowie State College (Maryland) and a psychologist in private practice. He is a frequent consultant specializing in mental health, corrections and education. He co-authored *Career Goals Counseling: A Holistic Approach.*

John Nield is associate professor of Psychology and Counselor Education at Pittsburg State University. Prior to moving to Kansas, John served as Director of Child Development and Family Counseling Center associated with the University of Nevada System.

Terrance D. Olson is an Associate Professor in the Department of Child Development and Family Relationships at Brigham Young University in Provo, Utah.

Mary Louise O'Phelan received a B.A. in Psychology from Hamline University and a M.A. in Community Counseling at the College of St. Thomas. Currently, she is Director of the West 7th Family Center in St. Paul, Minnesota.

Richard J. Riordan is Professor and Chairman of the Department of Counseling and Psychological Services at Georgia State University where he teaches in the rehabilitation and community counseling program.

Manford Sonstegard is a professor of counseling at the West Virginia College of Graduate Study. He is a consultant to family guidance centers and a psychologist in private practice. His most recent publication is *Living in Harmony With Your Children.*

Thomas Springer is Associate Professor of Behavioral Sciences at Louisiana Tech University. He teaches courses in physiological psychology, psychology of sexual behavior and computer science.

Jane Taylor completed her doctoral study at the University of South Carolina and is presently entering private in Washington, D.C. She received training in psychodrama at St. Elizabeth's Hospital and is interested in life style from the psychodrama aspects of interpersonal relations.

Adele Thomas is a Psychological Counselor at Ramapo College in New Jersey. She is also a student in the Psychotherapy Program at the Alfred Adler Institute in New York City.

Donald Ward is an assistant professor in the Department of Counseling and Psychology at Pittsburg State University (Kansas). He also has a part-time assignment in the Counseling Center where he specializes in group counseling and career development. He has previous teaching experience in England and at Ball State University.

John D. West is an Associate Professor Counseling at West Virginia Institute of Graduate Studies. He received his doctoral training at Idaho State University and has a private practice in counseling.

Robert Willhite is Director of the Centering Place in Minneapolis. He received training at the Alfred Adler Institute, Chicago, and has developed a unique method of interpreting early recollections.

John Zarski is an associate professor of counseling at the West Virginia College of Graduate Study and a psychologist in private practice. His current research involves measuring social interest and also assessing counseling effectiveness.

Appendix B

Early Recollections Instruction Sheet

Date _____ Sex _____ Social Security Number _____

Name (optional) _____

The purpose of this questionnaire is to find out what you can recall as your earliest childhood memories. The responses are to be used for research purposes and will be treated in a professional, confidential manner. Please keep the following points in mind:

(1) The early memory (recollection) must be a *specific* incident, event, occurrence, or happening that you can remember. Early memories which describe incidents that occurred over and over again (example: "We *used to* do such and such," or "I did this *many* times") are not true early recollections and, consequently, should not be written down.

(2) Write down any early recollection that comes to your mind, even if you are not sure the incident actually occurred.

(3) Report any specific recollection that you think of, regardless of how insignificant it may seem to you.

(4) Write down the recollections *in the order that you remember them,* even if you are not sure which ones really occurred earlier. It is not important that the recollections be reported in their true chronological order; rather, in the order that you remember them.

(5) Write down only those recollections which you think occurred approximately before age eight (8).

(6) Report six (6) early recollections.

(7) Be sure to complete all the descriptions of your six early recollections (pages 1, 2, 3) before you begin filling in the related questions (pages 4, 5) that follow.

Appendix C

Early Recollections Rating Scale

Counselor Number _____ E. R. Number _____

Behavior

	1	2	3	4	5	6	7	
Withdrawal								Gregarious
Passivity								Activity
Agression hostility								Benevolence kindness
Mistreated								Befriended treated well

Perception of Environment

	1	2	3	4	5	6	7	
Threatening frustrating								Friendly nurturing
Rejection								Acceptance
Inferiority								Self-confidence
Depressing								Cheerful
Dependence								Independence

Rater Number _____

Appendix D

Instructions to Early Recollections Raters

The rating scale for early recollections is a bipolar scale and is divided into two sections. The first section is concerned with the behavior of the person in the recollection, i.e., is more content oriented. The second section has to do with affect or how the person sees his environment. Please place a check in the appropriate space. If the category is not in the recollection, check box 4 (average).

Further explanations of the categories are given below:

Withdrawal: shy, lonely; avoids conflict by withdrawing from people
Gregarious: sociable, congenial, approaches people

Passivity: person is passive in his behavior
Activity: person is active in his behavior

Aggression; hostility: aggression or hostility may be expressed openly or by devious methods, or by passive resistance
Benevolence; kindness: treats objects or others in benevolent manner

Mistreated: person relating early recollection is mistreated
Befriended; treated well: person giving early recollection is treated well by others

Threatening; frustrating: sees environment as physically or emotionally threatening or is denied wants by the environment
Friendly; nurturing: sees the environment as friendly or helpful

Rejection: feels rejected by others or animals
Acceptance: feels accepted by others or animals

Inferiority: feels weak, helpless
Self-confidence: feels confidence in self

Depressing: objects or people seen as distant, sad, bleak
Cheerful: objects or people seen as pleasant, happy

Dependence: relies on others for help or approval
Independence: being able to stand on one's own two feet; feeling okay without relying on others

Appendix E

Revised Early Recollections Questionnaire

The purpose of this questionnaire is to find out what memories you can recall from your early childhood. Think back as far as you can and write down what you remember from this period in your life. The early memory (recollection) must be a *specific* incident, event, occurrence or happening that you remember. Early memories which describe incidents that occurred over and over again (example: "We used to do such and such every Sunday," or "I did this many times") are not true early recollections and, consequently, should not be written down.

Please consider that there are no right or wrong answers on this questionnaire so write down any recollection that comes to your mind, even if you are not sure the incident occurred or regardless of how unimportant it may seem to you.

You are requested to follow the four part sequence detailed below when writing your early recollections and the researchers would like for *at least three* early recollections and as many as *six* if possible.

.a. Describe your first recollection in detail.
b. What part of the recollection stands out the most?
   What part seems most significant to you?
c. Approximately how old were you when this incident occurred?
d. Describe how you were feeling (i.e., your emotions) during this incident.

Appendix F

Early Recollections, Inventory of Social Interest Rating Scale

1. Coping (Active)		vs		Avoidance (Passive)
5	4	3	2	1
definite seeking better ways of doing things, a self-starter	considerable	some	little	no initiation of activities

2. Friendly		vs		Hostility
5	4	3	2	1
definite movement to to seek out and enjoy others	considerable	some	little	movement away from another through anger or aggression

3. Altruistic		vs		Manipulative
5	4	3	2	1
definite engagement in helping behavior for benefit of others	considerable	some	little	interaction with another to achieve one's own ends

4. Accepting		vs		Rejecting
5	4	3	2	1
definite interest and understanding of others	considerable	some	little	no interest in understanding others

5. Flexibility		vs		Inflexibility
5	4	3	2	1
complete adaptability to one's environment	considerable	some	little	lacks insight into self and social relations

6. Interdependence		vs		Dependence
5	4	3	2	1
definite decision-making ability and seeks to co-operate with others in meeting life task	considerable	some	little	exhibits no decision-making or cooperative behavior

7. Optimistic   vs   Pessimistic

5	4	3	2	1
highly confident and self-assured of one's ability	considerable	some	little	no confidence and self-assurance, fails in task

8. Cooperative   vs   Competitive

5	4	3	2	1
definitely participates with another in common efforts	considerable	some	little	no cooperation with another, over-concern with one's status; how am I doing

9. Cheerful   vs   Depressing

5	4	3	2	1
enjoys life, accepts set-backs, perceives humor in situations	considerable	some	little	no enjoyment of life, uncertain and insecure, withdraws from life tasks

10. Encouraging   vs   Discouraging

5	4	3	2	1
accepts and has faith in individuals as they are (not their potential) and reacts optimistically to others	considerable	some	little	no acceptance of others, emphasizes evaluations of how others are doing, stresses comparisons with others

Appendix G

Life Style Interview Guide

(Reproduced from *Life Style: What It Is and How to Do It* by Eckstein, D.; Baruth, L.; and Mahrer, F. D., Dubuque, IA.: Kendall/Hunt Publishing Company, 1978.

Write the name and age of each sibling (including yourself) in descending order beginning with the oldest. Include deceased siblings. When you have listed all the siblings, describe each sibling again including yourself.

Sibling 1	Sibling 2	Sibling 3
Name:	Name:	Name:
Age:	Age:	Age:
Description:	Description:	Description:

Sibling 4	Sibling 5	Sibling 6
Name:	Name:	Name:
Age:	Age:	Age:
Description:	Description:	Description:

Further Sibling Descriptions

In relation to your family answer the questions below as accurately as possible.

Who was most different from you? How? If you are an only child, in your peer group who was the most different from you? How?

_____

_____

_____

Who was most like you? How?

_____

_____

_____

Did you have many or few friends? Describe your relationship with them.

_____
_____
_____
_____

Who fought and argued? _____
Who played together? _____
Who took care of whom? _____
Who had a handicap or prolonged illness? _____
What were the most important family values? _____
_____
_____

What was your family motto? _____
_____

Sibling Ratings

Following each adjective or description indicate which siblings demonstrated that characteristic most and least. If you are at neither extreme, show in which direction you were inclined by pointing an arrow. An example might be:

Characteristic	Most	Least
Idealistic	Sam	Rachel

This would indicate that regarding idealism, Sam was most idealistic, Rachel was least idealistic, and you tended to be on the least idealistic end of the continuum. If you are an only child, rate yourself in comparison to your peer group you associated with as a child. These ratings should focus on *your personal opinion* of your family situation during the first eight years of your life.

Now respond to each of the following characteristics:

Characteristic	Most	Least

1. Intelligence
2. Hardest Worker
3. Best Grades in School
4. Helping Around the House
5. Conforming
6. Rebellious
7. Trying to Please
8. Critical of Others
9. Considerateness
10. Selfishness
11. Having Own Way
12. Sensitive-Easily Hurt
13. Temper Tantrums
14. Sense of Humor
15. Idealistic
16. Materialistic
17. Standards of Accomplishment
18. Most Athletic
19. Strongest
20. Attractive

Most   Least

21. Spoiled
22. Punished
23. Spontaneous

Description of Parents

Father   Current Age:
                                Occupation

Father's Favorite? Why?

_____

_____

Description of Father: Ambitions for children?

_____   _____

_____   _____

_____   Relationship to children?

_____   _____

_____   _____

                                Sibling most like father? How?

                                _____

                                _____

Mother   Current Age:
                                Occupation:

Mother's Favorite? Why

_____

_____

Description of Mother: Ambitions for children?

_____   _____

_____   _____

_____   Relationship to children?

_____   _____

_____   _____

                                Sibling most like mother? How?

                                _____

                                _____

Describe the nature of your parent's relationship.

_____

_____

_____

_____

If there were other parental figures in your family, describe the effect they have had on your outlook on life.

_____

_____

_____

_____

Early Recollections

Think back as far as you can and describe the first specific incident that you remember. Describe what feeling you had at that time. Make sure it is a specific situation and not a generalization. When you have completed the information for the first incident, do the same with the second situation. Try to do this for at least five or six incidents. If you had a recurring dream when you were a child, describe the dream and discuss how you felt.

First Incident:
   Description:

   Your feeling:

Second Incident:
   Description:

   Your Feeling:

Third Incident:
   Description:

   Your feeling:

Fourth Incident:
   Description:

   Your feeling:

Fifth Incident:
   Description:

   Your feeling:

Sixth Incident:
   Description:

   Your feeling:

Recurring Dream:
   Description:

   Your feeling:

Appendix H

Interview Guide for Establishing the Life Style*

Betty Lowe
Raymond Lowe

Following is a guide intended to assist you in establishing the life style. The information appearing in parentheses makes reference to where information about the particular item may be found. The first digit refers to the textual source which may be found on page 197, and the second set of digits refers to the pages in the text.

---

1. Name   Date

2. The subjective situation   1 (4–5)
                                                                                                            1 (14–15)
                                                                                                            10 (105)

3. The objective situation   1 (4–5)
                                                                                                            1 (14–15)
   a. Work   1 5   2 (83–98)
                                                                                                            3 (237–238)
                                                                                                            4 (91–108)
                                                                                                            10 (103–110)
                                                                                                            10 (105)

   b. Society   1 5

   c. Sex   1 5

---

*It appears that Adler never intended to invent a single procedure for establishing the life style. Such a position probably would be in conflict with his point of view about holism. While the student may find a variety of "formats" for gathering and interpreting the life style, only one is proposed here. As a student gains confidence in thinking globally, if not holistically, s/he will develop his/her own particular approach to this process.

Reprinted by permission of the authors.

4. *The* question

1 (5–8)
5 (114–119)
3 (112)
10 (105–106)

5. Family influences

   a. Birth order/family constellation/family atmosphere

   List all siblings in descending order, including client (*) in his/her position. Give client's age, and after each sibling the years of age difference with the client (indicate with + or −). Indicate siblings now dead. Ask client to give a sentence or two description of each sibling including his/herself. If client is an only child, ask him/her to describe him/herself in relationship to peers. Children who lived with the client's family (e.g., cousins, foster children) may be included, depending on whether they were in the role of siblings.

Sibling	Age	∓	Description/Relationship to Client
_____	___	___	_____
			_____
_____	___	___	_____
			_____
_____	___	___	_____
			_____
_____	___	___	_____
			_____
_____	___	___	_____

1 (9–12)
1 (14–17)
2 (198–215)
3 (22–24)
3 (85–88)
4 (37–42)
6 (5–17)
7 (15–23)
7 (97–99)
8 (35–40)
8 (49–54)
9 (29–33)
9 (45–59)

   b. Family atmosphere

3 (24–25)
8 (41–47)

     (1) Parent's relationship

9 (33–34)

     (2) Quarrels: how started; how stopped

(3) Client's feelings about quarrels; taking sides

(4) Child raising ideas

(5) Dominance in decision making

c. Parents

(1) Father's name   Age   Vocation
Description   6 (15–16)

Favorite child; why

Relationship to children; general or particular

Ambitions for children; general or particular

Client's relationship

Sibling most like father and how

Attitude toward his and spouse's vocation

Attitude toward his and spouse's avocation

(2) Mother's name   Age   Vocation

Description

Favorite child; why

Relationship to children; general or particular

Ambitions for children; general or particular

Client's relationship

Sibling most like mother and how

Attitude toward her and spouse's vocation

Attitude toward her and spouse's avocation

6. Other adults closely involved with family

Name	Age	Description/Relationship

7. Family values   6 (15)

    Identify functional values generally held by family   8 (46)

                                                                      9 (34)

Who opposed family values the most

Did family have a family motto indicative of values held

8. Sibling relationship

Who took care of whom

Who played together

Who got along best with whom

Quarrels: who started; how; how stopped

9. Sibling ratings   6 (13–14)

Indicate sibling who comes closest to being the most and least for each attribute. If an only child, compare with other acquaintances as more or less for each sttribute.

Attribute	Most or More	Least or Less	In what way
Intelligent	_____	_____	_____
Hardest Worker	_____	_____	_____
Best grades in school	_____	_____	_____
Helpful around house	_____	_____	_____
Conforming	_____	_____	_____
Rebellious	_____	_____	_____
Trying to please	_____	_____	_____
Critical of others	_____	_____	_____
Considerate	_____	_____	_____
Selfish	_____	_____	_____
Have own way	_____	_____	_____
Sensitive, easily hurt	_____	_____	_____
Temper tantrums	_____	_____	_____
Sense of humor	_____	_____	_____
Idealistic	_____	_____	_____

Materialistic

Standards of achievement

Standards of morals

Athletic

Strongest

Attractive

Tallest

Masculine

Musical

Artistic

Spoiled

Punished

Friends

Leader

Follower

Handicapped/prolonged illness

Sibling most like client; how

Sibling least like client; how

10. Early recollections

Think as far back in your childhood as you can and tell me the first thing you can remember.

First early recollection description

Feeling

1 (93 in PP & C)
2 (60–75)
2 (144–152)
6 (18–19)
7 (72–82)
7 (92–95)
7 (135–144)
8 (55–60)

Second early recollection description

Feeling

Third early recollection description

Feeling

Fourth early recollection description

Feeling

Fifth early recollection description

Feeling

11. Dreams

    a. Childhood

        Do you recall as a child any particular dreams, especially dreams that were repeated?

        First dream description   4 (85–90)

                                          6 (19–20)

                                          7 (24–30)

                                        9 (60–80)

                                        11 (219–222)

        Feeling

        Second dream description

        Feeling

    b. Adulthood

        Recently have you been experiencing any particular kind of dream, one that is often repeated?

        First dream description

        Feeling

        Second dream description

        Feeling

c. Day dreams

When and where occur

Description of content and sequence

Feeling

12. Closing (metaphorical) questions as appropriate

Did client as a child have a favorite book, fairy tale, or character? What did s/he like about it?

Did client as a child have a nickname? (How did s/he feel about it?

Three wishes

References

1. Dreikurs, *The Psychological Interview in Medicine.*
2. Mosak, *On Purpose.*
3. Dinkmeyer, et al., *Adlerian Counseling and Psychotherapy.*
4. Dreikurs, *Fundamentals of Adlerian Psychology.*
5. Dreikurs, *A Reliable Differential Diagnosis of Disturbances.*
6. Eckstein, et al., *Life Style.*
7. Baruth, et al., *Life Style.*
8. Nikelly, *Techniques for Behavior Change.*
9. Shulman, *Contributions to Individual Psychology.*
10. Dreikurs, *Psychodynamic Diagnosis in Psychiatry.*
11. Dreikurs, *The Meaning of Dreams.*

Appendix I

Life Style Interpretation
Betty Lowe
Raymond Lowe

(For information concerning these references, see page 197.)

1. Name   Date

2. Summary   6 (21–31)
                                                                        6 (38)
                                                                        6 (49)
   a. The subjective situation   7 (31–33)
                                                                        7 (47–105)
                                                                        9 (35–39)
                                                                        9 (42–44)

   b. The objective situation

   c. Family constellation   6 (37)
                                                                        6 (49)
                                                                        7 (35–39)

   d. Family atmosphere

Reprinted by permission of the authors.

199

Appendix J

An Instrument for Assessing Competencies in Establishing the Life Style

Betty Lowe
Raymond Lowe

Instructions

Following are a number of items identified as characteristics or qualities considered essential to conducting a life style analysis. The instrument is intended as a training device to direct attention to specific strengths or specific areas in need of attention.

The instrument may be used in a variety of ways. It may be completed by a student counselor for purposes of self-evaluation, by a supervisor, or by observers who wish to learn more about the process. When a student and supervisor are involved, it is suggested that optimum growth will probably result when both the supervisor and the student counselor complete separate instruments and subsequently use these as a basis for conferring. In whatever capacity the instrument is used—by student, supervisor, or observer—it should be completed following, not during, the analysis session.

Indicate on the scale provided the level you think the student counselor performed on each item.

Scale

1. *Decidedly lacking in competence.* Counselor is sufficiently uninformed or inexperienced that s/he must confer with his/her supervisor for additional training.

2. *Lacking in competence.* Counselor will probably improve with additional information or experience. S/he may wish to confer with his/her supervisor or the supervisor may wish to confer with the counselor.

3. *Competent.* Counselor is qualified to function with minimal supervision.

4. *Decidedly competent.* Conferring with colleagues rather than supervisors is indicated.

5. *Insufficient information.* The competency is appropriate to the session, but information is unavailable or inadequate to evaluate the competency.

6. *Not applicable.* The competency is not appropriate to this particular session.

I am using this instrument:

( ) As a supervisor.
( ) As a peer/observer.
( ) For self-evaluation.

Name of Student: _____

Date: _____

PART I   ADLERIAN THEORY

Competencies expected of a counselor utilizing Adlerian Psychology as a theoretical basis for undertaking the life style analysis include:

PERSONAL CONGRUENCE

The counselor's posture, facial expressions, and gestures are congruent with   1   2   3   4   5   6
the client and the situation (1).

Reprinted by permission of the authors.

ASSUMPTIONS

The counselor articulates Adler's assumptions about human behavior as they relate to the client's behavior (2).   1 2 3 4 5 6

LIMITATIONS

The counselor recognizes the adequacy of her/his knowledge of Individual Psychology to the situation with which s/he is dealing (3).   1 2 3 4 5 6

GUESSING

The counselor:

integrates what s/he has learned (4), and   1 2 3 4 5 6

"guesses in the right direction" (5).   1 2 3 4 5 6

The counselor:

validates his/her "guesses (6), and   1 2 3 4 5 6

in the absence of validation readily shifts the guessing process (7).   1 2 3 4 5 6

PRIVATE LOGIC

The counselor is aware of the client's private logic and the purpose it serves (8).   1 2 3 4 5 6

SOCIAL INTEREST

The counselor utilizes the notion of social interest in the helping process (9).   1 2 3 4 5 6

PART II   ADLERIAN TECHNIQUE

Competencies expected of a counselor utilizing Adlerian techniques in the analysis process include:

INTRODUCTION

The counselor easily orients the client to the analysis session (10).   1 2 3 4 5 6

SUBJECTIVE SITUATION

The counselor solicits the subjective situation (11).   1 2 3 4 5 6

OBJECTIVE SITUATION

The counselor explores the objective (current) situation in terms of the client's approach to the life tasks:

Work (12).   1 2 3 4 5 6

Society (13).   1 2 3 4 5 6

Sex (14).   1 2 3 4 5 6

THE QUESTION

The counselor appropirately raises "The Question" (15).   1 2 3 4 5 6

FAMILY CONSTELLATION

The counselor establishes the family constellation and draws appropriate inferences (16).   1 2 3 4 5 6

FAMILY ATMOSPHERE

The counselor recognizes the importance of identifying the family atmosphere (17).   1 2 3 4 5 6

PARENTS

The counselor integrates information about the parents into the data gathering process (18).   1 2 3 4 5 6

SIBLINGS

The counselor seeks attributes of siblings and is aware of the implied relationships of each to the client (19).   1 2 3 4 5 6

EARLY RECOLLECTIONS

The counselor appropriately solicits early recollections (20).   1 2 3 4 5 6

DREAMS

The counselor appropriately solicits dreams or daydreams (21).   1 2 3 4 5 6

DIAGNOSIS

The counselor identifies maladaptive symtomatology as consistent with the notions of social interest (22).   1 2 3 4 5 6

INTERPRETATION

The counselor assists the client in recognizing his/her mistaken goals (23).   1 2 3 4 5 6

INITIATING REDIRECTION

The counselor explores with the client the alternatives to the mistaken goal (24).   1 2 3 4 5 6

CONFRONTATION

The counselor is able to utilize the technique of confrontation for purpose of:

keeping the client's attention on the problem being explored (25), and   1 2 3 4 5 6

assisting the client in understanding the apparent contradiction between statements and behaviors (26).   1 2 3 4 5 6

SUMMARY

The counselor assists the client in understanding his/her subjective views, mistaken beliefs, private logic, or destructive behavior (27).   1 2 3 4 5 6

The counselor summarizes the client's life style in a succinct phrase or statement intelligible to the client (28).   1 2 3 4 5 6